A Gathering of Light

"No one can ever set his foot upon the Path,
can turn toward that Light within himself,
and ever be the same again."

WESLEY LA VIOLETTE
The Creative Light

Praise

for

A Gathering of Light

"*A Gathering of Light: Eternal Wisdom for a Time of Transformation* is the essence of ancient and recent enlightening quotations showing humanity the guideposts of the new needed vision for the 21st century and new millennium. I hope this magnificent book will be on the desk of every head of state and chief executive of all major institutions, medias and corporations of this planet."

> **Robert Muller,** Former Assistant Under Secretary General of the United Nations; Chancellor, University For Peace

A Gathering of Light:

Eternal Wisdom
for a
Time of Transformation

Published by
Wings of Spirit
A *Gathering of Light* Foundation
6757 Arapaho, Suite 711, Box 345
Dallas, Texas 75248

ISBN# 1-887884-06-8 (pbk.): $24.95

Printed in USA
First Edition, 1st Printing

Compilation & Arrangement © 1998 John A. Price
See credits at end of book for special permissions

Wings of Spirit Foundation is a not-for-profit organization dedicated to the engagement of humankind in individual and collective prayer, surrendered to the Will of God [by whatever name], and to raising the consciousness of humanity to the realization of Oneness in Spirit. Through its endeavors, Wings of Spirit seeks to create an environment of harmony among all people and a world of peace.

" The day will come when, after harnessing the ether, the winds, the tides, gravitation, we shall harness for God the energies of love. And, on that day, for the second time in the history of the world, man will have discovered fire."

PIERRE TEILHARD de CHARDIN, "*The Evolution of Chastity*," *Toward the Future*

SPECIAL THANKS

I am eternally grateful to my wife, Diadra, without whom this book would not be a reality for her love, encouragement, and inspiration, as well as for her graphics design and layout of the book. I am deeply indebted to and thankful for Jean Blanton for all her countless hours of typing and editing of the materials. I also wish to thank Bob and Janice Carter for their generous contributions and support of this project.

DEDICATION

This book is dedicated to the ones who, throughout the ages, have kept the flame lit to light the way for the many to follow. Thanks to these dedicated "light bearers" whose words are memorialized in this book, humankind has survived to experience this exciting and tumultuous time of transformation long ago foretold. The torch now has been passed. At this time of the "Gathering of Light," it is imperative all of us in whom the Light is burning allow that Light to shine forth and to light the way for our fellow brothers and sisters.

PREFACE

The message of "light" is as old as civilization. It has been passed down from generation to generation, both orally and in writings of the major cultures and religions throughout time. It is a message of hope, joy and love which knows no boundaries (geographical, cultural, religious, racial or generational). It is a message which seeks to reunite us to our higher and true Self, to reenchant the world, to quicken the Spirit within, to unite our family of being, to serve as midwife to our spiritual rebirth, and to lead us through our dark night of fear and guilt and into the light of a new day. It is a message which has sometimes flickered dimly or been forgotten, but it is time to rekindle the flame to light a pathway for humankind's passage through this time of transformation.

"A Gathering of Light" is a book of timeless wisdom which speaks to the issues of our time, providing assistance and guidance to a seemingly dysfunctional world filled with doubt, fear, despair and hopelessness. It is a message of "light" gathered from ancient to modern times pointing us in the direction of a reunification with the infinite Source of power within us all. It is a road map for personal and global transformation, and it is a call to awake.

Many have long foretold the renewal and rebirth of the eternal Spirit of Light -- the "Second Coming", the "New Millennium," the "New Genesis." That time is upon us, as the stage is set for a rebirth and reawakening. The message of "light" can no longer be held secret, but must be spread to all those who are and will be the "light workers" of the coming new age. It is time for the flame to burn brightly and for the inner light within each one of us to come forth in full radiance. It is time for all peoples to come together. It is time to rediscover our common bonds, to honor our common heritage, to forgive our common failings, to rejoice in our common blessings, to bring to fruition our common dreams, to rekindle our common Spirit, and to rejoin in common vision and purpose for the co-creation of a brighter and more harmonious future for ourselves, our children, our communities and our Earth. It is time for "A Gathering of Light."

FOREWORD

"I quote others only to better express myself."

> MICHEL DE MONTAIGNE, *The Essays of Michel de Montaigne*

"All truly wise thoughts have been thought already thousands of times; but to make them truly ours, we must think them over again honestly, till they take root in our personal experience."

> JOHANN WOLFGANG VON GOETHE

"We ought . . . to read devout and simple books. . . . Let not the authority of the writer move thee, whether he be of small or great learning: but let the love of pure truth draw thee to read. Search not who said this, but mark what is said."

> THOMAS A. KEMPIS, *The Imitation of Christ*

"We are like dwarfs seated on the shoulders of giants. We see more things than the Ancients, and things farther away, but this is not due to the sharpness of our vision or the heights of our Build. It is because they carry us and raise us from their gigantic height."

> BERNARD de CHARTRES

CONTENTS

INTRODUCTION

"Each past cycle in the growth of man toward higher levels has been illumined by the few inspired messengers of the Light who have known God in themselves.

New inspired messengers who know God in themselves will likewise give the Light to this new cycle. And these few messengers of the Light must multiply to legions, for the need of a spiritual awakening is great. Man's whole reason for being is to gradually pass through his millions of years of physical sensing into his ultimate goal of spiritual knowing. Man has now reached a transition point in his unfolding where he must have that knowing. He can acquire that knowing only through greater awareness of the Light of the universal Self which centers him as One with God."

WALTER RUSSELL, *The Secret of Light*

"[I]n our first sleepy steps we can set our feet upon the footprints of all those great minds, those richer souls that have gone before. Then our thoughts and our desires are but lengthened shadows of their thoughts, and all we see is seen as if we had their eyes."

WESLEY LA VIOLETTE, *The Creative Light*

I.

$\mathscr{S}$TATE OF UNION

State of Union

"$\mathscr{T}$hese times of ours are serious and full of calamity, but all times are essentialy alike. As soon as there is life there is danger."
RALPH WALDO EMERSON,
"Public and Private Education"

A. ℰCOLOGY

"*W*here have all the flowers gone?"
                                    PETE SEEGER

"*I* can't conceive of any problem that the human mind can define that it can't also solve. I think that what makes the human race unique is its ability to do something for the first time. And for the first time we're called upon to meet a threat to the survival of the species."
                                    NORMAN COUSINS

"[*W*]e will have to realize, in our daily decisions and forms of behavior, that finally we are nothing but a little part of the history of nature. And either we learn to preserve nature -- or, if you wish, to preserve creation -- or we will not survive."

RICHARD VON WEIZSACKER, *An Agenda for the 21st Century*

"*T*he earth will not be reduced to abject servitude. After all man's assaults the majesty of the earth stands over against him with an inscrutable countenance. There are gathering signs of a response in the form of massive retaliation. The game is a game but only if it leads to larger life. Else the game is no longer a creative experience but a struggle to the death, a struggle which man cannot win."

THOMAS BERRY, "*The Human Venture*"

"The history of 'civilization' has been a steady process of estrangement from nature that has increasingly developed into outright antagonism."
MURRAY BOOKCHIN

"The world of today is sick to its thin blood for lack of elemental things, for fire before the hands, for water welling from the earth, for air, for the dear earth itself underfoot."
HENRY BESTON, *The Outermost House*

"Like winds and sunsets, wild things were taken for granted until progress began to do away with them. Now we face the question of whether a still higher 'standard of living' is worth its cost in things natural, wild and free."
ALDO LEOPOLD, *A Sand County Almanac*

"The crisis of our time and in our world anticipates a complete process of transformation which can but be transcribed by the phrase 'global catastrophe.' Evaluated from a point of view which is not merely anthropocentric, this state of affairs must present itself as a new array of planetary dimensions. Soberness is demanded of us; we must face the fact that there remain only a few decades until those conditions are fulfilled. The time of grace is fixed by the increase in technical possibilities, which is in exact proportion to the decrease in man's awareness to his responsibilities -- unless a new factor arises on the scene to overcome this threatening situation. ...

Either we overcome the crisis or it will overcome us. Only he who conquers himself will prevail. Either we are liquidated and cut to pieces, or we solve the problem and work toward wholeness. In other words, either time is fulfilled in us -- and that means the end and death of our earth and of present-day man -- or it is we who succeed in fulfilling time. This is tantamount to attaining wholeness and realizing the present, and synonymous with working to achieve the unification of our primordial Origin (ursprung) and our living Present (Gegenwart), and making it real."

JEAN GEBSER, *"The Foundations of the Aperspective World," Nature, Man, and Society: Main Currents in Modern Thought*

"*Because* the global ecosystem is a connected whole, in which nothing can be gained or lost and which is not subject to over-all improvement, anything extracted from it by human effort must be replaced. Payment of this price cannot be avoided; it can only be delayed. The present environmental crisis is a warning that we have delayed nearly too long."

BARRY COMMONER, *The Closing Circle: Nature, Man & Technology*

"*We're* flying blind into a highly uncertain future. These changes are going to affect every human being and every ecosystem on the face of the earth, and we only have a glimmer of what these changes will be. The atmosphere is supposed to do two things for us: maintain a constant chemical climate of oxygen, nitrogen and water vapor, and help maintain the radiation balance -- for example, by keeping out excess ultraviolet. The unthinkable is that we're distorting this atmospheric balance. We're shifting the chemical balance so that we have more poisons in the atmosphere-ozone and acid rain on ground level -- while we're also changing the thermal climate of the earth through the green-house effect and -- get this -- simultaneously causing destruction of our primary filter of ultraviolet light. It's incredible. Talk about the national-debt crisis -- we're piling up debts in the atmosphere, and the piper will want to be paid."

MICHAEL OPPENHEIMER

"*I* am utterly convinced that most of the great environmental struggles will be either won or lost in the 1990s. And that by the next century it will be too late."

THOMAS LOVEJOY

"[*D*]ealing with myriads of monumental human and ecological issues confronting the Earth, our task begins now and here. It is a task to create the Earth of our dreams in the not-too-far-distant future, for us and for our children for many millennia to come.

. . . A sea of changes have occurred universally -- in the mental, physical and emotional universe. For the first time in the history of our existence, we have created an earthly nightmare by our arrogance, foolishness and viciousness. Now with our courage and will, we must convert it into a dream of our heart. But, as we begin our journey . . ., we must recognize that we, 5.4 billion humans, along with 20 million other species, have a unique existence in a unique and sacred home whirling around the sun in the immense universe. The ultimate test . . . will be in how we succeed in harmonizing ourselves with the immutable laws of nature, which, through evolution, created a beautiful and enjoyable earth and life."

RASHMI MAYUR

"*New* in this age is an unparalleled awareness of the terrifying seriousness of the human situation. Questions we seriously ask today would have seemed utterly absurd twenty years ago, such as, for example: Are we the last generation? Is this the very last hour for . . . civilization?"

ABRAHAM JOSHUA HESCHEL

"Thank God, they cannot cut down the clouds!"

HENRY DAVID THOREAU, *Journal*

"Deep ecology recognizes that nothing short of a total revolution in consciousness will be of lasting use in preserving the life-support systems of our planet."

JOHN SEED, *Thinking Like A Mountain*

"Never before has humankind faced so many crises altogether at one time. We stumble over critical threshold after critical threshold in a long chain of events running parallel to one another which are destined to clash simultaneously any moment. Any one of these thresholds of pollution, population explosion, destruction of the ozone shield or other dramatic climatic changes brought about by the greenhouse effect is, even by itself, sufficient to detonate an evolutionary bomb which could totally change the direction of our species.

* * *

On close examination, the choice does not seem to be whether it will happen, but whether we will manage to destroy ourselves before it happens."

YATRI, *Unknown Man: The Mysterious
Birth of a New Species*

"The need for resurrection has increased in intensity in our time. We are living at the very edge of history, at a time when the whole planet is heading toward a global passion play, a planetary crucifixion. Great yellow clouds of pollution hover over major cities. The land is raped, the forests decimated. . . . We are truly experiencing a worldwide Golgotha."

JEAN HOUSTON, *Godseed: The Journey of Christ*

"Once green with perennial vegetation, pastures of the countryside have been diminished as the cattle of a thousand hills have been removed off the land. Once quiet and still with ecological health, waters of streams and ponds have gained a disquieting turbulence as they bear their wasteful loads. Creation's evangelical testimony is increasingly smogged and muted. Creation's song of praise -- its testimony -- is being impoverished by insatiable, grasping hands and machines."

SHANTILAL P. BHAGAT, *Creation in Crisis*

"The deteriorating condition of the planet is the most important issue of our time. Growth of the human population and expansion of destructive human activities have long since become the enemies of human progress and of the biosphere in general. The 'silent Armageddon' promised us decades ago by many voices in the scientific community is no longer a possibility among many possibilities lying over the horizon. It is here; we are living in its early phases."

BILL WILLERS, *Learning to Listen to the Land*

"How long will the land mourn, and the grass of every field wither?"

JEREMIAH 12:4

B. Human SUFFERING

"Never before has man had such capacity to control his own environment, to end thirst and hunger, to conquer poverty and disease, to banish illiteracy and massive human misery. We have the power to make this the best generation of mankind in the history of the world -- or to make it the last."

JOHN F. KENNEDY, *Address before the General Assembly of the United Nations, New York City (September 20, 1963)*

"Is not one of the problems of religious life today that we have separated ourselves from the poor and the wounded and the suffering? We have too much time to discuss and to theorize, and we have lost the yearning for God which comes when we are faced with the sufferings of people."

JANE VANIER, *Followers of Jesus*

"Our hope for creative living in this world house that we have inherited lies in our ability to reestablish the moral ends of our lives in personal character and social justice. Without this spiritual and moral reawakening, we shall destroy ourselves in the misuse of our own instruments."

MARTIN LUTHER KING, JR.

"*The* world will not endure half developed and half undeveloped, half healthy and half ill, half hungry and half fully fed, half clothed and half naked."

D. F. ANNAN, *Vice President of Ghana, Address to the United Nations Conference on Environment and Development in Rio de Janeiro (June 1992)*

"*We* waste the precious raw material of the earth all the time. Our haste and rivalry, our fear that somebody will get ahead of us in exploiting the rich deposits in the soil of the earth are squandering the limited stock of supplies, which ought to be handled with the utmost care and conserved for those who will come after us. But much more serious is the waste of human life. We exploit men and women and children as well as coal and oil. We build our cities for the ease and convenience of commerce, not for the promotion of life and happiness. The slum is an outrage against humanity. The narrow, treeless streets, without gardens and breathing spaces for the play of children, are marks of selfishness, ignorance and stupidity. The mills and factories and mines, where labour is massed, where initiative and creative qualities are eliminated, where a person is largely reduced to a mechanistic tool, involve a large sum total both of blunders and sins against palpitating human beings whom God has made."

RUFUS JONES, *The Faith and Practice of the Quakers*

C. INERTIA

"We will have to repent in this generation, not merely for the vitriolic words and actions of the bad people, but for the appalling silence of the good people."

MARTIN LUTHER KING, JR., *"Letter from the Birmingham Jail" (January 16, 1963)*

"It is too easy to find an excuse for inaction by pleading the decadence of civilization, or the imminent end of the world. This defeatism, whether it be innate or a mere affection . . . seems to be the besetting temptation of our time."

PIERRE TEILHARD de CHARDIN, *Building the Earth*

"Never before has humanity possessed as it does today the knowledge and the skills, the resources and the cohesion to shape a better world. This should generate a resounding hope for all people. Yet there is a widespread sense of unease and fear of impending changes which, in impinging on the still undigested changes of recent decades, will add to the uncertainty. This very uncertainty, together with the broken rigidities of the past and the new hopes for the future, is an enormous opportunity for reshaping the world society. The tragedy of the human condition is that we have not yet reached a position to realize our potential. We see the world and its resources being grossly mismanaged, yet we are lulled by the complacency of our leaders and our own inertia and resistance to change. Time is running out. Some problems have already reached a magnitude which is beyond the point of successful attack and the costs of delay are monstrously high. Unless we wake up and act quickly it could be too late."

The First Global Revolution, A Report by the Council of The Club of Rome

"*O*ur loss has been ontological, not psychological.   A deficiency in meaning and in being. A refusal to care for what matters, a limpness in the face of the challenge of our history. The challenges seem overwhelming, and we are understandably tempted to retreat . . . into private pleasures and high consumption. But let's call that what it is: moral cowardice, abdication of responsibility, voluntary myopia. And if we continue on this path we will continue to feel empty and devoid of meaning."

SAM KEEN, *Fire in the Belly: On Being a Man*

"[*I*]t is not inertia alone that causes the unspeakably monotonous unrenewed human condition to repeat itself again and again. It is the aversion to anything new, any unpredictable experience, which is believed to be untenable."

RAINER MARIA RILKE, *Letters To A Young Poet*

"*I*f the human family drifts into the future half-awake, then we are assured of a future with immense hardship and suffering for ourselves and our children. . . . It is imperative that we begin to deliberately choose our pathway into the future as a human family. If we do not muster the will and creativity to choose our future more consciously, we will become one of the unfortunate 'cosmic seeds' that has taken root, but is so crippled by self-destructive actions that it never flowers into the fullness of its potential."

DUANE ELGIN, "*Awakening Earth*"

"Each of us is in a profound trance, consensus consciousness, a state of partly suspended animation, of stupor, of inability to function at our maximum level."

CHARLES TART, *Waking Up:*
Overcoming the Obstacles to
Human Potential

"When our strategies are formed and informed by a larger context than our narrow ego selves, when we realize we are acting not just from our own opinions or beliefs, but on behalf of a larger Self -- the Earth -- with the authority of more than four billion years of our planet's evolution behind us, then we are filled with new determination, courage and perseverance, less limited by self-doubt, narrow self-interest and discouragement. The apathy from which many of us suffer, the sense of paralysis, is a product of our shriveled sense of self."

JOHN SEED, *Thinking Like a*
Mountain

"[T]he ordinary person is a shriveled, desiccated fragment of what a person can be. As adults, we have forgotten most of our childhood, not only its content, but its flavor. As men of the world, we hardly remember our dreams and make little sense of them when we do. As for our bodies we retain just sufficient proprioceptive sensations to coordinate our movements and to ensure the minimal requirements for bio-social survival -- to register fatigue, signals for food, sex, defecation, sleep: beyond that . . . little or nothing.

Our capacity to think, except in the service of what we are dangerously deluded in supposing is our self interest, and in conformity with common sense, is pitifully limited: our capacity even to see, hear, touch, taste and smell is so shrouded in veils of mystification that an intensive discipline of unlearning is necessary for anyone before one can begin to experience the world afresh, with innocence, truth and love."

> RONALD LAING, *The Politics of Experience and the Bird of Paradise*

D. *V*ISIONARY VACUUM

"*The* world is facing an awful crisis, . . . The very future of humanity is at stake. Mankind can be saved only by a group of men who are so centered in God at the source that their wisdom is a part of the All-Wisdom, and therefore so conscious of the cosmos and so integrated at the center that they will be able to think clearly in many fields and not be limited to one field alone. Such a group of men, if they could find each other out, and share their wisdom, might be able to chart a course that could save the world."

> DR. ALEXIS CARREL

"*Only* a giant leap of the imagination can project on to our mental screens the immensity and radicality of the impasse now confronting humanity."

> PAULOS MAR GREGORIOS, *The Human Presence: Ecological Spirituality and the Age of the Spirit*

"We have not yet developed technological wisdom, technological discipline, technological stewardship. Ecological destruction is not the result of science and technology, but of social decisions that allow scientific and technological institutions to grow in undisciplined ways."

SAM KEEN, *Fire in the Belly: On Being a Man*

"Are we as a species able to use the awesome power we have developed for the good of the universe? Do we have the intelligence to do it? If not, we fail the test -- and fail as a species. Moreover this test is one with a time limit, and I fear the time left is running out fast."

PETER RUSSELL, "*A Crisis of Consciousness*"

"We live in an age disturbed, confused, bewildered, afraid of its own forces, in search not merely of its road but even of its direction. There are many voices of counsel, but few voices of vision; there is much excitement and feverish activity, but little concert of thoughtful purpose. We are distressed by our own ungoverned, undirected energies and do many things, but nothing long. It is our duty to find ourselves."

WOODROW WILSON, *Baccalaureate Address, Princeton University (June 9, 1907)*

"Unless man can match his strides in weaponry and technology with equal strides in social and political development, our great strength, like that of the dinosaur, will become incapable of proper control, and man, like the dinosaur, will vanish from the earth."

JOHN F. KENNEDY, *Speech to the United Nations General Assembly (September 25, 1961)*

"*We* are still imprisoned in our cave, with our backs to the light, and can only watch the shadows on the wall."

SIR JAMES JEANS, *The Mysterious Universe*

"*Each* moment from all sides rushes to us the call to love. We are running to contemplate its vast green field. Do you want to come with us? This is not the time to stay at home, but to go out and give yourself to the garden. The dawn of joy has arisen, and this is the moment of union, of vision. . . ."

Jalal-ud-Din RUMI

E. *Poverty* OF SPIRIT

"*Our* God has become too small for us."

PIERRE TEILHARD de CHARDIN

"*Light* there was not: for the Flame of Spirit was not yet rekindled."

SECRET DOCTRINE OF THE
ROSICRUCIANS

"*If*, as I believe, health means wealth, then the earth is indeed becoming an increasingly impoverished place as we lay waste to its rich blessings of earth, air, fire and water. Where is our indignation amid all this suffering of the poor? Any liberation movement must possess the power to awaken moral indignation among its citizens for within that indignation lies the power to liberate."

MATTHEW FOX, *Creation Spirituality: Liberating Gifts for the Peoples of the Earth*

"*The* fundamental issues confronted by any civilization or by any person in his or her life are issues of meaning. . . . For more than 99 percent of human history, the world was enchanted, and man saw himself as an integral part of it. The complete reversal of this perception [in the modern Western world] has destroyed the continuity of human experience and the integrity of the human psyche. It has very nearly wrecked the planet as well. The only hope . . . lies in a reenchantment of the world."

MORRIS BERMAN, *The Enchantment of the World*

"*There* is hunger for ordinary bread, and there is hunger for love, for kindness, for thoughtfulness, and this is the great poverty that makes people suffer so much."

MOTHER TERESA OF CALCUTTA

"[*W*]ho looking dispassionately at the human race from Cro-Magnon to Auschwitz to the Gulag Archipelago can doubt that we are technological giants yet ethical pygmies."

CHARLES HAMPDEN-TURNER

"The crisis is in our consciousness, not in the world."
J. K. KRISHNAMURTI

"[The crisis which . . . man is undergoing is a metaphysical one. There is probably no more dangerous illusion than that of imagining that some readjustment of social or institutional conditions could suffice of itself to appease a contemporary sense of disquiet which rises, in fact, from the very depth of man's being."
GABRIEL MARCEL

"The root of our environmental crisis is an inner spiritual aridity."
PETER RUSSELL, "*A Crisis of Consciousness*"

"Turning and turning in the widening gyre
The falcon cannot hear the falconer;
Things fall apart; the center cannot hold;
Mere anarchy is loosed upon the world,
The blood-dimmed tide is loosed, and everywhere
The ceremony of innocence is drowned;
The best lack all conviction, while the worst
Are full of passionate intensity,

Surely some revelation is at hand. . . ."
W. B. YEATS, "*The Second Coming*"

"Our whole culture -- with its endless violence, homeless people on the streets, colossal nuclear arsenals, and global pollution -- is sick. It is sick because it is out of harmony with itself; it suffers from what Hopi Indians call koyaanisqatsi, which is rendered in English, 'crazy life, life in turmoil, life out of balance.' What is missing is the feminine dimension in our spiritual and psychological lives; that deep mystical sense of the earth and her cycles and of the very cosmos as a living mystery. We have lost our inner connection to that momentous power that used to be called the Great Mother of us all."

JENNIFER AND ROGER WOOLGER, *The Goddess Within: A Guide to the Eternal Myths That Shape Women's Lives*

"Though the problems in the world have many different forms, they are nothing but symptoms of one underlying condition: the emotional, moral, and spiritual state of modern humanity. . . . In the last analysis, they are the collective result of the present level of consciousness of individual human beings. The only effective and lasting solution to these problems, therefore, would be a radical inner transformation of humanity on a large scale and its consequent rise to a higher level of awareness and maturity."

CHRISTINA AND STANISLAV GROF, *The Stormy Search for the Self*

"If man had originally inhabited a world as blankly uniform as a high rise housing development, as featureless as a parking lot, as destitute of life as an automated factory, it is doubtful that he would have had a sufficiently varied experience to retain images, mold languages, or acquire ideas."

LOUIS MUMFORD, *The Myth of the Machine*

"The only courage that is demanded of us, is the courage for the most strange, the most singular, the most inexplicable that we may encounter. Mankind has in this sense been cowardly, has done life endless harm. The experiences that are called visions, the whole so-called spirit world, death, all these things that are so closely akin to us, have by daily paring been so crowded out of our life, that the senses with which we could have grasped them are atrophied, to say nothing of God."

RAINER MARIA RILKE

"*H*umankind is being brought to a moment where it will have to decide between suicide and adoration."

PIERRE TEILHARD de CHARDIN

"*The* core of our problem as human beings is that we are in a mass psychic depression. This depression is everywhere and it eats away at every resolve we take, at every passion, and every attempt at health. It is a massive worldwide depression and its cause is a fundamental loss of our identity, our memory of our Divine origin."

ANDREW HARVEY, *The Way of Passion, a Celebration of Rumi*

F. *I*NTERRELATEDNESS

"*B*ut war or peace; the destruction or protection of nature; the violation or promotion of human rights and democratic freedoms; poverty or material well-being; the lack of moral and spiritual values or their existence and development; the breakdown or development of human understanding, are not isolated phenomena that can be analyzed and tackled independently of one another. In fact, they are very much interrelated at all levels and need to be approached with that understanding."

TENZIN GYATSO, 14TH DALAI LAMA OF TIBET, *Nobel Peace Prize Lecture, Oslo, Norway (1989)*

"[M]odern man is 'unfinished,' his transition to a greater maturity retarded. One must recognize this as a cold fact. The current global crisis -- in which old and new problems of population, food, education, resources, energy, crowding, inflation, poverty, alienation, militarization, disorder, ecodegradation, injustice, etc., are growing and intertwining beyond recognition -- are a consequence of the difficulty people have in achieving the level of understanding and sense of responsibility demanded by their mutated universe. They have -- all of them, in all classes and nations throughout the planet -- remained confined within obsolete cultural boundaries which in the past could serve them well enough, but which nowadays are dangerously crippling, preventing them from living on par with the reality of their time and from controlling the mechanisms of change."

AURELIO PECCEI, *The Inner Limits of Mankind*

"At the beginning of the last two decades of our century, we find ourselves in a state of profound, world-wide crisis. It is a complex, multi-dimensional crisis whose facets touch every aspect of our lives -- our health and livelihood, the quality of our environment, and our social relationships, our economy, technology and politics. It is a crisis of intellectual, moral, and spiritual dimensions; a crisis of a scale and urgency unprecedented in recorded human history. For the first time we have to face the very real threat of extinction of the human race and of all life on this planet."

FRITJOF CAPRA, *The Turning Point: Science, Society, and the Rising Culture*

" The world and its environmental and developmental problems are totally indivisible. The globe is one and its people and problems are interconnected. Whether we like it or not, human society is internationalized."

RASHMI MAYUR

" Crucial for the survival of the world: because the only way to cure this horrific psychic agony that is freezing, paralyzing and destroying everyone in various ways on the earth is to awaken everyone, to give everyone the sense of what he or she really is, to bring back into the heart of the human race the glory of our Divine origin and the glory of the visionary truth that those who have lived in that origin, and who have become that origin, know to be real. . . . If we don't open to this testimony of our Divine origin and of the divinity of the earth, and of our secret interconnectedness with all things now, if we don't go on a journey to transform ourselves in the light of that knowledge, and if we don't succeed in transforming ourselves to an unprecedented extent to allow the Divine to act through us, there will be no human race, no habitable world."

ANDREW HARVEY, *The Way of Passion, a Celebration of Rumi*

II.

ᏆRANSFORMATION

"*We* live at the edge of the miraculous."

HENRY MILLER

A. WINDS OF CHANGE

"*If* you listen you will hear the sound of the kingdom of God in the air as no generation ever could before."

ALBERT SCHWEITZER, *Reverence for Life*

"*To* every thing there is a season, and time to every purpose under the Heaven:
A time to be born, and a time to die; a time to plant, and a time to pluck up that which is planted;
A time to kill, and a time to heal; a time to break down, and a time to build up;
A time to get, and a time to lose; a time to keep, and a time to cast away;
A time to rend, and a time to sew; a time to keep silence and a time to speak;
A time to love, and a time to hate; a time of war, and a time of peace."
ECCLESIASTES 3:1-8

"*We* are at a very exciting moment in history, perhaps a turning point."

ILYA PRIGOGINE, *Lecture at University of Texas (April 1978)*

"*It* was the best of times, it was the worst of times, it was the age of wisdom, it was the age of foolishness, it was the epoch of belief, it was the epoch of incredulity, it was the season of Light, it was the season of

Darkness, it was the spring of hope, it was the winter of despair, we had everything before us, we had nothing before us, we were all going directly to Heaven, we were all going directly the other way -- in short, the period was so far like the present period, that some of its noisiest authorities insisted on its being received, for good or for evil, in the superlative degree of comparison only."

CHARLES DICKENS, *A Tale of Two Cities*

"*Only* the supremely wise and abysmally ignorant do not change."

CONFUCIUS

"*No* matter how old you are in the year 2000, profound change will have been written into your life by the time you start the 21st century. None of us will be the same when the century turns. If the dramatic change of the sixties is not in the air these days, do not for one minute think that change is not on its way."

MARVIN CETRON and THOMAS O'TOOLE, *Encounters with the Future: A Forecast of Life into the 21st Century*

"*Do* not say, 'There are yet four months, then comes the harvest'? I tell you, lift up your eyes, and see how the fields are already white from harvest!"

JOHN 4:35

"Time, events, or the unaided individual action of the mind will sometimes undermine or destroy an opinion without any outward sign of change. . . . No conspiracy has been formed to make war on it, but its followers one by one noiselessly secede. As its opponents remain mute or only interchange their thoughts by stealth, they are themselves unaware for a long period that a great revolution has actually been effected."

ALEXIS DE TOCQUEVILLE,
Democracy in America

"In our time a secret manifesto is being written. Its language is a longing we read in one another's eyes. It is the longing to know our authentic vocation in the world, to find the work and the way of being that belong to each of us. . . . I speak of the Manifesto of the Person, the declaration of our sovereign right to self-discovery. I cannot say if those who have answered its summons are indeed millions, but I know that its influence moves significantly among us, a subterranean current of our history, that awakens in all those it touches an intoxicating sense of how deep the roots of the self reach, and what strange forces of energy they embrace. . . ."

THEODORE ROSZAK, *Lecture at
Claremont College, 1976*

"We are living at a time when history is holding its breath, and the present is detaching itself from the past like an iceberg that has broken away from its moorings to sail across the boundless ocean."
ARTHUR CLARKE

"We are engaged, if the transformational thinker is correct, in a process which has no parallel in human history -- an attempt to change the whole of a culture through a conscious process."
ROBERT THEOBALD

"All things are in the act of change; thou thyself in ceaseless transformation and partial decay, and the whole universe with thee."
                                    MARCUS AURELIUS

"[O]ur griefs . . . are the moments when something new has entered into us, something unfamiliar. Our feelings become mute in timid shyness. Everything within us steps back; a silence ensues, and the something new, known to no one, stands in the center and is silent.

* * *

We are alone with the strange thing that has stepped into our presence. For a moment everything intimate and familiar has been taken from us. We stand in the midst of a transition where we cannot remain standing.

[T]he something new within us, the thing that has joined us, has entered our heart, has gone into its innermost chamber and is no longer there either -- it is already in the blood. And we do not find out what it was. One could easily make us believe that nothing happened; and yet we have been changed, as a house is changed when a guest has entered it. We cannot say who came; we shall perhaps never know. But many signals affirm that the future has stepped into us in such a way as to change itself into us, and that long before it manifests itself outwardly."

                         RAINER MARIA RILKE, *Letters*
                    To A Young Poet

"The order is
Rapidly fadin'.
And the first one now
Will later be last
For the times they are a-changin'."

                    BOB DYLAN, "*The Times They*
               Are A-Changin'"

B. NEW EVOLUTIONARY STAGE

"Toto, I've a feeling we're not in Kansas anymore."

DOROTHY, *The Wizard of Oz*

> "The simple truth is that there has lived on Earth -- appearing at different intervals -- for thousands of years among ordinary people, the faint beginnings of another race, walking the Earth and breathing the air with us. . . . This new race is in the act of being born from us, and in the near future, will occupy and possess the Earth."
>
> EDMOND BUCKE, *Cosmic Consciousness*

"[A]t a deeper level in the structure of society we can find indications of a revolutionary shift in the most basic assumptions about the nature of reality -- assumptions that underlie modern society and all its institutions. It is a shift away from the materialism inherent in reductionist science, and toward a recognition that our picture is incomplete and misleading so long as it does not explicitly recognize the extent and magnificence of the potentialities of the human spirit."

WILLIS HARMAN AND JOHN HORMANN,
Creative Work -- The Constructive Role
of Business in a Transforming Society

"*We* stand, now, on the threshold of a new evolutionary step in the unfoldment of humankind. The keynote of this step is the new understanding of an ancient truth: <u>We are One</u>. Behind our nationalities, colors of skin, cultures, lifestyles, and histories, We are One. It is this unity, this common bond, that will be the hallmark of a new age on earth."

ALAN COHEN, *The Dragon Doesn't Live Here Anymore*

"*The* world will not evolve past its current state of crisis by using the same thinking that created the situation."

ALBERT EINSTEIN

"*This* is an exciting age, perhaps the most exciting in the history of humanity. We live at the precise moment when we are simultaneously becoming aware of the processes that evolve our societies and acquiring mastery of the technologies that determine how they evolve. We live at the conjunction of knowledge and power. Whether we also live at the moment of emerging wisdom remains to be seen."

ERWIN LASZLO, *Evolution, The Grand Synthesis*

"*The* coming of a spiritual age must be preceded by the appearance of an increasing number of individuals who are no longer satisfied with the normal intellectual, vital, and physical existence of man, but perceive that a greater evolution is the recognized goal of the race. In proportion as they succeed and to the degree to which they carry this evolution, the yet unrealized potentiality which they represent will become an actual possibility of the future."

SRI AUROBINDO GHOSE, *The Human Cycle*

"*No* one can see, even in outline, the shape of things to come. History has been stepped up incredibly and is now exceeding the speed limit. Still, it is my belief, in spite of old rancors, new envies, and the chaos of the hour, that we are entering the greatest era in the story of man, destined to see changes such as man has never seen."

JOSEPH FORT NEWTON

"*Our* species is . . . being given the chance to choose how it will learn, how it will evolve. This is the time for us as a species and as individuals to choose again. It is an opportunity for us as a species and as individuals to choose differently, to choose otherwise, to choose . . . to learn love through wisdom, to take the vertical path of clarity, of conscious growth and conscious life. . . ."

GARY ZUKAV, *The Seat of the Soul*

"[*T*]he modern world is undergoing a period of fundamental transformation, the extent and meaning of which we who are living through it are only beginning to grasp. . . .

* * *

[T]he perception of reality is . . . shifting at that . . . deep level of the most basic assumptions about the nature of man/woman in the cosmos, and about what is ultimately important. . . . [I]t means that the world of the 21st century will be as different from the present as the present is from the Middle Ages. . . . [W]e are striking out in a dramatically new direction.

* * *

[T]he scientific materialism which so confidently held forth . . . answers . . . a couple of generations ago, is a dying orthodoxy. It's basic positivistic and reductionistic premises are being replaced by some sort of transcendentalist beliefs that include increased faith in reason guided by deep intuition. In other words, a respiritualization of society is taking place, but one more experiential and noninstitutionalized, less fundamentalist and sacerdotal, than most of the historically familiar forms of religion. Science, in turn, is reassessing its foundation assumptions to better accommodate the human spirit and the conscious awareness that comprise our most direct link with reality. Such a change in basic assumptions must inevitably be accompanied by a long-term shift in value emphases and priorities.

* * *

The majority of people . . . are just becoming aware that forces for radical change have been mounting and may be close to . . . [a] critical mass. . . . [It] is not the classical revolutionary force . . . It is, rather, the revolutionary awareness we have been oppressing ourselves with a belief system that we bought into, a belief system on which our

whole techno-economic structure rests, which is not compatible with a viable future for human society on the planet. . . ."

WILLIS HARMAN

"*In* the very heart of the modern spirit there is a schism. The egg is breaking, the chromosomes are splitting to go forward with a new pattern of life. Those of us who seem most alien . . . are the ones who are going forward to create the life as yet inchoate.

We who are affected cannot make ourselves clear. . . . This is the era when apocalyptic visions are to be fulfilled. We are on the brink of a new life, entering a new domain."

HENRY MILLER, *The Wisdom of the Heart*

"One of the truths of our time is this hunger deep in people all over the planet for coming into relationship with each other.

Human consciousness is crossing a threshold as mighty as the one from the Middle Ages to the Renaissance. People are hungering and thirsting after experience that feels true to them on the inside, after so much hard work mapping the outer spaces of the physical world. They are gaining courage to ask for what they need: living interconnections, a sense of individual worth, shared opportunities. . . .

Our relationship to past symbols of authority is changing because we are awakening to ourselves as individual beings with an inner rulership. Property and credentials and status are not as intimidating anymore. . . . New symbols are rising: pictures of wholeness. Freedom sings within us as well as outside us. . . . Sages and seers have foretold this second coming. People don't want to feel stuck, they want to be able to change."

M. C. RICHARDS, *The Crossing Point*

"*We* are seemingly between two epochs: the dying Sensate [secular] culture of our magnificent yesterday and the coming [new] culture of the creative tomorrow. We are living, thinking and acting at the end of a brilliant six-hundred-year-long Sensate day. The oblique rays of the sun still illumine the glory of the passing epoch. But the light is fading, and in the deepening shadows it becomes more and more difficult to see clearly and to orient ourselves safely in the confusions of the twilight. The night of the transitory period begins to loom before us, with its nightmares, frightening shadows and heart-rending horrors. Beyond it, however, the dawn of a new great culture is . . . waiting to greet the men of the future."

PITIRIM A. SOROKIN, "Three Basic Trends of Our Times," *Nature, Man, and Society: Main Currents in Modern Thought*

"*We* are entering an era in which ancient dreams of peace and prosperity might at last be fulfilled. . . . [H]ere on the threshold, it doesn't feel like Utopia at all. It requires a conscious act of will to step back and see where we stand in history."

MARJORIE KELLY, "*The Million Hands of God*"

"[A] new reflective consciousness of planetary scope is rapidly emerging. We have already begun to create a conscious, planetary civilization. The earth is already awakening."

> DUANE ELGIN, *"Awakening Earth"*

"We do not understand, but somehow we are a part of a creative destiny, reaching backward and forward to infinity -- a destiny that reveals itself, though dimly, in our striving, in our love, our thought, our appreciation. We are the fruition of a process that stretches back to star-dust. We are material in the hands of the Genius of the universe for a still larger destiny that we cannot see in the everlasting rhythm of worlds. We fail and fall by the way, yet redeeming grace fashions us anew and eliminates our failures in the larger pattern."

> JOHN ELOF BOODIN, <u>Cosmic Evolution</u>

"Man is entering upon a new stage in his evolutionary development."

> JONAS SALK

"The age of analysis has done its work; the age of synthesis has begun."
ERWIN LASZLO, <u>Evolution, The Grand Synthesis</u>

"It is high time to realize that this is not one of the ordinary crises which happen almost every decade, but one of the greatest transitions in human history."

> PITIRIM A. SOROKIN, <u>Cultural and Social Dynamics</u>

"*We* suspect from past evidence that any evolutionary transformation of a species maybe is preceded by a crisis in the environment. It has also been shown that many of our present critical thresholds are destined to collide at any moment and that each hour brings us closer to that apocalyptic event. Each single critical pathway is, of itself, sufficient to trigger an evolutionary time-bomb which could detonate a transformation of our species. The magnitude and number of these thresholds compels us to conclude that something of a revolutionary nature is imminent."

YATRI, *Unknown Man: The Mysterious Birth of a New Species*

"*Every* stage of the life of a person carries a Beyond within it. Life itself of our kind has a principle of advance in the onward flow of it. The World that has given us our convictions of eternal values, the World that has impressed us with its Beauty and its Ends of Good, its Truth, and its Love, gives us ground to expect that there is more where that comes from. And our ineradicable belief in the final intelligibility of that World sends our minds 'on loft,' as Chaucer would say, with a profound conviction that the gates of the future are open."

RUFUS JONES, *Spirit in Man*

"*The* dark night of the soul comes just before revelation.

When everything is lost, and all seems darkness, then comes the new life and all that is needed."

JOSEPH CAMPBELL

"*We* stand on the brink of a new age: the age of an open world and of a self capable of playing its part in that larger sphere. An age of renewal, when work and leisure and learning and love will unite to produce a fresh form for every stage of life, and a higher trajectory for life as a whole. . . In carrying man's self-transformation to this further stage, world culture may bring about a fresh release of spiritual energy that will unveil new potentialities, no more visible in the human self today than radium was in the physical world a century ago, though always present . . . . For who can set bounds to man's emergence or to his power of surpassing his provisional achievements? So far we have found no limits to the imagination, nor yet to the sources on which it may draw. Every goal man reaches provides a new starting point, and the sum of all man's days is just a beginning."

LEWIS MUMFORD

"*Earth!* Invisible! What is your urgent command, if not transformation?"

RAINER MARIA RILKE, *The Duino Elegies*

"*There* is another way of looking at the world."

A COURSE IN MIRACLES

"*Never,* ever recover or even want to from the wound of Divine Love, of Divine Longing, so you will come to long with your whole being to participate now in the vast transformation that destination is demanding of the human race."

Jalal-ud-Din RUMI

C. PARADIGM SHIFTS

"The universe is home for us all. Each of us is a living part of a limitless, creative process, and, as children of the cosmos, at every instant we face both an awesome freedom and a responsibility for ourselves, for others, and for our world. If we believe in the endless subtlety and wholeness of nature, we will also see the need for a new ethic -- for a radically different way for society to act. In seeing ourselves as full participators in the great dance of the world, we will no longer seek to control and exploit nature for our ends. So a radical transformation in our way of being is called for, one involving a totally new form of response . . ."

> F. DAVID PEAT, *Philosopher's Stone: Chaos, Synchronicity, and the Hidden Order of the World*

"The unleashed power of the atom has changed everything except our way of thinking. Thus we are drifting toward a catastrophe beyond comparison. We shall require a substantially new manner of thinking if mankind is to survive."

> ALBERT EINSTEIN

"Before long, it seems, there will be reached the social 'critical mass' necessary for a revolutionary change in direction. May it come quickly; a change of revolutionary nature is long overdue."

> BILL WILLERS, *Learning to Listen to the Land*

"The potential for rescue at this time of crisis is neither luck, coincidence, nor wishful thinking. Armed with a more sophisticated understanding of how change occurs, we know that the very forces that have brought us to planetary brinkmanship carry in them the seeds of renewal. The current disequilibrium -- personal and social -- foreshadows a new kind of society. Roles, relationships, institutions, and old ideas are being reexamined, reformulated, redesigned.

For the first time in history humankind has come upon the control panel of change -- an understanding of how transformation occurs. We are living in the change of change, the time in which we can intentionally align ourselves with nature for rapid remaking of ourselves and our collapsing institutions.

The paradigm of the Aquarian Conspiracy sees humankind embedded in nature. It promotes the autonomous individual and decentralized society. It sees us as stewards of all our resources, inner and outer. It says that we are not victims, not pawns, not limited by conditions or conditioning. Heirs to evolutionary riches, we are capable of imagination, invention, and experiences we have only glimpsed."

MARILYN FERGUSON, *The Aquarian Conspiracy: Personal and Social Transformation in Our Time*

"Even if we believe that the time of our civilization is running out fast, like sugar spilled from a torn bag, we must wait. But while we are waiting, we can try to feel and think and behave as if our society were already beginning to be contained by religion. . . . as if we were finding our way home again in the universe. We can stop disinheriting ourselves. . . . We can challenge the whole de-humanizing, depersonalizing process that is taking the symbolic richness, the dimension of depth out of men's lives, inducing the anesthesia that demands violence, crudely horribly effects, to feel anything at all. Instead of wanting to look at the back of the moon, remote from our lives, we can try to look at the back of our own minds."

> J. B. PRIESTLEY, *Literature and Western Man*

"[We] hold the purpose of establishing a far-reaching transforming vision -- one that releases the human race from age-old tyrannies and creates and nurtures a new sense of what it is to be human. It requires a fundamental shift in our mode of thought. It involves a rite of passage from adolescence to mature adult. It requires a burgeoning world acceptance of our earth responsibilities. Now is the time for a coming together of all people who wish to support this great task -- to restore the earth and heal and uplift all life on earth."

> CAMPAIGN FOR THE EARTH, Pamphlet entitled "Gathering the Momentum"

"[The] most critical change that must take place is a transformation in our very relationship with the Earth. The Earth does not need to change in order to survive -- she will survive with or without us. If we are to continue, it is our values that need to change."

> ALLAN HUNT BADINER, *Dharma Gaia*

"[A]ny major transformation of the psyche involves a long process of the destructuring of the old self, before there can be any constructing of a new identity."

SAM KEEN, *Fire in the Belly: On Being a Man*

"The Perennial Philosophy is the only viewpoint broad enough to address our personal and planetary concerns. Its insistence that the inner and outer form one unified whole helps account for environmentally sound action based on the perception of our shared interdependence. If the basic assumptions of the perennial wisdom become the dominant vision of modern society, life a few generations from now will be as different from modern industrial society as our current lifestyle is from the Middle Ages."

WILLIS HARMAN, *Global Mind Change*

"Every era opens with its challenges, and they cannot be met by elaborating methods of the past."

CHARLES A. LINDBERG

"In the late twentieth century there is a growing awareness that we are doomed as a species and planet unless we have a radical change of consciousness. The re-emergence of the Goddess is becoming the symbol and metaphor for this transformation of culture."

ELINOR W. GADON, *The Once and Future Goddess*

"This new life is not very well defined, which is why we want to hold onto the past. The journey to this new life, a journey we must all make, cannot be made unless we let go of the past. The reality of living in space is that we are born anew; not born again to an old-time religion, but born to a new order of things: there are no horizons. That is the meaning of the space age. We are in a free fall into a future that is mysterious."

JOSEPH CAMPBELL

"Life is making us abandon established stereotypes and outdated views, and it is making us discard illusions. It would be naive to think that the problems facing mankind today can be solved by the means and methods that were applied or seemed to work in the past."

MIKHAIL GORBACHEV, *Address to the United Nations (1987)*

"Never before has the responsibility of the human being for the planetary process been greater. Never before have we gained power of such magnitude over the primordial issues of life and death. The density and intimacy of the global village, along with the staggering consequences of our new knowledge and technologies, make us directors of a world that, up to now, has mostly directed us. This is a responsibility for which we have been ill prepared and for which the usual formulas and stop-gap solutions will not work."

JEAN HOUSTON, *The Possible Human*

D. $\mathcal{S}$EEDS OF CHANGE

"$\mathcal{I}$t is no use trying to merely modify present forms. The whole great form of our era will have to go. And nothing will really help send it down but the new shoots of life springing up and slowly busting the foundations. And one can do nothing but fight tooth and nail to defend the new shoots of life from being crushed out, and let them grow."

D. H. LAWRENCE

"[$\mathcal{J}$ust beneath the surface of our society, a great historical tidal wave is on the move -- a set of monumental political, social, and economic impulses, which are carrying us relentlessly toward a rendezvous with the future."

GEORGE GALLUP JR., *Forecast 2000*

"$\mathcal{I}$ believe that the principles of universal evolution are revealed to us through our intuition. And I think that if we combine our intuition and our reason, we can respond in an evolutionary sound way to our problems. . . ."

JONAS SALK

"$\mathcal{W}$e are on the verge of a new age, a whole new world.
Human consciousness, our mutual awareness,
is going to make a quantum leap.
Everything will change . . .
All this is going to happen just as soon as you're ready."

PAUL WILLIAMS, *Das Energi*

"The healing of the Planet Earth will come, for indeed it <u>has</u> come within our hearts. This transformation is being accomplished not simply through talking about it, wishing for it, or waiting for it. The healing is coming through <u>living</u> it, and it is coming through people like you and me, people who believe that we are worthy of peace because we are born of a loving God."

ALAN COHEN, *Lifestyles of the Rich in Spirit*

"It is increasingly clear that a philosophical revolution is under way. A comprehensive system is swiftly developing, like a tree beginning to bear fruit on every branch at the same time."

ABRAHAM MASLOW

"Awakenings begin in periods of cultural distortion and grave personal stress, when we lose faith in the legitimacy of our norms, the viability of our institutions, and the authority of our leaders."

WILLIAM MCLOUGHLIN, *Revivals, Awakenings, and Reform*

"*A* new world is born. It is not the old world that is changing. It is a new world which is born. And we are right in the middle of the transition period, when the two overlap, when the old is still all-powerful and entirely controlling the ordinary consciousness. But the new slips in, still very modest and unnoticed -- so unnoticed that externally it disturbs hardly anything . . . For the moment, it is even absolutely imperceptible in the consciousness of most people. But it is working, it is growing."

THE MOTHER, *The Mind of the Cells*

"[*Y*]ou are in a period of transition and wish . . . to transform yourself. If some aspect of your life is not well . . . consider the illness to be the means for an organism to free itself from something foreign to it. . . . [H]elp it to be ill and have its whole illness, to let it break out. That is the course of its progress."

RAINER MARIA RILKE, *Letters To A Young Poet*

"[*T*]he human race stands on the brink of a major breakthrough. We have advanced to the point where we can put our hand on the hem of the curtain that separates us from an understanding of the nature of our minds. Is it conceivable that we will withdraw our hand and turn back through discouragement and lack of vision?"

PERCY W. BRIDGMAN

"Great are the dangers facing mankind. There are enough elements of confrontation, but the forces wishing and capable of stopping and overcoming that confrontation are growing in strength and scope before our very eyes."

MIKHAIL   GORBACHEV,
Perestroika

E. Metamorphosis

"Something is afoot in the universe, a result is working out which can best be compared to a gestation and birth: the birth of a new spiritual reality formed by souls and the matter they draw after them. Laboriously, by way of human activity and thanks to it, the new earth is gathering, isolating and purifying itself. No, we are not like flowers in a bunch, but the leaves and flowers of a great tree, on which each appears at its time and place, according to the demands of the All."

PIERRE TEILHARD de CHARDIN,
Human Energy

"*In* this eliminative period of world changes, of transformation through the power of transmutation . . . , we can begin to see a union of the visible world of matter with the invisible world of mind. All of us are suffering in the travail of a new world that is crying out in pain. It is struggling to be born into the light of perfect day."

WESLEY LA VIOLETTE, *The Creative Light*

"*Humanity* as an entity is only beginning to shape and to evolve: it begins to have common perceptions of reality, common feelings and common concerns; it begins to act and react as one body to common dangers and events, to evolve towards higher forms of coordinated action and fulfillment in total cosmic reality. In this evolution all former primitive groups and beliefs will have to adapt or perish."

ROBERT MULLER, *A Planet of Hope*

"*We* are the spark that will light the fire of change. The power for change is here and NOW -- in the present moment. A new way of thinking and a new way of being in unity and harmony here upon our planet is emerging in the minds and hearts of millions on every distant shore. During the days ahead, our collective spark will grow ever larger as it unites with others in a worldwide flame of passion for life, love and peace."

CAMPAIGN FOR THE EARTH

"*Beloved*, we are God's children now, but it does not yet appear what we shall become. ..."

1 JOHN 3:2

"The metamorphosis of a larva to become an adult insect begins with the degeneration of much of the larval tissue. Simultaneously there is a proliferation of growth around special cells called 'imaginal cells.' These colonies of new cells in effect create parts of the new creature that will eventually emerge from the pupal shell. When they grow large enough, they merge to form the adult insect, and the remainder of the larval tissue in between disintegrates. It may well be that the metamorphosis of industrial society has already begun, with thousands of 'new age' organizations and experimental communities in voluntary associations playing the role of 'imaginal cells' linked by a vaguely defined image of a sparkling new future."

WILLIS HARMAN, "*Where is Our Positive Image of the Future*"

"Ecologically, in the depths at least, we and the world are flowering simultaneously. As the world is fermenting, becoming resacralized, we are becoming as gods, but gods who must outgrow in patterns and in principle the archaic strata of previous ages lest we bring havoc and the twilight of the gods before a new day, a good day, a God day can dawn."

JEAN HOUSTON, "*The Promise of The New Millennium*"

F. CHARTING A NEW COURSE

"If you do not change direction, you may end up where you are heading."
LAO TZU

"Greater knowledge about the world will, I think, be the keynote of the immediate future. But greater knowledge alone will not be enough. There must also be greater love and understanding among men. And there must also be greater faith in humankind and in the purposes of the Creator of the Universe. Knowledge, love, faith -- with these three the atomic age, the age in which we live, can become an age of mercy, of joy, and of hope, one of the blessed periods of all history. . . .

We have great visions today. We are going to have more of them. From our strengths have come great actions. We can move forward to even greater achievements. In our hearts we know we have heard only the opening bars of the New World Symphony.

Ours is a time of great expectations. . . . There is open before us an unparalleled opportunity to build new and firmer foundations under our feet. We stand at the gateway of an age of expansion, of the flowering of modern imagination and new skills and knowledge of mankind.

The task ahead may prove to be the boldest and most stirring adventure of the human spirit since the circumnavigation of the globe. That will be true if it can release a flood of pent-up genius, not alone in our works of hands and skills in management but in the development of the free spirit."

DAVID E. LILIENTHAL

"The twentieth century is the bloodiest century in history, but we can yet retrieve it. The last half of the century could produce a world-wide flowering of the human spirit such as we have not known since the Renaissance -- or, more accurately, since the twelfth century -- a flowering that would be fertilized by the blood and sorrow of these last calamitous decades. We know that science and medicine are on the threshold of great events. It can be a time, too, of great literature, of creative art and drama. With intelligence and conscience to guide us, we can also make gigantic strides in social control, bringing our destructive weapons within the orbit of a world authority, and harnessing these powers to enhance the happiness of men and increase the dignity and worth of the human person.

This is not an idle dream. It's realization is distinctly possible, but only on the condition that we fight for it -- fight for it with undiscouraged faith and grim tenacity. If men . . . can develop the wisdom to use their technology only for constructive ends, if they will act on the principle that racial intolerance of every kind threatens the safety of the future, if they will move out into a new world society with decisiveness and daring, then the twentieth century can be redeemed."

RAYMOND B. FOSDICK

"The tasks facing us today are enormous, but it is the glory of human nature that there will always be those rare individuals who say, 'Let there be dangers, let there be difficulties -- whatever it costs, I want to live to the full height of my being, my feet still on the ground but my head crowned with stars.' According to Mahatma Gandhi, this can be done only by facing difficulties that appear almost impossible. If that is so, the 1990s offer an unparalleled opportunity."

EKNATH EASWARAN, The Compassionate
Universe: The Power of the Individual to
Heal the Environment

"Humanity at last has a unifying crisis -- our environment itself is threatened. In response to this crisis, it is time that we bring all the separate members of our planetary body together for a mighty uprising of creativity and love for our Earth."

BARBARA MARX HUBBARD

"The shift we need to make is both a shift in consciousness and a major restructuring of all the institutions of society. We need to engage in active, nonviolent resistance to the destruction being mounted all around us. At the same time, we need to develop and make real our alternative visions; start the businesses; live in the households; grow the gardens that embody our ideals. In so doing, we can experiment with our ideals on a small scale and find out if they actually work in practice."

STARHAWK

"In a world of global civilization, only those who are looking for a technical trick to save the civilization need feel despair. But those who believe, in all modesty, in the mysterious power of their own human Being, which mediates between them and the mysterious power of the world's Being, have no reason to despair at all."

VACLAV HAVEL, *Address to World Economic Forum (February 4, 1992)*

"Humanity groans half-crushed under the weight of the advances that it has made. It does not know sufficiently that its future depends on itself. It is for it, above all, to make up its mind if it wishes to continue to live."

HENRI BERGSON, *The Two Sources of Morality and Religion*

" *We* are living in . . . an age of apocalypse that is also an age of rebirth.
. . . What the human race needs now is not more religions or dogmas, but
witnesses to divine Reality and Glory, lovers of God and the world who
can speak out of their love clearly and guide us into our own Fire."

ANDREW HARVEY, *The Way of Passion, a*
Celebration of Rumi

"*A* total spiritual direction given to the whole life and the whole nature
can alone lift humanity beyond itself. ... It is only the full emergence of the
soul, the full descent of the native light and power of the Spirit ... that can
effect this evolutionary miracle.

...

... [W]hat evolutionary Nature presses for, is an awakening to the
knowledge of self, the discovery of self, the manifestation of the self and
spirit within us and the release of its self-knowledge, its self-power, its
native self-instrumentation. It is, besides, a step for which the whole of
evolution has been a preparation and which is brought closer at each crisis
of human destiny when the mental and vital evolution of the being touches
a point where intellect and vital force reach some acme of tension and
there is a need either for them to collapse, to sink back into a torpor of
defeat or a repose of unprogressive quiescence or to rend their way
through the veil against which they are straining. What is necessary is that
there should be a turn in humanity felt by some or many towards the vision
of this change, a feeling of its imperative need, the sense of its possibility,
the will to make it possible in themselves and to find the way. "

SRI AUROBINDO GHOSE, *The Life Divine*

"At the end of this heroic effort that we are called to make, there will be, if we prevail, the most extraordinary transformation of humankind. We know that it is possible because it is beating in all of our hearts. We know it is possible because our lives are full of yearning for it. We know it is possible because nothing else could possibly save our world now. So we also know the truth that when, finally, the dawn of our true humanity comes, . . . we'll be ashamed of the . . . old ideas, concepts, and fantasies. We will be finally what we are: divine children living a divine life on earth."

ANDREW HARVEY, *The Way of Passion, a Celebration of Rumi*

III.

₲AIA

Gaia

"ℳan can no longer live for himself alone. We must realize that all life is valuable and that we are united to all life. From this knowledge comes our spiritual relationship with the universe."

ALBERT   SCHWEITZER,   *Animals, Nature & Albert Schweitzer*

A. EARTH AS LIVING ORGANISM

> "*L*et us admit that this world is a living being who has a soul; that it is a spiritual being and that, in truth, it has been engendered by the Providence of God."
>
> PLATO, *Timaeus*

"*The* earth I tread on is not a dead, inert mass; it is a body, has a spirit, is organic and fluid to the influence of its spirit."

HENRY DAVID THOREAU, *The Writings of Henry Thoreau*

"*The* earth is a living organism, the body of a higher individual who has a will and wants to be well, who is at times less healthy or more healthy, physically and mentally. People should treat their own bodies with respect. It's the same thing with the earth. Too many people don't know that when they harm the earth they harm themselves, nor do they realize that when they harm themselves they harm the earth."

ROLLING THUNDER

"*The* old gods are dead or dying and people everywhere are searching, asking: What is the new mythology to be, the mythology of this unified earth as one harmonious being?"

JOSEPH CAMPBELL

"The Earth, its life am I
The Earth, its body is my body
The Earth, its thoughts are my thoughts."
                    NAVAJO SONG

"The earth is not a mere fragment of dead history . . . but a living earth; compared with whose central life all animal and vegetative life is merely parasitic."
                    HENRY DAVID THOREAU, *Walden*

"The cycles of Life need to be approached with reverence. They have been in place for billions of years. They are the reflection of the natural breathing of the soul of Gaia itself, the Earth consciousness, as it moves its force fields and guides the cycles of Life. If these are revered, how could we look at something as exquisite as our Earth's ecology and do one thing that would risk the balance of this system?"
                    GARY ZUKAV, *The Seat of the Soul*

"Call the world, if you please,
The veil of Soulmaking,
Then you will find out
the use of the world. . . ."
                    JOHN KEATS

"The earth is not . . . stratum upon stratum like the leaves of a book, to be studied by geologists and antiquaries chiefly, but living poetry like the leaves of a tree, which precede flowers and fruit -- not a fossil earth, but a living earth."

HENRY DAVID THOREAU, *Walden*

B. DEEP ECOLOGY

"The <u>deep</u> ecological task is . . . to awaken in human souls the sharpest possible awareness that belief in the existence of God absolutely demands the deepest respect and reverence for the rights of the Earth."

REVEREND VINCENT ROSSI, "*The Eleventh Commandment: A Christian Deep Ecology,*" *The Eleventh Commandment Newsletter*

"Deep ecology goes beyond a limited piecemeal shallow approach to environmental problems and attempts to articulate a comprehensive . . . philosophical worldview. . . . [Its] basic insight . . . of biocentric equality is that all things in the biosphere have an equal right to live and blossom and to reach their own individual forms of . . . self-realization."

GEORGE SESSIONS AND BILL DEVALL, *Deep Ecology: Living as if Nature Mattered*

"*Just* as we should cultivate gentle and peaceful relations with our fellow human beings, we should also extend the same kind of attitude towards the natural environment. Morally speaking, we should be concerned for our whole environment."

TENZIN GYATSO, 14TH DALAI LAMA OF TIBET,
Humanity and Ecology

"*Justice* does not require equality. It does require that we share one another's fate. The lesson of ecology is that we do share one another's fate in the shallow sense since we all share the fate of the earth. The message of deep ecology is that we ought to care as deeply and as compassionately as possible about that fate -- not because it affects us but because it is us."

WARWICK FOX, "*Deep Ecology: a New Philosophy of Our Time*," *Ecologist*

"*Joys* come from simple and natural things, mists over meadows, sunlight on leaves, the path of the moon over water. Even rain and wind and stormy clouds bring joy, just as knowing animals and flowers and where they live. Such things are where you find them, and belong to the aware and alive. They require little scientific knowledge, but bring in their train an ecological perspective, and a way of looking at the world."

SIGURD F. OLSON, *Open Horizons*

C. LAWS OF NATURE

"*If* you will stay close to nature, to its simplicity, to the small things hardly noticeable, those things can unexpectedly become great and immeasurable."

RAINER MARIA RILKE, *Letters To A Young Poet*

"*This* law of nature, being co-eval with mankind and dictated by God himself, is of course superior in obligation to any other. It is binding over all the globe, in all countries, and at all times: no human laws are of any validity, if contrary to this; and such of them as are valid derive all their force, and all their authority . . . . from this original."

WILLIAM BLACKSTONE, *Commentaries on the Laws of England*

"*Cultures* come -- and go. . . . [W]hen a society is in clash with the universe, once a society transgresses the laws of nature, it loses its survival value. So, as soon as we leave the basis of nature -- the universe and its laws -- . . . we lose the possibility of existence."

F. S. PERLS, *Gestalt Therapy Verbatim*

"*Countless* . . . ., unaware of nature's Law, think all these unseen, unheard and still withheld forces and expressions of Divine Idea are only phenomena, empty images, a meaningless mirage that glitters in a fevered brain. Yet he who knows himself as ancient beyond time, who is aware of consciousness expressed and manifested everywhere, who sees that every nook and cranny of the universe is soaked and drenched with life, who hears the breath of life sweep through the winds of deepest space, becomes master, striking off the chains of ignorance and knowing his part within the stream of life itself."

WESLEY LA VIOLETTE, *The Creative Light*

"Our ability to see the planet we live on with its various habitats and elements as Original Blessing is the key to its survival and our own. Instead of approaching nature as something to 'master' . . . or make profit from, we need a whole new way -- which is, in fact, the more ancient way -- of relating to nature: of subject to subject instead of subject to object. It is a way of awe, since awe is our response to blessing. It is a mystical way, a way of 'entering the mysteries' which surround us with beauty, grace, and unconditional love."

MATTHEW FOX, *Original Blessing*

"We live here with the permission of the Great Spirit. . . . [T]he supreme law of the land is the Great Spirit's, not Man's Law."

THOMAS BANYACYA *(Hopi Indian)*

"[A]ll beauty in animals and plants is a silent and enduring form of love and longing. We can see the animal just as we perceive the plant, patiently and willingly uniting, multiplying, and growing, not from physical desire, not from physical grief, rather from adapting to what has to be. That existing order transcends desire and grief and is mightier than will and resistance. The earth is full of this secret down to her smallest things."

RAINER MARIA RILKE, *Letters To A Young Poet*

"One day as I was passing through the Amazon forests, suddenly at dawn I had a vision. All life around me had just awakened. The sweet music of birds and animals filled the fresh air; the rays of the sun peeped through the trees and everywhere life seemed to dance and sing in joy. A truth and hope became apparent to me. I discovered that even though the world has many ills, humans need not be enemies of truth, and that truth is expressed in the laws of nature that govern earth, life and the future."

RASHMI MAYUR

"The question before the human race is whether the God of nature shall govern the world by His own laws, or whether priests and kings shall rule it by fictitious miracles."

THOMAS JEFFERSON, *Letter to John Adams*

"[The Book of Nature is a Holy Scroll . . . [T]each . . . how once again to read from the living pages of the Earthly Mother. For in everything that is life is the law written. It is written in the grass, in the trees, in rivers, mountains, birds of the sky and fishes of the sea; and most of all within the Son of Man. Only when he returns to the bosom of his Earthly Mother will he find everlasting life and the Stream of Life which leads to his Heavenly Father; only thus may the dark vision of the future come not to pass."

THE ESSENE GOSPEL OF PEACE

D. *N*ATURE'S PARTNER

> "*F*orget not that the earth delights to feel your bare feet and the winds long to play with your hair."
>
> KAHLIL GIBRAN, *The Prophet*

"*W*hat is proposed here is a broadening of value, so that nature will cease to be merely 'property' and become a commonwealth. . . . If we now universalize 'person,' consider how slowly the circle has enlarged . . . to include aliens, strangers, infants, children, Negroes, Jews, slaves, women, Indians, prisoners, the elderly, the insane, the deformed, and even now we ponder the status of fetuses. Ecological ethics queries whether we ought to again universalize, recognizing the intrinsic value of every ecobiotic component."

HOLMES ROLSTON

"[*T*]he religion of the future will be a belief in a Creed of Kinship, a charter of human and sub-human relationships."

HENRY S. SALT, *The Creed of Kinship*

"A theology of the natural world . . . asserts the intrinsic worth of the non-human world. Such a theology declares that the non-human world has just as much right to its internal integrity as does the human world, that human beings transgress their divine authority when they destroy or fundamentally alter the rocks, the trees, the air, the water, the soil, the animals -- just as they do when they murder other human beings."

ALLAN R. BROCKWAY

"There is a revolution coming. Its ultimate creation will be a new and enduring wholeness . . . a renewed relationship of man to himself, to other men, to society, to nature, and to the land."

CHARLES REICH, *The Greening of America*

"[Your breath, your blood, the fire of life within you, all are one with the Earthly Mother."

THE ESSENE GOSPEL OF PEACE

"[It is very clear the planet is our own house, and without this we can't survive. That's quite certain. Ultimately, we are the children of the mother Earth, so ultimately we are at the mercy of the mother planet concerning environment and ecology. This is not something sacred or moral. It is a question of our own survival. I think -- at least, I hope -- that it may not be too late if we realize the importance of the natural environment."

TENZIN GYATSO, 14TH DALAI LAMA OF TIBET, *In the Footsteps of Gandhi: Conversations With Spiritual Social Activists*

"*We* are sons of the earth: and, like Antaeus in the fable, if, in wrestling with a Hercules, we now and then receive a fall, the touch of our parent will communicate to us fresh strength and vigour to renew the contest."

BENJAMIN FRANKLIN, *Comfort for America*

"*Human* society is not an abstraction. The only real society is the complete society of the natural world. We are awkward at this manner of thinking because our religious as well as our humanist traditions carry a certain antagonism toward the natural world. But now the refusal of the human beings to become intimate members of the community of the earth is leading to their own destruction."

THOMAS BERRY, "*Our Children: Their Future*"

"*Humanity* participates by nature in all cosmic events, and is inwardly as well as outwardly interwoven with them."

RICHARD WILHELM, *The Secret of the Golden Flower*

"*There* must be new contact between men and the earth; the earth must be newly seen and heard and felt and smelled and tasted; there must be a renewal of the wisdom that comes with knowing clearly the pain and the pleasure and the risk and the responsibility of being alive in this world."

WENDELL BERRY

"*W*hen the Pleiades and the wind in the grass are no longer a part of the human spirit . . . man becomes . . . a kind of cosmic outlaw, having neither the completeness and integrity of the animal, nor the birthright of a true humanity."

HENRY BESTON, *The Outermost House*

"*T*o interpret Nature is not to improve upon her; it is to draw her out; it is to have an emotional intercourse with her, absorb her and reproduce her tinged with the colors of the spirit."

JOHN BURROUGHS, *Wake-Robin*

"*H*appy the man whose lot it is to know
The secrets of the earth. He hastens not
To work his fellows hurt by unjust deeds,
But with rapt admiration contemplates
Immortal Nature's ageless harmony,
And how and when her order came to be."

EURIPIDES

"*T*hrough intimate association with the living things around us, we reach beyond the narrow human sphere into the larger natural world that surrounds and sustains us. We develop toward this world an attitude, often intensely personal, that with time and thought may grow into a world view or philosophy of nature; possibly, if held with fervor and capable of strongly influencing our conduct, it might be called a religion. Perhaps to have developed such a comprehensive outlook, especially if it be hopeful and sustaining rather than gloomy or despairing, is the most important outcome of long association with nature."

ALEXANDER FRANK SKUTCH, *Nature
Through Tropical Windows*

"I went to the woods because I wished to live deliberately, to front only the essential facts of life, and see if I could not learn what it had to teach, and not, when I came to die, discover that I had not lived."

HENRY DAVID THOREAU, *Walden*

"The Grail is being in perfect accord with the abundance of nature, the highest spiritual realization, the inexhaustible vessel from which you get everything you want."

JOSEPH CAMPBELL

"Nature is a part of our humanity, and without some awareness and experience of that divine mystery, man ceases to be man."

HENRY BESTON, *The Outermost House*

"I was seeing in a sacred manner the shapes of all things in the spirit, and the shape of all things as they must live together, like one being. And I saw that the sacred hoop of my people was one of many hoops that made one circle, wide as daylight and as starlight, and in the center grew one mighty flowering tree to shelter all the children of one mother and one father."

SIOUX MEDICINE MAN *(Keeper of the Sacred Pipe)*

"As is the human body,
    so is the cosmic body.
As is the human mind,
    so is the cosmic mind.
As is the microcosm,
    so is the macrocosm.
As is the atom,
    so is the universe."

                        THE UPANISHADS

"[W]e must overcome our particular form of species selfishness, which has enabled us to separate ourselves from nature and to wantonly exploit the world's resources. We must rethink the Earth not as a collection of objects, but as a community of objects to whom we are committed by bonds of courtesy and compassion. Without this new spiritual orientation, the devastation of the Earth will continue to lead to the devastation of religion and our souls."

                        THOMAS BERRY

"PRAYER FOR THE HEALING OF THE EARTH

We join with the earth and with each other.

To bring new life to the land
To restore the waters
To refresh the air
      We join with the earth and with each other.

To renew the forests
To care for the plants
To protect the creatures
      We join with the earth and with each other.

To celebrate the seas
To rejoice in the sunlight
To sing the song of the stars
      We join with the earth and with each other.

To recreate the human community
To promote justice and peace
To remember our children
      We join with the earth and with each other.

We join together as many and diverse expressions
of one loving mystery for the healing of the
earth and the renewal of all life."

      U. N. ENVIRONMENTAL SABBATH
      PROGRAM

"*W*hen the Copernican Revolution superseded the ancient Ptolemaic worldview, the earth took its rightful place as one planet among many. Man was no longer the center of the universe and though his self-image was deflated, he grew in maturity. In the same way, we must take our rightful place in nature -- not as its self-centered and profligate 'master' with the divine right of kings of exploit and despoil, but as one species living in harmony with the whole."

R. D. LAING

"*H*ere is calm so deep, grasses cease waving . . . wonderful how completely everything in wild nature fits into us, as if truly part and parent of us. The rivers flow not past, but through us, thrilling, tingling, vibrating every fiber and cell of the substance of our bodies, making them glide and sing."

JOHN MUIR

E. *I*NTERCONNECTEDNESS

"*W*e know ourselves to be made from this earth.
We know this earth is made from our bodies.
For we see ourselves. And we are nature.
We are nature seeing nature.
We are nature with a concept of nature.
Nature weeping.
Nature speaking of nature to nature."

SUSAN GRIFFIN, *Women and Nature:*
The Roaring Inside Her

"Those who regard all things as one are companions of nature."
CHUANG TZU

"Every form of life, every form of consciousness is conditioned and depends on the totality of all that exists or ever came into existence. The more that we become conscious of this infinite interrelationship, the freer we become because we liberate ourselves from the illusion of separation."
LAMA ANAGARIKA GOVINDA, *Creative Meditation and Multi-Dimensional Consciousness*

"The deep ecology sense of self-realization goes beyond the modern Western sense of 'self' as an isolated ego striving for hedonistic gratification. . . . Self, in this sense, is experienced as integrated with the whole of Nature."
GEORGE SESSIONS AND BILL DEVALL, *Deep Ecology: Living as if Nature Mattered*

"We must ask how we relate to the rest of the universe? -- to the tiniest neutron and proton as well as to the whirling, whistling, ranting galaxies light years in advance of our own. ... [N]othing is trivial for nothing is unconnected to the whole. All is a source of awe, wonder, wisdom, and the presence of the divine. All is a revelation; all is unfinished. ..."
MATTHEW FOX, *The Coming of the Cosmic Christ*

"*What* man most passionately wants is living wholeness and his living unison, not an isolated salvation of his soul. I am part of the sun as my eye is part of me. That I am part of the earth, my feet know perfectly well, and my blood is part of the sea. There is no thing of me that is alone and absolute except my mind, and we shall find that the mind has no existence by itself. It is only the glitter of the sun on the surfaces of the waters."

D. H. LAWRENCE, *The Apocalypse*

"*Any* particular activity upon the earth must take its norm from the principles governing the total community."

THOMAS BERRY, "*Our Children: Their Future*"

"*In* all the universe around us, and in the secret regions of our own secret hearts, instinct everywhere pervades: profound unlearned impulsions giving guidance to the lives of ants and birds and beasts and men and all the creatures of the earth."

ALAN DEVOE, *Lives Around Us*

"*All* things by immortal power
Near or far
Hiddenly
To each other linked are,
That thou canst not stir a flower
Without troubling a star."

FRANCES THOMPSON, *The Mistress of Vision*

"[Ma]n will come to see that the world is the perennial miracle which the soul worketh, and be less astonished at particular wonders; he will learn that there is no profane history; that all history is sacred; that the universe is represented in an atom, in a moment of time."

RALPH WALDO EMERSON, *Essays*

"The Earth does not belong to man; man belongs to the Earth. All things are connected like the blood which unites one's family. All things are connected. Whatever befalls the Earth befalls the sons of the Earth. Man did not weave the web of life: he is merely a strand in it. Whatever he does to the web, he does to himself."

CHIEF SEATTLE

"Molecules don't have passports. All the creatures on Earth are in this together. We need a primary allegiance to the species and to the planet Earth."

CARL SAGAN

"To enlist ourselves in the struggle for the liberation of any of God's creation eventually renders us vulnerable to the struggle for the liberation of all creation. For compassion means, as the mystics have always known and as contemporary science is finding out, that 'all things are interdependent,' in Eckhart's words, and 'all things are penetrated with connectedness,' as Hildegard of Bingen said. Compassion is the working out of our interconnectedness; it is the praxis of interconnectedness."

MATTHEW FOX, *Creation Spirituality: Liberating Gifts for the Peoples of the Earth*

"Perfection of rhythm, <u>balanced</u> perfection of rhythm. Everything in Nature is expressed by rhythmic waves of light. Every thought and action is a light-wave of thought and action. If one interprets the God within one, one's thoughts and actions must be balanced rhythmic waves. Ugliness, fears, failures and diseases arise from unbalanced thoughts and actions. Therefore think beauty always if one desires vitality of body and happiness."

WALTER RUSSELL

"[The body does not consist of one member but of many. If the foot should say, 'Because I am not a hand, I do not belong to the body,' that would not make it any less a part of the body. And if the ear should say, 'Because I am not an eye, I do not belong to the body,' that would not make it any less a part of the body. If the whole body were an eye, where would be the hearing? If the whole body were an ear, where would be the sense of smell? But as it is, God arranged the organs in the body, each one of them, as he chose. If all were a single organ, where would the body be? As it is, there are many parts, yet one body. The eye cannot say to the hand, 'I have no need of you,' nor again the head to the feet, 'I have no need of you.' On the contrary, the parts of the body which seem to be weaker are indispensable, and those parts of the body which we think less honorable we invest with the greater honor, and our unpresentable parts are treated with greater modesty, which our more presentable parts do not require. But God has so composed the body, giving the greater honor to the inferior, that there may be no discord in the body, but that the members may have the same care for one another. If one member suffers, all suffer together; if one member is honored, all rejoice together."

I CORINTHIANS 12:14-26

"The great calling of our time that is worthy of men and women is to hold each other within our hearts, and to conspire to create a hearth within the earth household.

These three live or die together: The Heart. The Hearth. The Earth."

SAM KEEN, *Fire in the Belly: On Being a Man*

"Destiny itself is like a wonderful wide tapestry in which every thread is guided by an unspeakably tender hand, placed beside another thread, and held and carried by a hundred others."

RAINER MARIA RILKE, *Letters To A Young Poet*

"The awakening to our true self is the awakening to that entirety, breaking out of the prison-self separate ego. The one who perceives this is the bodhisattva -- and we all are bodhisattvas because we are all capable of experiencing that -- it is our true nature. We are profoundly interconnected and therefore we are all able to recognize and act upon our deep, intricate, and intimate inter-existence with each other and all beings. That true nature of ours is already present in our pain for the world."

JOANNA MACY, *"The Greening of the Self"*

"Everything depends on others for survival and nothing really exists apart from everything else. Therefore, there is no permanent self or entity independent of others. Not only are we interdependent, but we are an interrelated whole. As trees, rocks, clouds, insects, humans and animals, we are all equals and part of our universe."

SAMU SUNIM, *"Responding to the Global Crisis"*

"The heroic quest is not about power over, about conquest and domination; it is a quest to bring balance into our lives through the marriage of both feminine and masculine aspects of our nature. . . . [The modern-day heroine] brings us wisdom about the innerconnectedness of all species; she teaches us how to live together in this global vessel and helps us to reclaim the feminine in our lives."

MAUREEN   MURDOCK,   The
Heroine's Journey

"To be of the Earth is to know
the restlessness of being a seed
the darkness of being planted
the struggle toward the light
the path of growth into the light
the joy of bursting and bearing fruit
the love of being food for someone
the scattering of your seeds
the decay of the seasons
the mystery of death
and the miracle of birth."

JOHN SOOS

"When you walk across the fields with your mind pure and holy, then from all the stones, and all growing things, and all animals, the sparks of their soul come out and cling to you, and then they are purified and become a holy fire in you."

HASIDIC SAYING

"You cannot move a flower without troubling a star."

FRANCIS THOMPSON

"*Our* bodies are . . . communities in relationship with the earth. Our bodily fluids carry the same chemicals as the primeval seas. . . . Our bones contain the sugar that once flowed in the sap of now-fossilized trees. The nitrogen which binds our bones together is the same as that which binds nitrates to the soil."

JAMES M. NELSON, *Between Two Gardens*

"*In* a sense, human flesh is made out of stardust. Every atom in the human body, excluding only the primordial hydrogen atoms, was fashioned in stars that formed, grew old and exploded most violently before the Sun and Earth came into being."

NIGEL CALDER

"*The* universe is a Unity, an interacting and genetically related community of beings bound together in an inseparable relationship in space and time. The Unity of the planet earth is especially clear; each being of the planet is profoundly implicated in the existence and functioning of every other being of the planet."

THOMAS BERRY

F. FRUITS OF THE EARTH

"The first man who having enclosed a piece of ground, bethought himself of saying <u>This is mine</u>, and found people simple enough to believe him, was the real founder of civil society. From how many crimes, wars and murders, from how many horrors and misfortunes might not anyone have saved mankind, by pulling up the stakes, or filling up the ditches, and crying to his fellows, 'Beware of listening to this imposter; you are undone if you once forget that the fruits of the earth belong to us all, and the earth itself to nobody.'"

> JEAN JAQUES ROUSSEAU, <u>*Dissertation on the Origin and Foundation of the Inequality of Mankind*</u>

"We not only live on the earth but also are of the earth, and the thought of its death, or even of its mutilation, touches a deep chord in our nature."
> JONATHAN SCHELL, <u>*The Fate of the Earth*</u>

"Beauty is all about us, but how many are blind to it! People take little pleasure in the natural and quiet and simple things of life."
> PABLO CASALS, <u>*Joys and Sorrows*</u>

G. Mother Earth

"For ancient people, nature was not just a treasure-trove of natural resources. Nature was a goddess, Mother Earth; the whole environment was divine."

ARNOLD TOYNBEE

"We see on Mother Earth the running streams,
We see the promise of her fruitfulness
Truly, her power she gives us.
Our thanks to Mother Earth!"

HAKO CEREMONY SONG OF THE
PAWNEE PEOPLE

"Oh Mother Earth, you are the earthly source of all existence. The fruits you bear are the source of life for all the Earth peoples. . . . May the steps we take in life upon you be sacred and not weak."

PRAYER OF THE OGLALA SIOUX

"We travel together, passengers on a little space ship, dependent on its vulnerable reserves of air and soil; all committed for our safety to its security and peace; preserved from annihilation only by the care, the work, and, I will say, the love we give our fragile craft. We cannot maintain it half fortunate, half miserable, half confident, half despairing, half slave -- to the ancient enemies of man -- half free in a liberation of resources undreamed of until this day. No craft, no crew can travel safely with such vast contradictions. On their resolution depends the survival of us all."

ADLAI E. STEVENSON, Speech to the Economic and Social Council of the United Nations, Geneva, Switzerland (July 9, 1965)

"A beautiful soul dwells always in a beautiful world."

RALPH WALDO EMERSON, Society and Solitude

"A renaissance is taking place among Native American peoples. This renaissance is not of a material nature. It is a spiritual renaissance, a retrieving and reviving of our original covenant with the Creator. We are reaffirming our relationship and stewardship with our Mother the Earth. . . ."

EDDIE BENTON-BANAI (Ojibway Indian)

"To the trustee, the earth -- Mother Earth -- is a beloved friend. His abiding desire is to adorn her with all the things she loves: trees, clean water, a rich topsoil, and all she needs for countless generations of healthy, secure children. Such a person stands at the crown of life, a protector and safe refuge for all that lives. Is there a nobler goal for humanity to strive for?"

> EKNATH EASWARAN, *The Compassionate Universe: The Power of the Individual to Heal the Environment*

H. REVERENCE

"[E]very form of life is unique, warranting respect regardless of worth to man, and, to accord other organisms such recognition, man must be guided by a moral code of action."

> THE UNITED NATIONS WORLD CHARTER FOR NATURE, *Adopted by the General Assembly of the United Nations (1982)*

"[C]herish our fragile world as we do our children and our grandchildren."

> CARL SAGAN, *"Nuclear War and Climatic Catastrophe," The Long Darkness: Psychological and Moral Perspectives on Nuclear Winter*

"*U*ltimately, the decision to save the environment must come from the human heart. The key point is a call for a genuine sense of universal responsibility that is based on love, compassion and clear awareness."

TENZIN GYATSO, 14TH DALAI LAMA OF TIBET, *Humanity and Ecology*

"*T*here is as yet no ethic dealing with man's relation to land and to the animals and plants that grow upon it. . . . [Such] a 'land ethic' changes the role of <u>Homo sapiens</u> from conqueror of the land-community to plain member and citizen of it. It implies respect for his fellow-members, and also respect for the community as such. . . . No important change in ethics was ever accomplished without an internal change in our intellectual emphases, loyalties, affections and convictions."

ALDO   LEOPOLD, *A   Sand County Almanac*

"*W*hatever I dig from thee, Earth, may that have quick growth again. Oh purifier, may we not injure thy vitals or thy heart."

HYMN TO THE EARTH, *Atharva Veda (3000 B.C.)*

"*I*njury to the earth is like striking, cutting, maiming, or killing a blind man. . . . He who understands the nature of sin against the earth is called a true sage."

ACARANGA SUTRA

"Every part of this earth is sacred to my people. Every shining pine needle, every sandy shore, every mist in the deep woods, every clearing and humming insect is holy in the memory and experience of my people. The sap which courses through the trees carries the memory of the red man."

>   CHIEF SEATTLE, *"The Great Chief Sends
>   Word," Chief Seattle's Testament*

"Humanity has reached the biological point where it must either lose all belief in the universe or quite resolutely worship it. This is where we must look for the origin of the present crisis in morality. . . . Henceforth the world will only kneel before the organic centre of its evolution."

>   PIERRE TEILHARD de CHARDIN, *Human Energy*

"The truly wise person kneels at the feet of all creatures and is not afraid to endure the mockery of others."

>   MECHTILD OF MAGDEBURG

"They [the people] will think of Nature as 'something to go out and look at.' They will try to live wholly apart from her and forget they're her sons. Forget? They will even deny it, and declare themselves sons of God. In spite of her wonders they will regard Nature as somehow too humble to be the true parent of such prominent people as simians. They will lose all respect for the dignity of fair Mother Earth, and whisper to each other she is an evil and indecent old person. They will snatch at her gifts, pry irreverently into her mysteries, and ignore half the warnings they get from her about how to live."

>   CLARENCE SHEPARD DAY, JR.,
>   *This Simian World*

"*A* day will come when, after making progress upon progress, man will succumb, destroyed by the excess of what he calls civilization. Too eager to play the god, he cannot hope for the animal's placid longevity; he will have disappeared when the little Toad is still saying his litany, in company with the Grasshopper, the Scops-Owl and the others. They were singing on this planet before us; they will sing after us, celebrating what can never change, the fiery glory of the sun."

JEAN HENRI FABRE, *The Wonders of Instinct*

". . . *If* the world can no longer afford the luxury of natural beauty, then it will soon be overcome and destroyed by its own ugliness. I myself feel deeply that the fate of Man, and his dignity, are at stake whenever the earth's natural splendors are threatened with extinction. . . . We are forever condemned to be part of a mystery that neither logic nor imagination can fathom, and your presence among us carries a resonance that cannot be accounted for in terms of science or reason, but only in terms of awe, wonder, and reverence. You are our last innocence."

ROMAIN GARY, "*A Love Letter to an Old Companion*"

"*R*everence is engaging in a form and a depth of contact with Life that is well beyond the shell of form and into essence. Reverence is contact with the essence of each thing and person and plant and bird and animal. It is contact with the interior of its beingness. Even if you cannot sense the interior, it is enough to know that the form, the shell, is merely an outer layer, and that underneath it the true power and essence of who a person is, or what a thing is, is present. That is what is honored in reverence. . . .

Reverence is . . . the experience of accepting that all Life is, in and of itself, of value."

GARY ZUKAV, *The Seat of the Soul*

"In our way of life, in our government, with every decision we make, we always keep in mind the Seventh Generation to come. It's our job to see that the people coming ahead, the generations still unborn, have a world no worse than ours - and hopefully better. When we walk upon Mother Earth we always plant our feet carefully because we know the faces of our future generations are looking up at us from beneath the ground. We never forget them."

CHIEF OREN LYONS *(Onondaga Indian)*

"All life is <u>wakan</u>. So also is everything which exhibits power, whether in action, as the winds and drifting clouds or in passive endurance, as the boulder by the wayside. For even the commonest sticks and stones have a spiritual essence which must be reverenced as a manifestation of the all-pervading mysterious power that fills the universe."

PRAIRIE OSAGE SAYING

"[O]nly if one loves this Earth with unending passion can one release one's sadness. A warrior is always joyful because his love is unalterable and his beloved, the Earth, bestows upon him inconceivable gifts. Only the love for this splendorous being can give freedom to a warrior's spirit; and freedom is joy, efficiency, an abandon in the face of any odds."

CARLOS CASTANEDA, *Tales of Power (Don Juan)*

"Those who have the humility of a child may find again the key to reverence for, and kinship with, all of life."

J. ALLEN BOONE

"The care of rivers is not a question of rivers, but of the human heart."

TANAKA SHOZO

"This Earth has become a paradise,
   an honored place in the order of creation.
God's love is on this Earth,
   and the heavens forever bend over to greet Her."
GHALIB

I. GIFT OF LIFE

"[I]n our origins we are all poor, all born naked and dependent on others, all born gratuitously into this vast cosmic dance; not one of us has earned it. When we suffer, if all are not saved, none of us is saved, and the gift cannot go on being given."

MATTHEW FOX, *Creation Spirituality:*
Liberating Gifts for the Peoples of the
Earth

"We belong to the ground.
It is our power
And we must stay close to it
or maybe we will get lost."

NARRITJIN MAYMURU YIRRKALA,
Australian Aborigine

"The miracle is not to fly in the air, or to walk on the water, but to walk on the earth."
CHINESE PROVERB

IV.

$\mathscr{A}$RK OF PEACE

"$\mathscr{A}$nd ye shall judge among the nations, and ye shall rebuke many people: and they shall beat their swords into ploughshares, and their spears into pruninghooks: nations shall not lift up sword against nation, neither shall they learn war anymore."

ISAIAH 2:4.

A. OUTWARD PEACE

"With malice toward none; with charity for all; with firmness in the right, as God gives us to see the right, let us strive on to finish the work we are in; to bind up the nation's wounds; to care for him who shall have borne the battle, and for his widow, and his orphan -- to do all which may achieve and cherish a just, and a lasting peace, among ourselves, and with all nations."

> ABRAHAM LINCOLN, *Second Inaugural Address (March 4, 1865)*

"There will be no security in our world, no release from agonized intention, no genuine progress, no enduring peace, until, in Shelley's fine words, 'reason's voice, loud as the voice of nature, shall have walked the nations.'"

> RALPH J. BUNCHE

"We begin by touching our own essential natures, and then we open ourselves to friends, parents, and family. Eventually, we expand this feeling and share it with every living being, extending this openness to all of nature. . . . When we feel open to all existence, our relationships naturally become harmonious."

> TARTHANG TULKU, *Gesture of Balance*

"*Our* thinking must be world-wide. . . . There can be no peace for any part of the world unless the foundations of peace are made secure throughout all parts of the world."

WENDELL WILLKIE, *One World*

"*I* believe that our Great Maker is preparing the world, in His own good time, to become one nation, speaking one language, and when armies and navies will be no longer required."

ULYSSES SIMPSON GRANT

"*The* law of love and compassion for all living creatures is again a doctrine to which we are all too ready to pay lip-service. However, if it is to become a reality, it requires a process of education, a veritable mental renaissance. Once it has become a reality, national as well as international problems will fall into perspective and become easier to solve. Wars and conflicts, too, will then become a thing of the past, because wars begin in the minds of men, and in those minds love and compassion would have built the defenses of peace."

U THANT, *Speech in Toronto, Canada (1966)*

"*Freedom* to have a world which is permanently at peace will not come so easily. It is not a gift but an achievement, an achievement which each one of us must devoutly desire and earnestly seek to promote and continually pray for."

JOHN A. REDHEAD, *Putting Your Faith to Work*

"*Who* are the peacemakers?
So many are they -- the people of goodwill
Who act with compassion
And vision the oneness of life,
Whose hearts are open to the plight of others,
Who respond with wisdom to their needs.

And the paths to peace, where are they?
Wherever true service marks the way,
So easy to find, so hard to travel.

And when will peace come?
When real needs are met, only then.
For justice and trust set the pace
Of the human journey to peace,
Justice, trust and the spirit of unity,
These goals of the peacemakers
For peace through goodwill."

JAN NATION, "*Who Are the Peacemakers*"

B. *I*NNER PEACE

"*I*f every single soul upon the earth would solemnly vow that he would
let peace begin first in his own heart, in his own conscience and
consciousness, the dove of peace would flutter much more quickly and
much more freely over this benighted planet than anything that will ever
come from the efforts of nations at peace tables. . . ."

WESLEY LA VIOLETTE, *The Creative Light*

"*Peace* is a daily, a weekly, a monthly process, gradually changing opinions, slowly eroding old barriers, quietly building new structures."

> JOHN F. KENNEDY, *Speech to the United Nations General Assembly (September 20, 1963)*

"*Peace* can only last where human rights are respected, where the people are fed, and where individuals and nations are free. True peace with ourselves and with the world around us can only be achieved through the development of mental peace. . . . "

> TENZIN GYATSO, 14TH DALAI LAMA OF TIBET, *Nobel Peace Prize Lecture, Oslo, Norway (1989)*

"*Lord*, make me a channel of your peace.
Where there is hatred, let me bring love.
Where there is offense, forgiveness.
Where this is discord, reconciliation.
Where there is doubt, faith.
Where there is despair, hope.
Where there is sadness, joy.
Where there is darkness, your light.
If we give, we are made rich.
If we forget ourselves, we find peace.
If we forgive, we receive forgiveness.
If we die, we receive eternal resurrection.
Give us peace, Lord."

> ST. FRANCIS OF ASSISI, *Francis: Bible of the Poor*

"Peace is an awareness of reserves from beyond ourselves, so that our power is not so much in us as through us."
                    HARRY EMERSON FOSDICK

"We can never obtain peace in the world if we neglect the inner world and don't make peace with ourselves. World peace must develop out of inner peace. Without inner peace it is impossible to achieve world peace, external peace."
                    TENZIN GYATSO, 14TH DALAI LAMA OF TIBET

"There is a stream of compassionate wisdom of which we are all a part. From the flowing heart comes a great wisdom to which each of us is attuned. . . . So peace is alive within us as a seed, as a song. To call it forth is a practice of clear vision and clear speech. See the beauty and praise the beauty, and wisdom's stream shall flow abundantly in our heart."
                    DHYANI YWAHOO (Cherokee)

"Peace does not rest in charters and covenants alone. It lies in the hearts and minds of all people. And if it is cast out there, then no act, no pact, no treaty, no organization can hope to preserve it. . . . So let us not rest all our hopes on parchment and on paper. Let us strive to build . . . a desire for peace . . . in the hearts and minds of all . . . people."
                    JOHN F. KENNEDY, Speech to the United Nations General Assembly (September 20, 1963)

"*If* ever there is truly peace on earth, goodwill to men, it will be because of women like Mother Teresa. Peace is not something you <u>wish</u> for; it's something you <u>make</u>, something you <u>do</u>, something you <u>are</u>, and something you <u>give away</u>!"

ROBERT FULGHUM, *All I Really Need to Know I Learned in Kindergarten*

"*We* can say 'Peace on Earth,' we can sing about it, preach about it, or pray about it, but if we have not internalized the mythology to make it happen inside of us, then it will not be."

BETTY SHABAZZ

"[*T*]here can never be peace between nations until there is first known that true peace which, as I have often said, is within the souls of men."

BLACK ELK *(Oglala Sioux)*

"*If* we are to create a peaceful world in the future we must begin with the experience of inner peace, the experience of God. God is not somewhere else; we are God. We are God and we are in God. It's simply a matter of acceptance."

BABA HARI DASS, *"God is Peace"*

"*Together* with material development, we need spiritual development so that inner peace and social harmony can be experienced. Without inner peace, without inner calm, it is difficult to have lasting external peace."

TENZIN GYATSO, 14TH DALAI LAMA OF TIBET

C. SANCTITY OF LIFE

"The ultimate end of all revolutionary social change is to establish the sanctity of human life, the dignity of man, the right of every human being to liberty and well-being."

EMMA GOLDMAN, *My Further Disillusion*

"You can't make any kind of laws or system to control nature or to control man's inner nature, his consciousness or his natural behavior -- the way he thinks and feels. That cannot be controlled. No individual or group can block another individual's path or change it against what fits his nature and his purpose. . . . Nature is sovereign and man's inner nature is sovereign. Nature is to be respected. All life and every single living being is to be respected. . . ."

ROLLING THUNDER

"[E]very creature is a word of God, and a book about God."

MEISTER ECKHART

"Now let me say that the next thing we must be concerned about if we are to have peace on earth and good will toward men is the nonviolent affirmation of the sacredness of all human life. Every man is somebody because he is a child of God."

MARTIN LUTHER KING, JR.

"The great fault of ethics hitherto has been that they believed themselves to have to deal only with the relations of man to man. In reality, however, the question is what is his attitude to the world and all life that comes within his reach. A man is ethical only when life, as such, is sacred to him, and that of plants and animals as that of his fellow men, and when he devotes himself helpfully to all life that is in need of help. Only the universal ethic of the feeling of responsibility in an ever-widening sphere for all that lives -- only that ethic can be founded in thought. . . The ethic of Reverence for Life, therefore, comprehends within itself everything that can be described as love, devotion, and sympathy whether in suffering, joy or effort."

ALBERT SCHWEITZER, *Out of My Life and Thought*

D. Non-Violence

"Non-violence is not a garment to be put on and off at will. Its seat is in the heart, and it must be an inseparable part of our very being."

MOHANDAS K. (MAHATMA) GANDHI, *Non-Violence in Peace and War*

"Non-violence is a powerful and just weapon. It is a weapon unique in history, which cuts without wounding and ennobles the man who wields it. It is a sword that heals."

MARTIN LUTHER KING, JR.

"*I* have learnt through bitter experience the one supreme lesson: to conserve my anger, and as heat conserved is transmuted into energy, even so our anger controlled can be transmuted into a power which can move the world."

MOHANDAS K. (MAHATMA) GANDHI

E. *R*EVERENCE FOR LIFE

"*R*everence for human suffering and human life, for the smallest and most insignificant, must be the inviolable law to rule the world from now on. In so doing, we do not replace old slogans with new ones and imagine that some good may come out of high-sounding speeches and pronouncements. We must recognize that a deep-seated change of heart, spreading from one man to another, can achieve such a thing in this world."

ALBERT SCHWEITZER, *Reverence for Life*

"*G*od started his show a good many millions years before he had any men for audience. . . . and . . . it is just barely possible that God himself likes to hear birds sing and see flowers grow."

ALDO LEOPOLD, *Some Fundamentals of Conservatism*

"[*M*]an will never be at peace with his own kind until he has recognized the . . . ethic that embraces decent consideration for all creatures -- a true reverence for life."

RACHEL CARSON, *Silent Spring*

"Anyone who is intending to claim his own right to walk the path of peace must take also his share of the heavy burden of trying to build a world in which the gentler forces of kindness, love, sympathy and co-operation are put into function."

RUFUS JONES, *The Faith and Practice of the Quakers*

"Reverence for life is more than solicitude or sensitivity for life. It is a sense of the whole, a capacity for inspired response, a respect for the intricate universe of individual life. It is the supreme awareness of awareness itself."

NORMAN COUSINS, *The Courage of Conviction*

F. FELLOW CREATURES

"True happiness comes not from a limited concern for one's own well-being, or that of those one feels close to, but from developing love and compassion for all sentient beings. Here, love means wishing that all sentient beings should find happiness, and compassion means wishing that they should all be free from suffering. The development of this attitude gives rise to a sense of openness and trust that provides the basis for peace."

TENZIN GYATSO, 14TH DALAI LAMA OF TIBET, *Universal Responsibilities and Human Rights*

". . . Only that kind of love for animals is beautiful and edifying which arises from the broader and more general love of the whole world of living creatures, a love whose most important and central feature must always be the love of mankind. . . ."

KONRAD Z. LORENZ, *Man Meets Dog*

"It is an absolute mercy and a complete bounty, the illumination of the world, fellowship and harmony, love and union; nay, rather, mercifulness and oneness, the elimination of discord and the unity of whosoever are on earth in the utmost of freedom and dignity. The Blessed Beauty said: 'All are the fruits of one tree and the leaves of one branch.' . . . They must purify their sight . . . and must always be thinking of doing good to someone, of love, consideration, affection and assistance to somebody. They must see no enemy and count no one as an ill wisher. They must consider everyone on the earth as a friend; regard the stranger as an intimate, and the alien as a companion. . . . These are the commands of the Blessed Beauty, these are the counsels of the Greatest Name. . . . The herald of peace, reformation, love and reconciliation is the Religion of the Blessed Beauty."

BAHA'U'LLAH OF PERSIA, *Selected Writings of Baha'u'llah and 'Abdu'l-Baha*

"I look upon all creatures equally; none are less dear to me and none more dear. But those who worship me with love live in me, and I come to life in them."

BHAGAVAD-GITA

"Every single creature has, in human nature, a stake in the eternal."

MEISTER ECKHART

"Today it is thought an exaggeration to state that a reasonable ethic demands constant consideration for all living things down to the lowliest manifestations of life. The time is coming, however, when people will be amazed that it took so long for mankind to recognize that thoughtless injury to life was incompatible with ethics."

ALBERT SCHWEITZER, *The Animal World of Albert Schweitzer*

G. End TO WAR

"One day the people of the world will want peace so much that the governments are going to have to get out of their way and let them have it."

PRESIDENT DWIGHT D. EISENHOWER

"If you have a nation of men who have risen to that height of moral cultivation that they will not declare war or carry arms, for they have not so much madness left in their brains, you have a nation of lovers, of benefactors, of true, great, and able men."

RALPH WALDO EMERSON, "War," *Miscellanies*

"We cannot accept the doctrine that war must be forever a part of man's destiny."

FRANKLIN D. ROOSEVELT, *Campaign Speech in Cleveland, Ohio (November 2, 1940)*

"What difference does it make to the dead, the orphans and the homeless, whether the mad destruction is wrought under the name of totalitarianism or the holy name of liberty or democracy?"

> MOHANDAS   K.   (MAHATMA) GANDHI, *Non-Violence in Peace and War*

"Let us call a truce to terror. Let us invoke the blessings of peace. And, as we build an international capacity to keep peace, let us join in dismantling the national capacity to wage war."

> JOHN F. KENNEDY, *Speech to the United Nations General Assembly (September 25, 1961)*

"I believe without a shadow of doubt that science and peace will finally triumph over ignorance and war, that the nations of the earth will ultimately agree not to destroy but to build up."

> LOUIS PASTEUR

"[P]erhaps the great day will come when a people, distinguished by wars and victories and by the highest development of a military order and intelligence, and accustomed to make the heaviest sacrifice for these things, will exclaim of its own free will, 'We break the sword,' and will smash its military establishment down to its lowest foundations. Rendering oneself unarmed when one has been the best armed, out of a height of feeling -- that is the means to real peace, which must always rest upon a peace of mind. . . ."

> NIETZSCHE

"The sword will always be conquered by the spirit."

> NAPOLEON BONAPARTE

V.

Communion

"*We* must not forget that the human soul, however independently created our philosophy represents it as being, is inseparable, in its birth and in its growth, from the universe into which it was born."

PIERRE TEILHARD de CHARDIN,
The Divine Milieu

A. ONE FAMILY

"The strongest bond of human sympathy outside the family relation should be one uniting all working people of all nations and tongues and kindreds."

ABRAHAM LINCOLN, *Letter to New York Workingman's Association (March 21, 1864)*

"The realization that we are all basically the same human beings, who seek happiness and try to avoid suffering, is very helpful in developing a sense of brotherhood and sisterhood -- a warm feeling of love and compassion for others. This, in turn, is essential if we are to survive in this ever-shrinking world we live in. For if we each selfishly pursue only what we believe to be in our own interests, without caring about the needs of others, we not only may end up harming others but also ourselves. . . . As individuals and nations are becoming increasingly interdependent we have no other choice than to develop what I call a sense of universal responsibility.

Today, we are truly a global family. What happens in one part of the world may affect us all. . . ."

TENZIN GYATSO, 14TH DALAI LAMA OF TIBET, *Nobel Peace Prize Lecture, Oslo, Norway (1989)*

"*S*urely it is not too idealistic to imagine a future global commonwealth in which each of Earth's citizens has a reasonable chance to create through his or her own efforts a decent life for self and family; in which men and women live in harmony with the Earth and its creatures, cooperating to create and maintain a wholesome environment for all; in which there is an ecology of different cultures, the diversity of which is appreciated and supported; in which war and flagrant violation of human rights in the name of the state has no legitimacy anywhere, and there is universal support of the rule of law throughout the world; in which throughout the entire human family there is a deep and shared sense of meaning in life itself."

WILLIS HARMAN, *Global Mind Change*

"*M*an is a Worm worried with joy he seeks the caves of sleep
Among the Flowers of Beulah in his Selfish cold repose
Forsaking Brotherhood & Universal love in selfish clay
Folding the pure wings of his mind seeking the places dark
Abstracted from the roots of Science then inclosd around
In Walls of Gold we cast him like a Seed into the Earth
Till times & spaces have passd over him duly every morn
We visit him covering with a Veil the immortal seed
With windows from the inclement sky we cover him & with
    walls
And hearths protect the selfish terror till divided all
In families we see our shadows born & thence we know
That Man subsists by Brotherhood & Universal Love
We fall on one anothers necks more closely we embrace
Not for ourselves but for the Eternal family we live
Man liveth not by Self alone but in his brother's face
Each shall behold the Eternal Father & love & joy abound."

WILLIAM BLAKE, *The Four Zoas: The Torments of Love & Jealousy in the Death and Judgment of Albion the Ancient Man*

"*We* are struck by the important difference between the way cartographers make our planet and the way it can be seen, given the perspective of the universe. There are no boundaries on the real planet Earth. No United States, no Soviet Union, no China, Taiwan, East Germany or West. Rivers flow unimpeded across the swaths of continents. The persistent tides -- the pulse of the sea -- do not discriminate; they push against all the varied shores on earth."

JACQUES   COUSTEAU, *The Cousteau Almanac*

"*The* vision of an emergent planetary culture involves the broadening and deepening of our individual and collective perspectives and assumptions so that we embrace ourselves as a species, as humankind, rather than as separate factions. It involves, moreover, seeing ourselves as sensitive, interdependent members of a community of life that transcends the human and embraces the whole of planetary ecology, including the Earth itself as a living being."

DAVID SPANGLER, *Revelations: The Birth of a New Age*

"*See* the world with global eyes.
Love the world with a global heart.
Understand the world with a global mind.
Merge with the world through a global spirit."

ROBERT MULLER, *A Planet of Hope*

"Perhaps the great renewal of the world will consist of this, that man and woman, freed of all confused feelings and desires, shall no longer seek each other as opposites, but simply as members of a family and neighbors, and will unite as human beings, in order to simply, earnestly, patiently, and jointly bear the heavy responsibility . . . that has been entrusted to them."

RAINER MARIA RILKE, *Letters To A Young Poet*

"The expansion of human power has hardly begun, and what we are going to do with our power may either save or destroy our planet. The earth may be of small significance within the infinite universe. But if it is of some significance, we hold the key to it. In our own age we have been forced into the realization that there will be either one world, or no world."

ABRAHAM JOSHUA HESCHEL

B. Unity OF ALL

"What Christ is saying always, what he never swerves from saying, what he says a thousand times and in a thousand different ways, but always with a central unity of belief, is this: 'I am my father's son, and you are my brothers.' And the unity that binds us all together, that makes this earth a family, and all men brothers and so the sons of God, is love."

THOMAS WOLFE, "*The Anatomy of Loneliness,*" *American Mercury (October 1941)*

"What we are trying to do is help people live a life of contemplative stillness out of which enlightened action may come. . . . Communication means nothing if there is no communion."

> MOTHER TESSA BIELECKI,
> *Naropa Institute*

"Whenever I meet a 'foreigner' I have always the same feeling: 'I am meeting another member of the human family.' This attitude has deepened my affection and respect for all beings. May this natural wish be my small contribution to world peace. I pray for a more friendly, more caring, and more understanding human family on this planet. For all who dislike suffering, who cherish lasting happiness -- this is my heartfelt appeal."

> TENZIN GYATSO, 14TH DALAI
> LAMA OF TIBET, *A Human*
> *Approach to World Peace*

"There is enough creative light forever burning in each one of us, enough understanding, that if we all united in intelligence and power of mind, it would transform not only our barren lives, but that of everyone who willingly would share and bear his part."

> WESLEY LA VIOLETTE, *The*
> *Creative Light*

"If we are going to do justice to the lower races [i.e., animals], we must get rid of the antiquated notion of a 'gulf' fixed between them and mankind, and must recognize the common bond of humanity that unites all living beings in one universal brotherhood."

> HENRY S. SALT, *Animals' Rights*
> *Considered in Relation to Social*
> *Progress*

"The world, we are told, was made especially for man -- a presumption not supported by all the facts. . . . Why should man value himself as more than a small part of the one great unit of creation?"
JOHN MUIR

"The poet says the proper study of mankind is man. I say, study to forget all that; take wider views of the universe."

HENRY DAVID THOREAU, *The Writings of Henry Thoreau*

"One's small song -- 'I like, I dislike,' . . . -- creates dissonance with the large song. Today we are called to sing a unity song."
DHYANI YWAHOO, *The Voices of our Ancestors*

"For men upon earth, all the earth, to learn to love one another, it is not enough that they should know themselves to be members of one and the same thing; in 'planetising' themselves, they must acquire the consciousness, without losing themselves, of becoming one and the same person."
PIERRE TEILHARD de CHARDIN

"This time on earth is about putting into action our new understanding of our place in the cosmos. It is about practicing living in Oneness with all people. It is about bringing together the forces we hold in our hands, ones which could ultimately destroy us, but, if used wisely, can unite us. From the point of view of the person who thinks in terms of the past, it is a painful breakdown of the familiar. From the viewpoint of the aspiring soul, it is the herald of a new and better life, one of drawing together and sharing. It is a promise of friendship, mutual support, and community. It is the end of 'Them' which never existed, and the affirmation of an 'Us' that has always been."

ALAN COHEN, *The Dragon Doesn't Live Here Anymore*

"When in Eternity Man converses with Man they enter
Into each others Bosom (which are Universes of delight)
In mutual interchange. . . .
When Souls mingle & join thro all the Fibres of Brotherhood
Can there be any secret joy on Earth greater than this?"

WILLIAM BLAKE, *Jerusalem*

"Civilization will not last, freedom will not survive, peace will not be kept, unless a very large majority of mankind unite together to defend them and show themselves possessed of a constabulary power before which barbaric and atavistic forces will stand in awe."

WINSTON CHURCHILL

"From my own unforgettable experience I know very well that there is a state in which the bonds of the personal nature of life seem to have fallen away from us and we experience an undivided unity."

MARTIN BUBER, *Between Man and Man*

"No man is an Iland, intire of it selfe. . . . every man is a peece of the Continent, a part of the maine; if a Clod bee washed away by the Sea, Europe is the lesse, as well as if a Promontorie were, as well as if a Mannor of thy friends or of thine own were; any man's death diminishes me, because I am involved in Mankinde; And therefore never send to know for whom the bell tolls; It tolls for thee."

JOHN DONNE, *Devotions Upon Emergent Occasions*

"Until you have become really, in actual fact, as brother of every one, brotherhood will not come to pass."

FYODOR DOSTOYEVSKI, *The Brothers Karamazov*

"I do not believe . . . that an individual may gain spiritually while those who surround him suffer. I believe in advita, I believe in the essential unity of man and for that matter, of all that lives. Therefore, I believe that if one man gains spiritually, the whole world gains with him and if one man falls the whole world falls to that extent."

MOHANDAS K. (MAHATMA) GANDHI

"To see a World in a Grain of Sand
And a Heaven in a Wild Flower,
Hold Infinity in the palm of your hand
And Eternity in an hour."

WILLIAM BLAKE, *Auguries of Innocence*

"[O]ur consciousness, rising above the growing (but still much too limited) circles of family, country and race, shall finally discover that the only truly natural and real human unity is the spirit of the earth."

PIERRE TEILHARD de CHARDIN,
Human Energy

"Gandhi held to the Buddhist and Jain view that all sins are modifications of himsa, that the basic sin, the only sin in the ultimate analysis, is the sin of separateness, or attavada. According to a Jain maxim, he who conquers this sin conquers all others."

RAGHAVAN IYER, *The Moral and Political Thought of Mahatma Gandhi*

"I am a part and parcel of the whole, and I cannot find God apart from the rest of humanity."

MOHANDAS K. (MAHATMA) GANDHI

"Awakening to the cosmic/earth/human process whereby all things have a genetic relationship with each other is the most significant intellectual achievement of humankind since the higher civilization came into being some 2500 years ago. Nothing can be itself without being in communion with everything else, nor can anything truly be the other without first acquiring a capacity for interior presence to itself."

THOMAS BERRY, "*Contemplation and World Order*"

"[T]he heart in thee is the heart of all; not a valve, not a wall, not an intersection is there anywhere in nature, but one blood rolls uninterruptedly, an endless circulation, through all men, as the water of the globe is all one sea, and, truly seen, its tide is one."

RALPH WALDO EMERSON, *Essays*

"A human being is part of the whole, called by us 'Universe'; a part limited in time and space. He experiences himself, his thoughts, and feelings as something separated from the rest -- a kind of optical delusion of his consciousness. This delusion is a kind of prison for us, restricting us to our personal desires and to affection for a few persons nearest to us.

Our task must be to free ourselves from this prison by widening our circle of compassion to embrace all living creatures, and the whole of nature in its beauty."

ALBERT EINSTEIN

"When you meet anyone, remember it is a holy encounter. As you see him you will see yourself. As you treat him you will treat yourself. As you think of him you will think of yourself. Never forget this, for in him you will find yourself or lose yourself. Whenever two Sons of God meet, they are given another chance at salvation. Do not leave anyone without giving salvation to him and receiving it yourself."

A COURSE IN MIRACLES

"I do not see a delegation
For the Four-footed.
I see no seat for the eagles.

We forget and we consider
Ourselves superior.

But we are after all
A mere part of the Creation.

And we must consider
To understand where we are.

And we stand somewhere between
The mountain and the Ant.

Somewhere and only there
As part and parcel
Of the Creation."

CHIEF OREN LYONS (Onondaga Indian),
Address to the Non-Governmental Organizations
of the United Nations, Geneva, Switzerland,
1977

"Wholeness, interconnectedness, unity -- these are central. We're recognizing that we've fragmented everything and that it doesn't work that way. We're alienated from our institutions, we're alienated from ourselves; . . . everything is divided up into separate departments and disciplines. And yet there's a wholeness underneath all of this, and we have got to get the wholeness back."

WILLIS HARMAN

"There is one universe, and modern understanding requires that all experience and knowledge be seen as a consistent part of the whole. Unity is possible because the reality is non-material and continuous and therefore universally present. That reality is the ultimate environment."

F. L. KUNZ, "The Reality of the Non-Material," *Nature, Man, and Society: Main Currents in Modern Thought*

"[H]umanity, perfectly unified yet preserving individual freedom, will constitute a new being for individual men, as man does for each of the cells of his body. This unified mankind must be regarded, from now on, not as a fiction nor even as an ideal, but as the inevitable reality toward which we are inexorably on the move. As soon as that future state is experienced by each one of us as an existential reality, it will become a true 'boundary condition' . . ."

JEAN E. CHARON, "Dissymmetry and the End of Time," *Nature, Man, and Society: Main Currents in Modern Thought*

"Nations beware:

people will form themselves into one humanity whatever you may think or do. No one can stop evolution."

ROBERT MULLER, *A Planet of Hope*

"*S*cience will not discover its true purpose until it is guided and controlled by an image of humanity huge enough in its conception, simple enough in its message and sense of unity, to satisfy the aspirations and needs of humanity as a whole."

WILLIAM ANDERSON, *Ancient Futures: Learning from Ladakh*

"*Y*ou never enjoy the world aright, till the sea itself flowest in your veins, till you are clothed with the heavens, and crowned with the stars; and perceive yourself to be the sole heir of the whole world, and more than so, because men are in it who are every one sole heirs as well as you. Till you can sing and rejoice and delight in God, as misers do in gold, and Kings in sceptres, you never enjoy the world."

THOMAS TRAHERNE

"*Th*e simple truth, which we have conspired to forget during the last century, is that the human species is an integral part of an incomprehensible unity of being in the process of becoming: a single organ in the body of Gaia; a cell through which universal history flows like fluid through a membrane; an Aeolian harp the spirit of life moves like the wind; a character within the dream of God; a citizen within the commonwealth of sentient beings."

SAM KEEN, *Fire in the Belly: On Being a Man*

"*L*ife need not be tragic. We can hope that what we do will make a difference, that we can build an earth from our fondest dreams and visions. Our purpose is to dedicate our lives to regenerating the earth and building a new human order. Our vision is to integrate ourselves with the larger web of life. Nature teaches us the lessons of simplicity, reverence, and unity. Therefore, let us build a world of recycling, renewable energy, non-exploitation, equity, sharing, and creative purposes."

RASHMI MAYUR

"*We* must learn anew to envisage the great, invisible solidarity of all living beings in universal life, of all minds in the eternal spirit -- and at the same time the mutual solidarity of the world process and the destiny of its supreme principle, and we must not just accept this world unity as a mere doctrine, but practice and promote it in our inner and outer lives."

MAX SCHELER

"*When* the boundaries of individual existence have been worn away, you and I, instead of being absolutely separate beings, are aspects of the same unity."

MILAREPA

"*What* we want is to reestablish the living organic connections, with the cosmos, the sun and earth, with mankind and nation and family."

D. H. LAWRENCE

"*Unless* we each find a way to chime in as one note in the organic whole, we shall only observe ourselves observing the interplay of its thousand components in a harmony outside our experience of it as harmony."

DAG HAMMARSKJOLD, <u>*Markings*</u>

"*As* is the inner, so is the outer;
as is the great, so is the small;
as it is above, so it is below;
there is but One Life and
Law: and he that worketh it
is ONE. Nothing is inner,
nothing is outer; nothing is
great, nothing is small;
nothing is high, nothing is
low, in the Divine Economy."

HERMETIC AXIOM

"In the ultimate depth of being, we find ourselves no longer separate but, rather, a part of the unity of the universe. That unity includes the sufferer and the suffering, and the healer and that which heals. Therefore, all acts of healing are ultimately ourselves healing our Self."

BABA RAM DASS

"[L]ife is no longer seen as an isolated phenomenon, briefly flaring up in what otherwise is a dying, entropy-filled universe, but as part of a whole living organism. Dissipative structures live or occur by allowing matter and energy to flow through them like the vortex in a stream of water. In this new vision the Infinite Endless Livingness is viewed as a flowing through everything, which is also 'Itself.' Man is both the flow and the flow-er, observer and observed, a wave within an infinite ocean. The cosmos begins to look more like an elaborate artwork as we live and flow as an ever transmuting order of creativity."

YATRI, *Unknown Man: The Mysterious Birth of a New Species*

"So we say deep down the consciousness of mankind is one. This is a virtual certainty because even in the vacuum, matter is one; and if we don't see this it is because we are blinding ourselves to it."

DAVID BOHM

"For man, the vast marvel is to be alive. For man, as for flower and beast and bird, the supreme triumph is to be most vividly, most perfectly alive. Whatever the unborn and dead may know, they cannot know the beauty, the marvel of being alive in the flesh. The dead may look after the afterwards. But the magnificent here and now of life in the flesh is ours, and ours alone and ours only for a time. We ought to dance with rapture that we should be alive and in the flesh, and part of the living incarnate cosmos. I am part of the sun as my eye is part of me. That I am part of the earth my feet know perfectly, and my blood is part of the sea. My soul knows that I am part of the human race, my soul is an organic part of the great human soul, as my spirit is part of my nation. In my very own self, I am part of my family. There is nothing of me that is alone and absolute except my mind, and we shall find that the mind has no existence by itself, it is only the glitter of the sun on the surface of the waters."

D. H. LAWRENCE, *Apocalypse*

"The Philosophy of Nature is the science of the eternal transformation of God into the world."

OKEN, *Lehrbuch der Naturphilosophie*

"Constantly remind yourself, 'I am a member of the whole body of conscious things.' If you think of yourself as a mere 'part,' then love for mankind will not well up in your heart; you will look for some reward in every act of kindness and miss the boon which the act itself is offering. Then all your work will be seen as a mere duty and not as the very porthole connecting you with the Universe itself."

MARCUS AURELIUS, *Meditations*

"Human unity is . . . a many stranded texture, with color and depth."

NORMAN COUSINS, *The Courage of Conviction*

"We must be still and still moving
Into another intensity
For a further union, a deeper communion. . . ."

DANAH ZOHAR, *The Quantum Self: Human Nature and Consciousness Defined by the New Physics*

"We live our lives inscrutably included within the streaming mutual life of the universe."

MARTIN BUBER, *I and Thou*

"Lead us from the individual to the Universal."

ALICE A. BAILEY, *Discipleship in the New Age*

"Look at a stream flowing from its source to the Ocean; it is an unbroken current, it is a complete whole. Yet the mind can conceive it as made up of an infinite number of drops of water, each perfect in itself, having individual identity, being a complete whole. And the mind can conceive each individual drop of water influenced as to its identity, modified as to its character, by the nature of the current, its rapidity, its slowness, its stagnation, and being clean or unclean according to the quality of the soil and land which contains the current and influences its course.

Look now at the Stream of the Soul of Humanity. It is likewise an unbroken whole flowing from the Unity and returning to the Unity; and this stream is formed of the Souls of Men; the drops of water, each possessed of identity and individuality, and clean or unclean according to the nature of the current around them, and the quality of the soil over which they pass and the influence exerted on them by the constraining land, the Phenomenal World through which the Stream of the Soul of Humanity passes and whose Law governs the progress of its flow."

HAJI IBRAHIM OF KERBELA, *The Mystic Rose from the Garden of the King*

C. CITIZENS OF WORLD

"Our true nationality is mankind."

H. G. WELLS, *The Outline of History*

"He who would not wish his own country to be bigger or smaller, richer or poorer, would be a citizen of the universe."

PATRIE VOLTAIRE, *Dictionnaire Philosophique*

"Our secret creative will divines its counterpart in others, experiencing its own universality."

DAG HAMMARSKJOLD, *Markings*

"We are at the dawn of an age in which extreme political concepts and dogmas may cease to dominate human affairs. We must use this historic opportunity to replace them by universal human and spiritual values and ensure that these values become the fiber of the global family which is emerging."

TENZIN GYATSO, 14TH DALAI LAMA OF TIBET, *Universal Responsibilities and Human Rights*

"It may be long before the law of love will be recognized in internal affairs. The machineries of governments stand between and hide the hearts of one people from those of another."

MOHANDAS   K.   (MAHATMA)
GANDHI

"It is almost a commonplace today to find people who, quite naturally and unaffectedly, live in the explicit consciousness of being an atom or a citizen of the universe. This collective awakening must inevitably have a profound religious reaction on the mass of mankind -- either to cast down or to exalt."

PIERRE TEILHARD de CHARDIN,
The Divine Milieu

"For I dipt into the future, far as human eye can see,
Saw the vision of the world, and all the wonder that would
    be,
Saw the heavens fill with commerce, argosies of magic sails,
Pilots of the purple twilight dropping down with costly
    bales. . . .
Heard the heavens filled with shouting, and there rained a
    ghastly dew
From the nation's airy navies grappling in the central blue.
    . . .
Far along the world wide whisper of the south wind rushing
    warm
With the standards of the peoples plunging through the
    thunder storm
Till the war drum throbbed no longer, and the battle flags
    were furled
In the parliament of man -- the federation of the world."
ALFRED, LORD TENNYSON

"*L*ove of one's country is a fine thing, but why should love stop at the border?"

PABLO CASALS

"*W*e must delight in one another, make others' conditions our own, rejoice together, mourn together, labor . . . together, always having before our eyes our community as members of the same body."

JOHN WINTHROP

"*W*e shall all be alike -- brothers of one father and one mother, with one sky above us and one country around us, and one government for all. Then the Great Spirit Chief who rules above will smile upon this land, and send rain to wash out the bloody spots from the face of the earth that were made by brothers' hands. . . ."

CHIEF JOSEPH (Nez Perce)

"*A*s you pass from sunlight into darkness and back again every hour and a half, you become startlingly aware how artificial are the thousands of boundaries we've created to separate and define. And for the first time in your life you feel in your gut the precious unity of the Earth and all the living things it supports. The dissonance between this unity you see and the separateness of human groupings that you know exists is starkly apparent."

RUSTY SCHWEICHART, *U.S.*
Astronaut, Lecture in Kyoto,
Japan (1982)

"One morning I woke up and decided to look out the window, to see where we were . . . I saw snow, the first snow we ever saw from orbit. Light and powdery, it blended with the contours of the land, with the veins of the rivers. I thought -- autumn, snow -- people are getting ready for winter. . . . I imagined that the arrival of autumn and winter is the same . . . in [all] places, and the process of getting ready for them is the same. And then it struck me that we are all children of our Earth. It does not matter what country you look at. We are all Earth's children, and we should treat her as our Mother."

ALEKSANDR   ALEKSANDROV,
Soviet Cosmonaut, The Home Planet

"To the wise man every land is eligible as a place of residence; for the whole world is the country of the worthy soul."
JOANNES STOBAEUS

"God grant that not only the love of liberty but a thorough knowledge of the rights of man may pervade all the nations of the earth, so that a philosopher may set his foot anywhere on its surface and say, 'This is my country.'"

BENJAMIN FRANKLIN, *Letter to David Hartley (December 4, 1789)*

"My country is the world; to do good is my religion."
THOMAS PAINE

D. $\mathscr{S}$OVEREIGNTY

"$\mathscr{T}$hus I am led to my first axiom: the quest of international security involves the unconditional surrender by every nation, in a certain measure, of its liberty of action, its sovereignty that is to say, and it is clear beyond all doubt that no other road can lead to such security."

> ALBERT EINSTEIN, *Letter to Dr. Freud (July 30, 1932). -- Published by The International Institute for Cultural Cooperation (1933)*

> "$\mathscr{I}$n our time, a secret manifesto is being written. It will not go out to the world as print on the page. No mass movement will ever raise it as a banner. Rather, its language is a longing we read in one another's eyes as the longing to know our authentic vocation in the world, to find the work and the way that belongs uniquely to each of us. And its authors, even if they should come to number millions, will never care to know themselves as an army on the march, but only as the few who can come together here and there in true companionship. I speak of the manifesto of the person, the declaration of our sovereign right to self-discovery."
>
> THEODORE ROSZAK

"$\mathscr{W}$hen the soul of a man is born in this country there are nets flung at it to hold it back from flight. You talk to me of nationality, language, religion. I shall try to fly by those nets."

> JAMES JOYCE, *A Portrait of the Artist as a Young Man*

E. RESPECT FOR DIVERSITY

"*So*, let us not be blind to our differences -- but let us also direct attention to our common interests and to the means by which those differences can be resolved. If we cannot end now our differences, at least we can help make the world safe for diversity."

JOHN F. KENNEDY, *Commencement Address at The American University (June 10, 1963)*

"*Only* a peace between equals can last. Only a peace the very principle of which is equality in a common participation in a common benefit."

WOODROW WILSON, *Speech to the U.S. Senate (January 22, 1917)*

"*Revolution* is not a one-time event. It is becoming always vigilant for the smallest opportunity to make a genuine change in established, outgrown responses; for instance, it is learning to address each other's difference with respect."

AUDRE LORDE

"*If* we cannot . . . end our differences, at least we can help make the world safe for diversity. For, in the final analysis our most basic common link is the fact that we all inhabit this planet. We all breathe the same air. We all cherish our children's future, and we are all mortal."

JOHN F. KENNEDY, *Speech at the American University, Washington, D.C. (June 10, 1963)*

F. INTERDEPENDENCY

"When will we learn, when will the people of the world get up and say, Enough is enough. God created us for fellowship. God created us so that we should form the human family, existing together because we were made for one another. We are not made for an exclusive self-sufficiency but for interdependence, and we break the law of our being at our peril."

                    DESMOND M. PILO TUTU

"Because we all share this small plant earth, we have to learn to live in harmony and peace with each other and with nature. It is not just a dream, but a necessity. We are dependent on each other in so many ways that we can no longer live in isolated communities and ignore what is happening outside those communities. We need to help each other when we have difficulties, and we must share the good fortune that we enjoy."

                    TENZIN GYATSO, 14TH DALAI
                    LAMA OF TIBET, *Nobel Peace
                    Prize Lecture, Oslo, Norway
                    (1989)*

"All ethics rest upon a single premise: that the individual is a member of a community of interdependent parts."

                    ALDO   LEOPOLD, *A Sand
                    County Almanac*

"[T]he whole idea of compassion is based on a keen awareness of the interdependence of all these living things, which are all part of one another and all involved in one another."

THOMAS MERTON, *A Vow of Conversation: Journals*

"We have begun to realize that our actions affect all people everywhere, and that the earth and all of her inhabitants are really one great living, breathing organism. This consciousness is a major breakthrough . . . -- it is our only hope for survival. We will survive only through our common identity, through our acknowledgement of our mutual selfhood. The highest good of each of us is the highest good of all; my success is the achievement of all, my pain is the hurt of all, and humanity's well-being is one with my own. . . ."

ALAN COHEN, *The Dragon Doesn't Live Here Anymore*

"All things are interdependent."

MEISTER ECKHART

"The immediate prospect for fragmented Western man encountering the electric implosion within his own culture is his steady and rapid transformation into a complex person. . . . emotionally aware of his total interdependence with the rest of human society. . . .

Might not the current translation of our entire lives into the spiritual form of information make of the entire globe, and of the human family, a single consciousness?"

MARSHALL   MCLUHAN, *Understanding Media*

"*We* are members of a vast cosmic orchestra in which each living instrument is essential to the complimentary and harmonious playing of the whole."

J. ALLEN BOONE, *Kinship With All Life*

"*Our* prophets have sought it. Our poets have dreamed of it. But it is only in our own day that astronomers, physicists, geologists, chemists, biologists, anthropologists, ethnologists, and archaeologists have all combined in a single witness of advanced science to tell us that, in every alphabet of our being, we do indeed belong to a single system, powered by a single energy, manifesting a fundamental unity under all its variations, depending for its survival on the balance and health of the total system."

BARBARA WARD and RENE' DUBOS, *Only One Earth: The Care and Maintenance of a Small Planet*

"*Synergy* means the behavior of whole systems unpredicted by any part of the system as considered only separately. The eternally regenerative Universe is synergetic. Humans have been included in this cosmic design as local Universe information gatherers and local problem solvers in support of the integrity of the eternal, 100 percent efficient, self-generative Universe."

BUCKMINSTER FULLER

VI.

$\mathcal{L}$IBERTY AND JUSTICE

"$\mathcal{W}$here, after all, do universal human rights begin? In small places, close to home -- so close and so small that they cannot be seen on any map of the world. Yet they <u>are</u> the world of the individual person: the neighborhood he lives in; the school or college he attends; the factory, farm or office where he works. Such are the places where every man, woman and child seeks equal justice, equal opportunity, equal dignity without discrimination. Unless these rights have meaning there, they have little meaning anywhere. Without concerted citizen action to uphold them close to home, we shall look in vain for progress in the larger world."

ELEANOR ROOSEVELT, *Remarks at Presentation of Booklet on Human Rights, In Your Hands, To the United Nations Commission on Human Rights, United Nations, New York (March 27, 1958)*

A. HUMAN JUSTICE

"Any religion which professes to be concerned about the souls of men and is not concerned about the social and economic conditions that can scar the soul, is a spiritually moribund religion only waiting for the day to be buried."

> MARTIN LUTHER KING, JR.,
> *Strive Toward Freedom*

"[W]hat of those to whom life is not an ocean, and man-made laws are not sandtowers,

But to whom life is a rock, and the law a chisel with which they would carve it in their own likeness?

What shall I say of these save that they . . . stand in the sunlight, but with their backs to the sun?

They see only their shadows, and their shadows are their laws.

And what is the sun to them but a caster of shadows?

And what is it to acknowledge the laws but to stoop down and trace their shadows upon the earth?"

> KAHLIL GIBRAN, *The Prophet*

"*True* peace is not merely the absence of tension; it is the presence of justice."   MARTIN LUTHER KING, JR.

B. *Geo* JUSTICE

"*War* is an invention of the human mind. The human mind can invent peace with justice."

NORMAN COUSINS, *Who Speaks for Man?*

"*It* is important to recall that justice is a cosmic category as well as a human one. All creation is ruled by justice or homeostasis, the quest for equilibrium that is intrinsic to all atoms, galaxies, the earth, the whole history of the universe. The human called to compassion and justice is not a burden and has nothing to do with feelings of righteousness. It is a matter of the human species joining the dance of all creation in the quest for balance."

MATTHEW FOX, *Creation Spirituality: Liberating Gifts for the Peoples of the Earth*

"*The* Golden Rule applies not only to the dealings of human individuals and human societies with one another, but also to their dealings with other living creatures and with the planet upon which we are all traveling through space and time."

ALDOUS HUXLEY, *Literature and Science*

"At this time when our world is becoming smaller and more interdependent, when populations are growing rapidly and contacts among peoples and their governments are increasing, it is important to consider and reassess the position, rights and responsibilities of individuals, nations and peoples with respect to each other and to the planet as a whole."

TENZIN GYATSO, 14TH DALAI LAMA OF TIBET, *Universal Responsibilities and Human Rights*

"During the past few decades, we have seen the rays of light of this new age beginning to make clear our next step. Like the first faint glimmering of dawn on the eastern horizon. These initial heartbeats of the child to be born to all have taken the form of sharing, joining together, in the affirmation of our collective unity as one family of human beings. Those who have heard the call of the conch, have let go of old, taught patterns of separateness and hiding, and stepped into the freedom of sharing. If there is any hope for mankind, it is in the sense of community that is rapidly maturing on the planet."

ALAN COHEN, *The Dragon Doesn't Live Here Anymore*

"Creation spirituality . . . insists not just on justice among humans but on geo-justice -- justice between humans and the earth and all her creatures. We cannot have authentic human justice without engaging equally in the struggle for justice toward our home, the planet earth. There is no need to choose in an either/or fashion between the human and the nonhuman. In the struggle for justice, justice toward the rain forest cannot wait until justice among humans is accomplished. We are too interdependent for that."

MATTHEW FOX, *Creation Spirituality: Liberating Gifts for the Peoples of the Earth*

C. FREEDOM FOR ALL

"If men and women are in chains anywhere in the world, then freedom is in danger everywhere."

JOHN F. KENNEDY, *Campaign Speech in Washington, D.C. (October 2, 1960)*

"Because I have confidence in the power of truth and in the power of spirit, I believe in the future of mankind."

ALBERT SCHWEITZER, *Out of My Life and Thought*

"We all know the immensity of the challenges facing our generation: the problem of overpopulation, the threat to our environment and the dangers of military confrontation. As this dramatic century draws to a close, it is clear that the renewed yearning for freedom and democracy sweeping the globe provides an unprecedented opportunity for building a better world. Freedom is the real source of human happiness and creativity. Only when it is allowed to flourish can a genuinely stable international climate exist."

> TENZIN GYATSO, 14TH DALAI LAMA OF TIBET: *Initial Remarks on Being Awarded the Nobel Peace Prize (October 5, 1989)*

"The real democratic idea is, not that every man shall be on a level with every other, but that everyone shall have liberty, without hindrance, to be what God made him."

> HENRY WARD BEECHER, *The Dishonest Politician*

"The wave of the future is not the conquest of the world by a single dogmatic creed but the liberation of the diverse energies of free nations and free men."

> JOHN F. KENNEDY, *Speech at the University of California, Berkeley (March 23, 1962)*

"May it [The Declaration of Independence] be to the world what I believe it will be (to some parts sooner, to others later, but finally to all): the signal of arousing men to burst the chains under which monkish ignorance and superstition have persuaded them to bind themselves and assume the blessings and security of self-government. That form which we have substituted restores the free right of the unbounded exercise of reason and freedom of opinion. All eyes are opened or opening to the rights of man. The general spread of the light of science has already laid open to every view the palpable truth that the mass of mankind has not been born with saddles on their backs, nor a favored few booted and spurred ready to ride them legitimately by the grace of God. These are grounds of hope for others."

THOMAS JEFFERSON, *Letter to Roger C. Weightman (June 24, 1826) (the 50th Anniversary of the Declaration and 10 days before Jefferson's death)*

"The American war is over: but this is far from being the case with the American revolution. On the contrary, nothing but the first act of the great drama is closed."

BENJAMIN RUSH

"The oppressed must realize that they are fighting not merely for freedom from hunger, but for . . . freedom to create and to construct, to wonder and to venture."

PAULO FREIRE, *Pedagogy of the Oppressed*

"My Father-God, who was and is and evermore shall be. . . . Who in the boundlessness of love has made all men to equal be. The white, the black, the yellow and the red can look up in thy face and say, Our Father-God. . . .

The Holy One has said that all His children shall be free; and every soul is child of God. The sudras shall be as free as priests; the farmers shall walk hand in hand with king, for all the world will own the brotherhood of man.

O men, arise! Be conscious of your powers, for he who wills need not remain a slave. Just live as you would have your brother live; unfold each day as does the flower; for earth is yours, and heaven is yours, and God will bring you to your own."

LEVI, *The Aquarian Gospel of Jesus The Christ*

"The law will never make men free; it is men who have got to make the law free."

HENRY DAVID THOREAU, *Slavery in Massachusetts*

"All men were made by the same Great Spirit Chief. They are all brothers. The earth is the mother of all people, and all people should have equal rights upon it. You might as well expect the rivers to run backward as that any man who was born a free man should be contented with penned up and denied liberty to go where he pleases."

CHIEF JOSEPH *(Nez Perce)*

"[L]iberty without learning is always in peril; and learning without liberty is always in vain. . . .

Any educated citizen who seeks . . . to suppress freedom, or to subject other human beings to acts that are less than human, degrades his heritage, ignores his learning, and betrays his obligations."

JOHN   F.   KENNEDY, *Address at Vanderbilt University (May 1963)*

"When we view liberation as a scarce resource, something only a precious few of us can have, we stifle our potential, our creativity, our genius for living, learning and growing."

ANDREA CANAAN

D. EQUALITY

"All men are by nature equal, made, all, of the same earth by the same Creator, and however we deceive ourselves, as dear to God is the poor peasant as the mighty prince."

PLATO

"Each of us is inevitable;
Each of us limitless -- each of us with his or her right
  upon the earth;
Each of us allow'd the eternal purports of the earth;
Each of us here as divinely as any is here."

WALT   WHITMAN,   Salut au
Monde

"And you who would understand justice, how shall you unless you look upon all deeds in the fullness of light?

Only then shall you know that the erect and the fallen are but one man standing in twilight between the night of his pygmy-self and the day of his god-self,

And that the corner-stone of the temple is not higher than the lowest stone in its foundation."

KAHLIL GIBRAN, The Prophet

"The reward of the adventure of life is freedom. The irony of the adventure is that we were free before we set out, but we needed to learn that freedom was not to be found where we fantasized it to be. We needed to learn, like our old friend Dorothy from Kansas, that there's no place like home, because there is no place but Home. When we learn that God is everywhere, that Love fills all space, and that Truth is the very Ground of our Being, we may surely release the little to embrace the All."

ALAN COHEN, The Dragon
Doesn't Live Here Anymore

"We have not yet developed technological wisdom, technological discipline, technological stewardship. Ecological destruction is not the result of science and technology, but of social decisions that allow scientific and technological institutions to grow in undisciplined ways."

SAM KEEN, Fire in the Belly: On
Being a Man

"I do not say that all men are equal in their ability, their character or their motivation, but I say they should be equal in their chance to develop their character, their motivation and their ability. They should be given a fair chance to develop all the talents that they have . . . not merely for reasons of economic efficiency, world diplomacy and domestic tranquility -- but, above all, because it is right."

JOHN F. KENNEDY, Civil Rights
Message to U. S. Congress (June
19, 1963)

"Who ever walked behind anyone to freedom? If we can't go hand in hand, I don't want to go."

HAZEL SCOTT

"One day in this lifetime, we will reach freedom's gate together and pass through to a land where we will all be judged by our fellow beings for the content of our character rather than the color of our skin."
DAVID DINKINS

E. HUMAN RIGHTS

"The fundamental source of all your errors, sophisms, and false reasonings, is a total ignorance of the natural rights of mankind. Were you once to become acquainted with these, you could never entertain a thought, that all men are not, by nature, entitled to a parity of privileges. You would be convinced, that natural liberty is a gift of the beneficent Creator, to the whole human race; and that civil liberty is founded in that; and cannot be wrested from any people, without the most manifest violation of justice. Civil liberty is only natural liberty, modified and secured by the sanctions of civil society. It is not a thing, in its own nature, precarious and dependent on human will and caprice; but it is conformable to the constitution of man, as well as necessary to the well-being of society."

ALEXANDER HAMILTON, "*The Farmer Refuted*," *The Works of Alexander Hamilton*

"Upon the standard to which the wise and honest will now repair it is written: 'You have lived the easy way; henceforth, you will live the hard way... You came into a great heritage made by the insight and the sweat and the blood of inspired and devoted and courageous men; thoughtlessly and in utmost self-indulgence you have all but squandered this inheritance. Now only by the heroic virtues which made this inheritance can you restore it again.... You took the good things for granted. Now you must earn them again.... For every right that you cherish, you have a duty which you must fulfill. For every hope that you entertain, you have a task that you must perform. For every good that you wish to preserve, you will have to sacrifice your comfort and your ease. There is nothing for nothing any longer.'"

> WALTER LIPPMANN, Speech to the Harvard Class of 1910 at Their Thirtieth Reunion (June 8, 1940). -- Walter Lippmann Papers, Yale University Library

"Freedom is indivisible, and when one man is enslaved, all are not free."

> JOHN F. KENNEDY, Speech in West Berlin (June 26, 1963)

"I say the time has come to walk out of the shadow of states' rights and into the sunlight of human rights."

> HUBERT H. HUMPHREY, Speech to the Democratic National Convention (August 1948)

"'Freedom from fear' could be said to sum up the whole philosophy of human rights."

DAG HAMMARSKJOLD, *On the 180th Anniversary of the Virginia Declaration of Human Rights (May 20, 1956)*

"The existence and validity of human rights are not written in the stars. . . . Those ideals and convictions which resulted from historical experience, from the craving for beauty and harmony, have been readily accepted in theory by man -- and at all times, have been trampled upon by the same people under the pressures of their animal instincts. A large part of history is therefore replete with the struggle for those human rights, an internal struggle in which a final victory can never be won. But to tire in that struggle would mean the ruin of society.

In talking about human rights today, we are referring primarily to the following demands: protection of the individual against arbitrary infringement by other individuals or by the government; the right to work and to adequate earnings from work; freedom of discussion and teaching; adequate participation of the individual in the formation of his government. These human rights are nowadays recognized theoretically, although, by abundant use of formalistic, legal maneuvers, they are being violated to a much greater extent than even a generation ago."

ALBERT EINSTEIN, *Address, Chicago Decalogue Society (February 20, 1954)*

"There is so much talk of rights, of basic human rights as well as of rights of particular groups, minorities, privileged and underprivileged people -- and almost never of responsibility. . . . Rights constitute a static and defensive, structure-oriented concept, whereas <u>the acceptance of responsibility implies creative participation in the design of the human world</u>. The ethics which dominates in the Western world is therefore an individualistic ethics in the guise of a socially committing behavioural code. It is not a multilevel ethics in the true sense."

ERICH JANTSCH, *Universe*

F. ℛIGHTS OF NATURE

"What is crucial to recognize is that the human capacity for empathy and identification is not static; the very process of recognizing <u>rights</u> in those higher vertebrates with whom we already empathize could well pave the way for still further extensions as we move upward along the spiral of moral evolution. It is not only the human liberation movements . . . that advance in waves of increased consciousness."

LAURENCE TRIBE

"[T]he blackness of the skin is no reason why a human being should be abandoned without redress to the caprice of a tormentor. It may come one day to be recognized, that the number of legs, the villosity of the skin, or the termination of the <u>os sacrum</u> [i.e., spinal base], are reasons equally insufficient for abandoning a sensitive being to the same fate."

JEREMY BENTHAM, *An Introduction to the Principles of Morals and Legislation*

"[I]t is not human life only that is lovable and sacred, but all innocent and beautiful life: the great republic of the future will not confine its beneficence to man."

HENRY S. SALT, *Animals' Rights Considered in Relation to Social Progress*

"There was an eighty-seven year hiatus from the Declaration of Independence to the Emancipation Proclamation and the freeing of American blacks from slavery. . . . The idea of an inalienable right of self-determination has moved with irresistible force to become what Jefferson claimed it was in 1776: a self-evident truth. . . . It is now nature's turn to be liberated."

DONALD WORSTER

"Animals aren't wild, they're just free."

CHIEF LEON SHENANDOAH (*Grand Council of the Six Nations Iroquois Confederacy*)

G. *Spirit* OF LIBERTY

"Liberty lies in the hearts of men and women; when it dies there, no constitution, no law, no court can save it; no constitution, no law, no court can even do much to help it.   The spirit of liberty is the spirit which is not too sure that it is right; the spirit of liberty is the spirit which seeks to understand the minds of other men and women; the spirit of liberty is the spirit which weighs their interests alongside its own without bias; the spirit of liberty remembers that not even a sparrow falls to earth unheeded; the spirit of liberty is the spirit of Him who, near two thousand years ago, taught mankind that lesson it has never learned, but has never quite forgotten; that there may be a kingdom where the least shall be heard and considered side by side with the greatest."

> LEARNED HAND, *"The Spirit of Liberty," Speech at "I Am an American Day" Ceremony, Central Park, New York City (May 21, 1944)*

"For the saddest epitaph which can be carved in memory of a vanished liberty is that it was lost because its possessors failed to stretch forth a saving hand while yet there was time."

> SUTHERLAND, J. *Associated Press v. N.L.R.B.*, 301 U.S. 103 (1937)

H. HUMAN SPIRIT

"I am certain that after the dust of centuries has passed over our cities, we, too, will be remembered not for victories or defeats in battles or politics, but for our contribution to the human spirit."

> JOHN F. KENNEDY, *Closed Circuit Television Broadcast (November 29, 1962)*

"Only when the human spirit grows powerful within us and guides us back to a civilization based on humanitarian ideal; only <u>then</u> will it act, through our intermediacy, upon those other peoples. All men . . . are endowed with the faculty of compassion, and for this reason can develop the humanitarian spirit. There is inflammable material within them: let there come a spark, and it will burst into flame."

ALBERT   SCHWEITZER,   *The Problem of Peace in the World of Today*

"We are indeed witnessing a tremendous and popular movement for the advancement of human rights and democratic freedoms in the world. This movement has such moral force that even determined governments and armies are incapable of suppressing it. It is an encouraging indication of the triumph of the human spirit for freedom."

TENZIN GYATSO, 14TH DALAI LAMA   OF   TIBET,   *Universal Responsibilities   and   Human Rights*

"Your clothes conceal much of your beauty, yet they hide not the unbeautiful.

And though you seek in garments the freedom of privacy you may find in them a harness and a chain.

Would that you could meet the sun and the wind with more of your skin and less of your raiment,

For the breath of life is in the sunlight and the hand of life is in the wind."

KAHLIL GIBRAN, *The Prophet*

"How can the bird that is born for joy,
Sit in a cage and sing.
How can a child when fears annoy,
But droop his tender wing,
And forget his youthful spring."

WILLIAM BLAKE, *Songs of Experience*

"The dignity of man requires obedience to a higher law -- to the strength of the spirit."

MOHANDAS K. (MAHATMA) GANDHI

"The creation of the world is not only a process which moves from God to humanity. God demands newness from humanity; God awaits the works of human freedom."

NIKOLAI BERDYAEV

"Fate is a very real aspect of our lives as long as we remain in ignorance, as real as the other aspect of freedom. What we call fate is the pulling and moulding of our lives from sources of which we are unconscious. Where there is the Light of consciousness all is freedom; wherever to us that Light does not penetrate is Fate. To the adept Siddha whose consciousness enfolds the whole range of manifested being there is no fate at all."

SRI KRISHNA PREM, *The Yoga of the Kathopanishad*

I. *L*ET FREEDOM RING

"*I*f a beachhead of cooperation may push back the jungles of suspicion, let both sides join in creating a new endeavor -- not a new balance of power, but a new world of law, where the strong are just and the weak secure and the peace preserved."

JOHN F. KENNEDY, *Inaugural Address (January 20, 1961)*

"*W*hen we let freedom ring, we let it ring from every village and every hamlet, from every state and every city, we will be able to speed up that day when all of God's children, black men and white men, Jews and Gentiles, Protestants and Catholics, will be able to join hands and sing in the words of the old Negro spiritual, 'Free at last! Free at last! Thank God Almighty, we are free at last!'"

MARTIN LUTHER KING, JR., *Speech at Gathering of the Civil Rights March on Washington, D.C. (August 28, 1963)*

"Great meanwhile is the moment, when tidings of Freedom reach us; when the long-enthralled soul, from amid its chains and squalid stagnancy, arises, were it still only in blindness and bewilderment, and swears by Him that made it, that it will be <u>free</u>! Free? Understand that well, it is the deep commandment, dimmer or clearer, of our whole being, to be <u>free</u>. Freedom is the one purport, wisely aimed at, or unwisely, of all man's struggles, toilings and sufferings, on this Earth."

THOMAS CARLYLE, <u>The French Revolution</u>

"The day will come when . . . victorious nations will plan and build in justice and freedom a house of many mansions, where there will be room for all."

WINSTON CHURCHILL

VII.

GOVERNANCE

"The century on which we are entering can be and must be the century of the common man."

HENRY WALLACE, *Speech in New York City (May 8, 1942)*

A. ROLE OF GOVERNMENT

"Those who say religion has nothing to do with politics do not know what religion means."

MOHANDAS K. (MAHATMA) GANDHI, An Autobiography

"A nation that continues year after year to spend more money on military defense than on programs of social uplift is approaching spiritual death."
MARTIN LUTHER KING, JR.

"I heartily accept the motto, -- 'That government is best which governs least;' and I should like to see it acted up to more rapidly and systematically. Carried out, it finally amounts to this, which I also believe, -- 'That government is best which governs not at all;' and when men are prepared for it, that will be the kind of government which they will have."

HENRY DAVID THOREAU, Civil Disobedience

"The main objects of all science, the freedom and happiness of man . . . [are] the sole objects of all legitimate government."

THOMAS JEFFERSON, Letter to General Thaddeus Kosciusko (February 26, 1810)

"The ultimate aim of government is not to rule, or restrain, by fear, nor to exact obedience, but contrariwise, to free every man from fear, that he may live in all possible security; in other words, to strengthen his natural right to exist and work without injury to himself or others.

No, the object of government is not to change men from rational beings into beasts or puppets, but to enable them to develop their minds and bodies in security, and to employ their reason unshackled; neither showing hatred, anger, or deceit, nor watched with the eyes of jealousy and injustice. In fact, the true aim of government is liberty."

> BENEDICTUS DE SPINOZA,
> *Writings on Political Philosophy,*
> *"Tractatus Theologico-Politicus"*

"Government should not be made an end in itself; it is a means only, -- a means to be freely adapted to advance the best interests of the social organism. The State exists for the sake of Society, not Society for the sake of the State."

> WOODROW WILSON, *The State:*
> *Elements of Historical and*
> *Practical Politics*

B. *D*UTY OF GOVERNMENT

"*A* state is not a mere society, having a common place, established for the prevention of mutual crime for the sake of its change. . . . Political society exists for the sake of noble actions, and not of mere companionship."

ARISTOTLE, *Politics*

"*The* care of human life and happiness, and not their destruction, is the first and only legitimate object of good government."

THOMAS JEFFERSON, *Letter to the Republican Citizens of Maryland (March 31, 1809)*

"*P*olitical sovereignty is but a mockery without the means of meeting poverty and illiteracy and disease. Self-determination is but a slogan if the future holds no hope."

JOHN F. KENNEDY, *Speech to the United Nations General Assembly (September 25, 1961)*

"*There* are seven sins in the world: wealth without work, pleasure without conscience, knowledge without character, commerce without morality, science without humanity, worship without faith, and politics without principle."

MOHANDAS   K.   (MAHATMA) GANDHI

"In dealing with the state, we ought to remember that its institutions are not aboriginal, though they existed before we were born: that they are not superior to the citizen: that every one of them was once the act of a single man: every law and usage was a man's expedient to meet a particular case: that they are all imitable, all alterable; we may make as good: we may make better."

RALPH WALDO EMERSON, *Essays*

"The world is filled with people who want to dream, to love, and to be happy. Yet happiness, love, and dreams are nowhere to be found on the agendas of governments and of world affairs. There must be something wrong in this planet's politics."

ROBERT MULLER, *A Planet of Hope*

"The chief duty of governments, insofar as they are coercive, is to restrain those who interfere with the inalienable rights of the individual, among which are the right to life, the right to liberty, the right to the pursuit of happiness and the right to worship God according to the dictates of one's conscience."

WILLIAM JENNINGS BRYAN, *Speech at Baltimore, Maryland (April 24, 1915)*

C. LIMITS OF POWER

"Wild liberty develops iron conscience. Want of liberty, by strengthening law and decorum, stupefies conscience."

RALPH WALDO EMERSON,
Essays

"The mind is the expression of the soul, which belongs to God and must be let alone by government."

ADLAI E. STEVENSON, JR., *Speech in Salt Lake City, Utah (October 14, 1952)*

"It is only the novice in political economy who thinks it is the duty of government to make citizens happy. -- Government has no such office. To protect the weak and the minority from the impositions of the strong and the majority -- to prevent any one from positively working to render the people unhappy . . . to do the labor not of an officious inter-meddler in the affairs of men, but of a prudent watchman who prevents outrage -- these are rather the proper duties of a government."

WALT WHITMAN, *Editorial, Brooklyn Eagle (April 4, 1846)*

"Whatever crushes our individuality is despotism."

JOHN STUART MILL, *On Liberty*

"*If* . . . the machine of government . . . is of such a nature that it requires you to be the agent of injustice to another, then, I say, break the law."
HENRY DAVID THOREAU

"*We* live in a very low state of the world, and pay unwilling tribute to governments founded on force. There is not, among the most religious and instructed men of the most religious and civil nations, a reliance on the moral sentiment, and a sufficient belief in the unity of things to persuade them that society can be maintained without artificial restraints, as well as the solar system; or that the private citizen might be reasonable, and a good neighbor, . . . [T]here never was in any man sufficient faith in the power of rectitude to inspire him with the broad design of renovating the State on the principle of right and love."
RALPH WALDO EMERSON, *Essays*

"*Humanity* is one living body made of human beings,
not of lifeless governments and institutions.
The latter are only the servants of life, not
life itself."
ROBERT MULLER, *A Planet of Hope*

"*The* question before the human race is whether the God of nature shall govern the world by his own laws, or whether priests and kings shall rule it by fictitious miracles."
JOHN ADAMS, *Letter to Thomas Jefferson (June 20, 1815)*

"*Power* is a word often on the lips of Jesus; never used, it should be said, in the sense of extrinsic authority or the right to command and govern, but always in reference to an intrinsic and interior moral and spiritual energy of life."

RUFUS JONES, *Spiritual Energies in Daily Life*

"[*A*]ll great advances have involved illegality. The early Christians broke the law; Galileo broke the law; the French revolutionaries broke the law; early trade unionists broke the law. The instances are so numerous and so important that no one can maintain as an absolute principle obedience to constituted authority."

BERTRAND RUSSELL, *Which Way to Peace?*

"*In* all that the people can individually do as well for themselves, government ought not to interfere."

ABRAHAM LINCOLN

D. *G*OVERNANCE BY THE PEOPLE

"*If* I were to attempt to put my political philosophy into a single phrase, it would be this: Trust the people. Trust their good sense, their decency, their fortitude, their faith. Trust them with the facts. Trust them with the great decisions, and fix as our guiding star the passion to create a society where people can fulfill their own best selves -- where no . . . [one] is held down by race or color, by worldly condition or social status, from gaining what his character earns him as . . . [a] citizen, as a human being, and as a child of God."

> ADLAI E. STEVENSON, *Speech at Harrisburg, Pennsylvania (September 13, 1956)*

"Democratic institutions are never done -- they are, like the living tissue, always a-making. It is a strenuous thing this of living the life of the free people: and we cannot escape the burden of our inheritance."

> WOODROW WILSON, *Speech in Middletown, Connecticut (April 30, 1889)*

"Democracy, is not a static thing. It is an everlasting march."

> FRANKLIN D. ROOSEVELT, *Speech in Los Angeles, California (October 1, 1935)*

"There is only one source of intelligent guidance. It lies within an awakened consciousness of the majority of the people. There and there alone lies the hope of all mankind."

> WESLEY LA VIOLETTE, *The Creative Light*

"[The less government we have, the better -- the fewer laws, and the less confided power. The antidote to . . . abuse of formal government is the influence of private character, the growth of the individual; the appearance of the principal to supersede the proxy; the appearance of the wise man, of whom the existing government is, it must be owned, a shabby imitation."

RALPH WALDO EMERSON, *Essays*

"Democracy cannot be saved by supermen, but only by the unswerving devotion and goodness of millions of little men."

ADLAI E. STEVENSON, JR., *Speech (1955)*

"A charter of Anachronism. It was not an instrument of government: it was a guarantee to the whole American nation that it never should be governed at all."

GEORGE   BERNARD   SHAW *(Speaking of the United States Constitution)*

"Democracy is a process, not a static condition. It is becoming, rather than being. It can easily be lost, but never is fully won. Its essence is eternal struggle."

WILLIAM H. HASTIE

"Is a democracy, such as we know it, the last improvement possible in government? Is it not possible to take a step further towards recognizing the rights of man? There will never be a free and enlightened State until the State comes to recognize the individual as a higher and independent power, from which all its own power and authority are derived, and treats him accordingly."

HENRY DAVID THOREAU, *On the Duty of Civil Disobedience*

"The new politics will speak for the millions -- one by one."

THEODORE ROSZAK

"[G]overnments will not change this world, but individuals of integrity, freely joining together."

BUCKMINSTER FULLER

"Democracy is not simply a political system; it is a moral movement and it springs from adventurous faith in human possibilities."

HARRY EMERSON FOSDICK, *Adventurous Religion*

"[I]f you give people a thorough understanding of what confronts them and the basic causes that produce it, they'll create their own program, and when the people create a program, you get action."

MALCOLM X

"*It* is appalling how few people regard themselves as citizens, as society makers. Instead they regard society as a pre-established machinery of institutions and authorities . . . The result must be and has been . . . standardization, . . . neglect, . . . injustice, and a base common denominator of valuation. There is no remedy except large numbers of authentic citizens, alert, concerned, intervening, deciding on all issues and all levels."

PAUL GOODMAN, *The Society I Live in Is Mine*

"*The* tendency of the times favor the idea of self-government, and leave the individual, for all code, to the rewards and penalties of his own constitution, which work with more energy than we believe, while we depend on artificial restraints. The movement in this direction has been very marked in modern history. . . . It separates the individual from all party, and unites him, at the same time, to the race. It promises a recognition of higher rights than those of personal freedom, or the security of property. A man has a right to be employed, to be trusted, to be loved, to be revered.

The power of love, as the basis of a state, has never been tried."

RALPH WALDO EMERSON, *Essays*

VIII.

*W*E THE PEOPLE

"*H*umanity is the shepherd of the world."
MARTIN HEIDEGGER

A. HUMAN RESPONSIBILITIES

i. Responsibility to Others

> "It is [the] loss of individual responsibility that has helped to bring the chaos in which mankind is wallowing today."
>
> WESLEY LA VIOLETTE, *The Creative Light*

"Just as the wave does not exist for itself, but is ever a part of the heaving surface of the ocean, so must I never live my life for itself, but always in the experience which is going on around me. It is an uncomfortable doctrine which the true ethics whisper into my ear. You are happy they say; therefore you are called upon to give much."

ALBERT SCHWEITZER, *Civilization and Ethics*

"Be ashamed to die until you have won some victory for humanity."

HORACE MANN, *Commencement Address at Antioch College (1859)*

"There is no cause half so sacred as the cause of a people. There is no idea so uplifting as the idea of the service of humanity."

WOODROW WILSON, *Campaign Speech in New York City (October 31, 1912)*

"The problems we face today, violent conflict, destruction of nature, poverty, hunger, and so on, are human created problems which can be solved through human effort, understanding and the development of a sense of brotherhood and sisterhood. We need to cultivate a universal responsibility for one another and the planet we share. . . .

***

I pray for all of us, oppressor and friend, that together we succeed in building a better world through human understanding and love, and that in doing so we may reduce the pain and suffering of all sentient beings."

TENZIN GYATSO, 14TH DALAI LAMA OF TIBET, *Nobel Peace Prize Acceptance Speech, Oslo, Norway (December 10, 1989)*

"Without a global revolution in the sphere of human consciousness, nothing will change for the better in the sphere of our being as humans, and the catastrophe toward which this world is headed -- be it ecological, social, demographic or a general breakdown of civilization -- will be unavoidable. If we are no longer threatened by world war or by the danger that the absurd mountains of accumulated nuclear weapons might blow up the world, this does not mean we have definitely won. We are still incapable of understanding that the only genuine backbone of all our actions, if they are to be moral, is responsibility. Responsibility to something higher than my family, my country, my company, my success -- responsibility to the order of being where all our actions are indelibly recorded and where and only where they will be properly judged."

VACLAV HAVEL, *President of Czechoslovakia, Speech to Joint Meeting of Congress (February 1990)*

"*I* wonder if the time has not come, in our efforts to move humanity to a fuller expression of its destiny, to begin asking the most basic of all moral questions: How can we honor one another? For 'honor' is another word for 'reverence,' and reverence comes from awe. If we have begun to intuit the awesomeness of the universe and the awesomeness of our being here, then it is time to honor one another."

MATTHEW FOX, *Creation Spirituality: Liberating Gifts for the Peoples of the Earth*

"*You* bring me the deepest joy that can be felt by a man whose invincible belief is that Science and Peace will triumph over Ignorance and War, that nations will unite, not to destroy, but to build, and that the future will belong to those who will have done most for suffering humanity."

LOUIS PASTEUR

"*This* is what you should do: love the earth and sun and animals, despise riches, give alms to everyone that asks, and devote your income and labor to others . . . and your very flesh shall become a great poem."

WALT WHITMAN, *Preface to Leaves of Grass*

"*All* things whatsoever you would have that men should do to you, do so to them."

MATTHEW 7:12

"Every man takes care that his neighbor shall not cheat him. But a day comes when he begins to care that he does not cheat his neighbor. Then all goes well. He has changed his market-cart into a chariot of the sun."

RALPH WALDO EMERSON, *From an Essay, Worship, Conduct of Life*

"We cannot live only for ourselves. A thousand fibers connect us with our fellow men; and among those fibers, as sympathetic threads, our actions run as causes, and they come back to us as effects."

HERMAN MELVILLE

"Those whose lives are fruitful to themselves, to their friends or to the world are inspired and sustained by joy; they see in imagination the things that might be and the way in which they are to be brought into existence. In their private relations they are not preoccupied with anxiety lest they should lose such affection and respect as they receive; they are engaged in giving affection and respect, freely, and the reward comes of itself without their seeking. In their work they are not haunted by jealousy of competitors, but are concerned with the actual matter that has to be done. In politics they do not spend time and passion defending unjust privileges of their clan or nation, but they aim at making the world as a whole happier, less cruel, less full of conflict between rival creeds and more full of human beings whose growth has not been dwarfed and stunted by oppression."

BERTRAND RUSSELL

"If I can stop one heart from breaking,
I shall not live in vain;
If I can ease one life the aching,
Or cool one pain,
Or help one fainting robin
Unto his nest again,
I shall not live in vain."

EMILY DICKINSON

"The law of love ordains that one should be harmless in thought and action. Treat others as you would have them treat you. . . . We sacrifice when we deprive the self of what it holds dear, to serve others and to serve a good cause. . . . To give what one needs for one's self to another, whose need is greater, is an act of sacrifice."

GURU NANAK

"The human heart readily responds to the opportunity, freely and spontaneously given, to be of help to another."

GARDNER MURPHY, "The Enigma of
Human Nature," Nature, Man, and
Society: Main Currents in Modern
Thought

"One is great only through the cause one serves. And in our time the greatest cause can only be the peace and happiness of all humanity."

ROBERT MULLER, A Planet of
Hope

"The most effective way to achieve right relations with any living thing is to look for the best in it, and then help that best into its fullest expression."

J. ALLEN BOONE, *Kinship With All Life*

"We have to take the whole universe as the expression of the one Self. Then only our love flows to all beings and creatures in the world equally."

SWAMI RAMDAS

"Let us not be justices of the peace, but angels of peace."

SAINT TERESA OF LISIEUX

"For one human being to love another is perhaps the most difficult task of all, the epitome, the ultimate test. It is that striving for which all other striving is merely preparation."

RAINER MARIA RILKE, *Letters To A Young Poet*

"You have not done enough, you have never done enough, so long as it is still possible that you have something of value to contribute."

DAG HAMMARSKJOLD, *Markings*

"[T]o discern that all points in the world are equally centres and that the true centre is outside the world, this is to consent to the rule of mechanical necessity in matter -- and of free choice at the centre of each soul. Such consent is love. The face of this love which is turned toward thinking persons is the love of our neighbour; the face turned towards matter is love of the order of the world."

SIMONE WEIL, *Gravity and Grace*

"For us to regard the Bomb (or the dying seas, the poisoned air) as a monstrous injustice to us would suggest that we never took seriously the injunction to love. Perhaps we thought all along that Gautama and Jesus were kidding, or their teachings were meant only for saints. But now we see, as an awful revelation, that we are all called to be saints -- not good necessarily, or pious or devout -- but saints in the sense of just loving each other."

JOANNA MACY

"It is a serious thing to live in a society of possible gods and goddesses, to remember that the dullest and most uninteresting person you can talk to may one day be a creature which, if you saw it now, you would be strongly tempted to worship, or else a horror and a corruption such as you now meet, if at all, only in a nightmare. All day long we are, in some degree, helping each other to one or other of these destinations. It is in the light of these overwhelming possibilities, it is with the awe and the circumspection proper to them, that we should conduct all our dealings with one another, all friendships, all loves, all play, all politics. There are no ordinary people. You have never met a mere mortal. Nations, cultures, arts, civilisations -- these are mortal, and their life is to ours as the life of a gnat. But it is immortals whom we joke with, work with, marry, snub, and exploit -- immortal horrors or everlasting splendours."

C. S. LEWIS, *The Weight of Glory*

"There is . . . only a single categorical imperative, and it is this: Act only on that principle which you could wish to become a universal law."

IMMANUEL   KANT,   *The Metaphysic of Morals*

"Genuine greatness is marked by . . . a hearty interest in others, a feeling of brotherhood with the human family, and respect for every intellectual and immortal being as capable of progress toward its own elevation."

WILLIAM ELLERY CHANNING

"Love is a high inducement to individuals to ripen, to strive to mature in the inner self, to manifest maturity in the outer world, to become that manifestation for the sake of another. This is a great, demanding task: it calls one to expand one's horizon greatly. . . . It is the final goal, perhaps one which human beings as yet hardly ever seek to attain."

RAINER MARIA RILKE, *Letters To A Young Poet*

"No person is your friend who demands your silence, or denies your right to grow."

ALICE WALKER

ii. Responsibility to Earth and Nature

"The scientific worldview established the notion that there is sense and purpose in the development of the universe when it recognized the evolution from the primal explosion to matter, life, and humanity. In humans, nature begins to recognize itself. The awareness of that recognition carries with it a responsibility to maintain and not destroy what has been created."

VICTOR WEISSKOPF, *The Joy of Insight*

"In the depth of my soul I believe -- and consider this belief to be natural to any human soul -- that this earth has a central significance in the universe. In the depth of my soul I entertain the presumption that the act of creation which called forth the inorganic world from nothingness and the procreation of life from the inorganic world, was aimed at humanity; a great experiment was initiated whose failure by human irresponsibility would mean the failure of the act of creation itself, its very refutation. Maybe it is so, maybe it is not. It would be good if humanity behaved as if it were so."

THOMAS MANN, *Lob der Vergänglichkeit (In Praise of Impermanence)*

"To advocate the rights of animals is far more than to plead for compassion or justice towards the victims of ill-usage; it is not only, and not primarily, for the sake of the victims that we plead, but for the sake of mankind itself. Our true civilization, our race-progress, our <u>humanity</u> . . . are concerned in this development; it is ourselves . . . that we wrong, when we trample on the rights of the fellow-beings, human or animal, for whom we chance to hold jurisdiction."

> HENRY S. SALT, <u>*Animals' Rights Considered in Relation to Social Progress*</u>

"Thou shalt inherit the holy earth as a faithful steward, conserving its resources and productivity from generation to generation. Thou shalt safeguard thy fields from soil erosion, thy living waters from drying up, thy forests from desolation, and protect the hills from overgrazing by thy herds, that thy descendants may have abundance forever. If any shall fail in this stewardship of the land, thy fruitful fields shall become sterile stony ground and wasting gullies, and thy descendents shall decrease and live in poverty or perish from off the face of the earth."

> WALTER C. LOWDERMILK, "The Eleventh Commandment," <u>*American Forests*</u>

"It is our collective and individual responsibility to protect and nurture the global family, to support its weaker members and to preserve and tend to the environment in which we all live."

> TENZIN GYATSO, 14TH DALAI LAMA OF TIBET, <u>*Universal Responsibilities and Human Rights*</u>

"[U]nderstanding begins with love and respect. It begins with respect for the Great Spirit, and the Great Spirit is the life that is in all things -- all the creatures and the plants and even the rocks and minerals. All things -- and I mean all things -- have their own will and their own way and their own purpose; this is what is to be respected.

Such respect is not a feeling or an attitude only. It's a way of life. Such respect means that we never stop realizing and that we never neglect to carry out our obligations to ourselves and our environment."

ROLLING THUNDER

"Creation spirituality teaches that the human race is entrusted with the history of this planet and the children to come upon it. Therefore, our spiritual and ethical ways of living need to be worthy of the beauty that is to come. All are entrusted with this sense of history; all have their gift to return to the cosmos."

MATTHEW FOX, Creation Spirituality: Liberating Gifts for the Peoples of the Earth

"The responsibility for living harmoniously on Planet Earth rests with each individual. As each person spiritually and cosmically comes of age, claiming his attunement and therefore his involvement in the business of all mankind, a beautiful new energy will be released which will gradually swing the earth into alignment with the universal forces of harmony and peace. This period of awareness will happen, but only when each man and woman looks beyond the exterior to the interior of their being to discover their own personal power through their connection to the Ultimate of All Energies."

MEREDITH   LADY   YOUNG, Agartha: A Journey to the Stars

"No poem, no painting, no work of man's hand or brain is as marvelous a thing as the least of the species of living beings that inhabit the earth. Each one . . . is a miracle as far beyond our comprehension as the stars. We cannot make them, we cannot understand how they were made. To destroy one . . . to wipe out a whole species . . . for all eternity, is to do so colossal a thing that the mind falters at the thought. Yet we have done it again and again and again, thoughtlessly, needlessly, wantonly, cruelly . . . many of the species that we have destroyed . . . or are now destroying . . . were among the noblest and most beautiful."

HERBERT RAVANEL SASS, *On the Wings of a Bird*

"A man should wonder about treating all creatures as he himself would be treated."

SUTRA-KRITANGA SUTRA 1:11:33

"The challenge to each human is creation. Will you create with reverence, or with neglect?"

GARY ZUKAV, *The Seat of the Soul*

"The Creator will guide our thoughts and strengthen us to be faithful to our sacred trust and restore harmony among all peoples, all living creatures, and Mother Earth. . . . We were instructed to carry a love for one another and to show a great respect for all the beings of this earth. . . . In our ways, spiritual consciousness is the highest form of politics. . . . When people cease to respect and express gratitude for these many things, then all life will be destroyed, and human life on this planet will come to an end. These are our times and our responsibilities. Every human being has a sacred duty to protect the welfare of our Mother Earth, from whom all life comes. In order to do this we must recognize the enemy -- the one within us. We must begin with ourselves. . . . We must live in harmony with the Natural World and recognize that excessive exploitation can only lead to our own destruction. We cannot trade the welfare of our future generations for profit now. We must abide by the Natural Law or be victim of its ultimate reality. We must stand together, the four sacred colors of man, as the one family that we are in the interest of peace. . . . We must raise leaders of peace. We must unite the religions of the world as the spiritual force strong enough to prevail in peace. It is no longer good enough to cry <u>peace</u>. We must act <u>peace</u>, live <u>peace</u>, and march in <u>peace</u> in alliance with the people of the world. We are the spiritual energy . . . Our energy is the combined will of <u>all</u> people with the spirit of the Natural World, to be one body, one heart, and one mind for <u>peace</u>. . . ."

CHIEF LEON SHENANDOAH *(Grand Council of the Six Nations Iroquois Confederacy), Address to the General Assembly of the United Nations, October 25, 1985*

"There are no passengers on Spaceship Earth. Everybody's crew."

MARSHALL MCLUHAN

"The tree which moves some to tears of joy is in the eyes of others only a green thing that stands in the way."

WILLIAM BLAKE

"It is an historic call to humanity that we, the humans, who today control everything on the Earth, and who have enormous powers to do or undo the future, must now become stewards of the Earth. We must accept our modest responsibility to bow down to the larger values and higher purposes which would unite us with 20 million other species sharing this home. In our arrogance we cannot think of being alone, nor can we alone survive life's evolutionary process. . . . [W]e finite human beings must . . . integrate ourselves with the larger principles of nature which determine the processes of the universe."

RASHMI MAYUR

"*We* can have justifiable pride only if we face the monumental issues of changing the social and ecological systems that have brought us to the edge of degradation. How can we stand tall and rejoice in our strength if we do not become earth-honoring? How can we respect ourselves if we do not care enough to husband and pass on the heritage of earth's fullness to our children?"

SAM KEEN, *Fire in the Belly: On Being a Man*

"*Continue* to contaminate your own bed, and you will one night suffocate in your own waste."

CHIEF SEATTLE

"*We* can listen to the voice of the Earth as she shakes and sings her song expressing her tiredness. She is calling us to attention, to be alert, to recognize that now is the time to transform selfish thought and action to compassionate caretaking. Do we want a world of peace and harmony? Are we willing to make the peace within ourselves? Will we call it forth? It is your choice. Your thought and action make a difference."

DHYANI YWAHOO

"*Don't* ever apologize for crying for the trees burning in the Amazon or for the water polluted from mines in the Rockies. . . . Don't apologize for the sorrow, grief and rage you feel. It's a measure of your humanity and your maturity. It is a measure of your open heart, and as your heart breaks open, there will be room for the world to heal."

JOANNA MACY, *Dharma Gaia*

"*In* our enchantment with technological growth, we have extinguished so many species that by all reckoning the Cenozoic Age is over. . . . Yet in its ashes, the Ecozoic Age is struggling to be born, guided by a vision we can no longer call utopian, since our survival depends on it. Recognizing human life as derivative and the natural world as primary, we'll grant all species their habitats and freedom of life expression. As we cease assaulting the planet in a frenzied attempt to find salvation through technology and consumerism, we'll learn to treat the Earth as a self-organizing community deserving of our respect and courtesy."

THOMAS BERRY, *The Dream of the Earth*

"The world is not to be put in order, the world is order incarnate. It is for us to put ourself in unison with this order."

HENRY MILLER

"When you heal yourself and assist others with their self-healing, you heal the earth. For the earth is one with everyone and every creature. . . .

The simple loving of the earth is healing. When you love the earth you bring energy for her healing. There is interconnectedness between earth energy and personal energy, and use of that energy is what the transition is all about."

EARTH MOTHER, *Earth Changes Channelling*

"Whatever befalls the Earth
befalls the sons of the Earth.
Man did not weave the web of life,
he is merely a strand in it.
Whatever he does to the web,
he does to himself."

CHIEF SEATTLE

"The choice is each person's . . . to use personal and group power as it can be used for the advancement of humanity or to use one's Goddess-potential for the destruction . . . and the disruption of the Earth. It is the responsibility of all who are awake to make this tenuous balance known, that none may later say they did not understand all that was being held in the balance."

MEREDITH LADY YOUNG, *Agartha: A Journey to the Stars*

"When the animals come to us,
  asking for our help,
  will we know what they are saying?

When the plants speak to us
  in their delicate, beautiful language,
  will we be able to answer them?

When the planet herself
  sings to us in our dreams,
  will we be able to wake ourselves, and act?"

GARY LAWLESS

"Together we shall save our planet or together we shall perish in its flames. Save it we can, and save it we must, and then shall we earn the eternal thanks of mankind and, as peace-makers, the eternal blessing of God."

JOHN F. KENNEDY, *Speech to the United Nations General Assembly (September 25, 1961)*

> "He who regards the world as he does the fortune of his own body can govern the world. He who loves the world as he does his own body can be entrusted with the world."
>
> TAO TE CHING

"We are made from Mother Earth and we go back to Mother Earth. We can't 'own' Mother Earth. We're just visiting here. We're the Creator's guests. He's invited us to stay for awhile, and now look what we've done to His Creation. . . . I'm working for the Creation. I refuse to take part in its destruction."

CHIEF   LEON   SHENANDOAH
(Grand   Council   of   the   Six
Nations Iroquois Confederacy)

iii. Responsibility to Self

"To be free is simply not to follow our ever-changing wants wherever they may lead. To be free is to choose what we shall want, what we shall value, and therefore what we shall be."

LAURENCE TRIBE, "Ways Not to
Think About Plastic Trees: New
Foundations for Environmental
Law," 83 Yale L.J. 1315,
1326-27 (1974)

"[Man's sin is in his failure to live what he is."

> ABRAHAM JOSHUA HESCHEL, *The Earth Is The Lord's*

"Become aware of what is in you. Announce it, pronounce it, produce it, and give birth to it."

> MEISTER ECKHART

"We cannot blame God for withholding providence from us; it is <u>we</u> who must be prepared to <u>accept</u> it. If we can just hold on long enough not to act on fear or luck, abundance on earth will be manifest in the fullness that was originally intended."

> ALAN COHEN, *The Dragon Doesn't Live Here Anymore*

"Be what you is, not what you ain't, 'cause if you ain't what you is, you is what you ain't."

> LUTHER D. PRICE

"To be a philosopher is not merely to have subtle thoughts, nor even to found a school, but so to love wisdom as to live according to its dictates, a life of simplicity, independence, magnanimity and trust."

> HENRY DAVID THOREAU, *Walden*

"The object of the man is to make daylight shine through him, to suffer the law to traverse his whole being without obstruction, ..."

> RALPH WALDO EMERSON, Essays

"Man is asked to make himself what he is supposed to become to fulfill his destiny."

> PAUL TILLICH

"We alone decide the kind of God that manifests through us."

> WESLEY LA VIOLETTE, *The Creative Light*

"This above all: to thine own self be true,
And it must follow, as the night the day,
Thou canst not then be false to any man."

> WILLIAM SHAKESPEARE, *Hamlet I.iii*

"The greatest human quest is to know what one must do in order to become a human being."

> IMMANUEL KANT

"Action springs not from thought, but from a readiness for responsibility."

> DIETRICH BONHOEFFER

"Sovereignty is something that goes in ever-widening circles, beginning with yourself. In order . . . to attain sovereignty, each of us has to be sovereign in ourselves. . . . Sovereignty isn't something someone gives you. You can't give us our sovereignty. Sovereignty isn't a privilege someone gives you. It's a responsibility you carry inside yourself. In order for my people to achieve sovereignty, each man and woman among us has to be sovereign. Sovereignty begins with yourself."

> EDDIE BENTON-BANAI *(Ojibway Indian)*

"Freedom is neither waywardness nor lawlessness, but the expression of one's inner law. Freedom and law do not exclude each other . . . Freedom consists in the right application of laws, in making the right use of them, and this depends . . . on the degree of our knowledge or insight into the nature of things, i.e., into our own nature. It is only there that freedom can be found. To express one's own inner law, one's character, in one's actions, is true self-expression, and self-expression is the hallmark of freedom."

LAMA ANAGARIKA GOVINDA, "*The Problem of Past and Future,*" *Nature, Man, and Society: Main Currents in Modern Thought*

"Each soul must meet the morning sun, the new, sweet earth, and the Great Silence alone!"

CHARLES ALEXANDER EASTMAN (*Santee Sioux*)

"Man's faith is inadequate if his whole existence is determined by something less than ultimate. Therefore, he must always try to break through the limits of his finitude and reach what never can be reached, the ultimate itself."

PAUL TILLICH, *Dynamics of Faith*

"If you do not feel free, it is because you have not yet declared your own freedom, you are waiting for it to be given to you.

You will wait forever."

PAUL WILLIAMS, *Das Energi*

"[O]ur deeds must express our freedom above all, otherwise we become like wheels revolving because compelled. There is a harmony between doing and not doing, between gaining and renouncing, which we must attain."

RABINDRANATH   TAGORE,
Sadhana

"We are told by Spirit that we have to build a belief system in which we carry the law in our hearts -- not one where we look over our shoulder to somebody else. We have to learn to take direct responsibility for our lives on an everyday basis."

SUN BEAR

"If you bring forth what is within you, what you bring forth will save you. If you do not bring forth what is within you, what you do not bring forth will destroy you."

THE GOSPEL OF THOMAS 70

"[E]verything can be taken away from a man but one thing: the last of the human freedoms -- to choose one's attitude in any given set of circumstances, to choose one's own way."

VIKTOR FRANKL

"Freedom is not something that anybody can be given; freedom is something people take and people are as free as they want to be."

JAMES BALDWIN

iv. *R*esponsibility to Children

"*A*ll children are born a genius, they just get de-geniused quickly."
BUCKMINSTER FULLER

"*The* senses you created in us are on the side of spirit.
Lord, creation-callousness
is not separate from Kingdom-callousness!
Blunting, dulling, and deadening
the senses of Child
killing the sentient Child,
is not only a sin against nature --
It is a sin against the Kingdom."

EDNA HONG, *Clues to the Kingdom*

"[*T*]he ultimate goal of education should be the attainment of 'full humanity,' . . . By 'full humanity' I mean the highest, integrated development of the bio-physical, emotional, intellectual, and spiritual activity of which the individual human being is capable, . . ."

DAVID WHITE, "*Toward Education for Full Humanity,*" *Nature, Man, and Society: Main Currents in Modern Thought*

"*W*hen will we teach our children in school what they are? We should say to each of them: Do you know what you are? You are a marvel. You are unique. In all of the world there is no other child exactly like you. In the millions of years that have passed there has never been another child like you. Look at your body -- what a wonder it is! your legs, your arms, your cunning fingers, the way you move! You may become a Shakespeare, a Michelangelo, a Beethoven. You have the capacity for anything. Yes, you are a marvel. And when you grow up, can you then harm another who is, like you, a marvel?"

PABLO CASALS, *Joys and Sorrows*

"*W*e enter into this life with the total knowledge we have learned to help the Mother Earth. Our purpose is to protect the Earth. This is why our children must be born to this world in warmth and love, and raised with such. They must be allowed to keep their Spirit memories and use them to aid the Mother."

BUCK GHOSTHORSE

"[*E*]ducation . . . should be directed to the development of as many heroes, saints, and sages as possible."

DAVID WHITE, "*Toward Education for Full Humanity*," *Nature, Man, and Society: Main Currents in Modern Thought*

"The child must know that he is a miracle,
that since the beginning of the world there hasn't
  been
and until the end of the world
there will not be another child like him.
He is a unique thing,
from the beginning to the end of the world.
Now, that child acquires a responsibility:
'Yes, it is true, I am a miracle.
I am a miracle like a tree is a miracle,
like a flower is a miracle.
Now, if I am a miracle, can I do a bad thing?
I can't, because I am a miracle'."
PABLO CASALS

"In the end we will conserve only what we love; we will love only what we understand; and we will understand only what we are taught."
BABA DIOUM *(Senegal Indian)*

"Good children are defined as meek, considerate, unselfish and perfectly law-abiding. Such rules leave no place for vitality, spontaneity, inner freedom, inner independence and critical judgment."
JOHN BRADSHAW

"No one has yet fully realized the wealth of sympathy, kindness and generosity hidden in the soul of a child. The effort of every true education should be to unlock that treasure."
EMMA GOLDMAN, *Living My Life*

"*We* cannot obtain right human relations if we do not give the children an honest view of the world into which they are born. We must give them a global view of the planet's marvels and conditions, of the human family and its rich diversity, we must give them to understand that they are a cosmos of their own endowed with the miracle of life among innumerable brethren and sisters on our planet. We must tell each child that he is a unique happening in the universe which will never be repeated in exactly the same form. Right human relations require that we tell the children how they should relate to the skies, to the stars, to the sun, to the infinite, to time, to the human family, to their planet and to all their human brethren and sisters. . . . We must tell them a story which no longer has anything to do with idealism but which reflects common facts derived from the collective efforts of the human family to learn, to understand and to elevate itself."

ROBERT MULLER, *New Genesis:*
Shaping a Global Spirituality

"*The* . . . goal of education . . . is a highly developed and developing person who works effectively in one or more of those areas of human achievement known as heroic action, selfless love, and humane wisdom."

DAVID WHITE, "*Toward Education*
for Full Humanity," *Nature,*
Man, and Society: Main Currents
in Modern Thought

"*There* are heroes in the seaweed,
There are children in the morning,
They are leaning out for love,
And they will lean that way forever."

LEONARD COHEN, "*Suzanne*"

"There should be no economy in education. Money should never be weighed against the soul of a child."

WILLIAM ELLERY CHANNING

"If you do not bend the twig of a vine when it is young, you cannot bend it when it hardens."

TALMUD

"What youth needs is a sense of significant being, a sense of reverence for the society to which we all belong."

ABRAHAM JOSHUA HESCHEL, *The Wisdom of Heschel*

"You must teach your children that the ground beneath their feet is the ashes of our grandfathers. So that they will respect the land, tell your children that the earth is rich with the lives of our kin. Teach your children what we have taught our children, that the earth is our mother."

CHIEF SEATTLE

v. Responsibility to Future Generations

"God has lent us the earth for our life; it is a great entail. It belongs as much to those who are to come after us, and whose names are already written in the book of creation, as to us; and we have no right, by anything we do or neglect, to involve them in unnecessary penalties, or deprive them of benefits which it was in our power to bequeath."

JOHN RUSKIN, "The Lamp of Memory," *The Seven Lamps of Architecture*

"It is our task in our time and in our generation to hand down undiminished to those who come after us, as was handed down to us by those who went before, the natural beauty which is ours."

JOHN F. KENNEDY, Speech Dedicating The National Wildlife Federation (March 3, 1961)

"Many of the earth's habitats, animals, plants, insects and even micro-organisms that we know to be rare may not be known at all by future generations. We have the capability and the responsibility to act; we must do so before it is too late."

TENZIN GYATSO, 14TH DALAI LAMA OF TIBET, Humanity and Ecology

"The young today are, more than ever, the last great hope for the planet. We cannot waste them to a system that is so narrow that it defines economics (which means keeping a household) by facile numbers about stocks, bonds, capital, and money. The economics of the future must be defined by the wealth, which is the health, of Mother Earth and her children, especially the children yet to come."

MATTHEW FOX, Creation Spirituality: Liberating Gifts for the Peoples of the Earth

"The revolt from Great Britain and the formations of our new governments at that time, were nothing compared to the great business now before us; there was then a certain degree of enthusiasm, which inspired and supported the minds; but to view, through the calm, sedate medium of reason the influence which the establishment now proposed may have upon the happiness or misery of millions yet unborn, is an object of such magnitude, as absorbs, and in a manner suspends the operation of the human understanding."

GEORGE MASON

"*Let* us develop the resources of our land, call forth its powers, build up its institutions, promote all its great interests, and see whether we also, in our day and generation, may not perform something worthy to be remembered."

DANIEL WEBSTER, *The Writings and Speeches of Daniel Webster*

"*If* we are to reach real peace in this world and if we are to carry on a real war against war, we shall have to begin with children; and if they will grow up in their natural innocence, we won't have to struggle; we won't have to pass fruitless idle resolutions, but we shall go from love to love and peace to peace, until at last all the corners of the world are covered with that peace and love for which consciously or unconsciously the whole world is hungering."

MOHANDAS K. (MAHATMA) GANDHI

"*We* who now live are parts of a humanity that extends into the remote past, a humanity that has interacted with nature. The things in civilization we most prize are not ourselves. They exist by grace of the doings and sufferings of the continuous human community in which we are a link. Ours is the responsibility of conserving, transmitting, rectifying, and expanding the heritage of values we have received that those who come after us may receive it more solid and more secure, more widely accessible, and more generously shared than we have received it."

JOHN DEWEY

"Think not forever of yourselves, O Chiefs, nor of your own generation. Think of continuing generations of our families, think of our grandchildren and of those yet unborn, whose faces are coming from beneath the ground."

PEACEMAKER *(Founder of the Iroquois Confederacy)*

"We give thanks to the Creator for . . . [the] fruits of the sea. We ask his blessings on the food that we eat and on all the generations that follow us down to the Seventh Generation. May the world we leave them be a better one that was left to us. Amen."

HARRIETT   STARLEAF   GUMBS *(Shinnecock Indian)*

"In our way of life, in our government, with every decision we make, we always keep in mind the Seventh Generation to come. It's our job to see that the people coming ahead, the generations still unborn, have a world no worse than ours - and hopefully better. When we walk upon Mother Earth we always plant our feet carefully because we know the faces of our future generations are looking up at us from beneath the ground. We never forget them."

CHIEF   OREN   LYONS *(Onondaga Indian)*

"The choice is ours. It can only be made by each of us, one at a time, one day at a time, but the results will shape the lives of our children and our children's children for centuries to come. Our choice, I hope, will ensure that those centuries will come in peace and harmony and those children will flourish."

EKNATH EASWARAN, *The Compassionate Universe: The Power of the Individual to Heal the Environment*

"*We* seek a renewed stirring of life for the earth,
We plead that what we are capable of doing is
not always what we ought to do.
We urge that all people now determine
that a wide untrampled freedom shall remain
to testify that this generation has love for the next.
If we want to succeed in that, we might show, meanwhile,
a little more love for this one, and for each other."

NANCY NEWHALL

B. *Power* OF ONE

i. *Power* of Individual

"*First*, is the danger of futility; the belief there is nothing one man or one woman can do against the enormous array of the world's ills -- against misery and ignorance, injustice and violence. Yet many of the world's great movements, of thought and action, have flowed from the work of a single man."

SENATOR ROBERT F. KENNEDY, "*Day of Affirmation*," *Address Delivered at the University of Capetown, South Africa (June 6, 1966)*

"If we desire sincerely and passionately the safety, the welfare and the free development of the talents of all men, we shall not be in want of the means to approach such a state. Even if only a small part of mankind strives for such goals, their superiority will prove itself in the long run."

ALBERT EINSTEIN, *Out of My Later Years*

"Never doubt that a small group of thoughtful committed citizens can change the world. Indeed, it's the only thing that ever has."

MARGARET MEAD

"Strength of numbers is the delight of the timid. The valiant in spirit glory in fighting alone."

MOHANDAS   K.   (MAHATMA) GANDHI

"Every revolution was once a thought in one man's mind, and when the same thought occurs to another man, it is the key to that era."

RALPH WALDO EMERSON, *History*

"I long to accomplish a great and noble task, but it is my duty to accomplish humble tasks as though they were great and noble. The world is moved along, not only by the mighty shoves of its heroes, but also by the aggregate of the tiny pushes of each honest worker."

HELEN KELLER

"I believe sincerely that every man has consummate genius within him. Some appear to have it more than others only because they are aware of it more than others are, and the awareness or unawareness of it is what makes each one of them into masters or holds them down to mediocrity. I believe that mediocrity is self-inflicted and that genius is self-bestowed.

Every successful man I have ever known, and I have known a great many, carries with him the key which unlocks that awareness and lets in the universal power that has made him into a master."

WALTER RUSSELL

"*We* have found a strange footprint on the shores of the unknown. We have devised profound theories, one after another, to account for its origin. At last, we have succeeded in the reconstruction of the creature that made the footprint. And lo: It is our own."

SIR ARTHUR STANLEY EDDINGTON

"*Few* will have the greatness to bend history itself; but each of us can work to change a small portion of events, and in the total of all those acts will be written the history of this generation."

SENATOR ROBERT F. KENNEDY, *"Day of Affirmation," Address Delivered at the University of Capetown, South Africa (June 6, 1966) -- Congressional Record, June 6, 1966, Vol. 112, p. 12430.*

"*One* man with courage makes a majority."

ANDREW JACKSON

"*In* a gentle way, you can shake the world."

MOHANDAS K. (MAHATMA) GANDHI

"*This* soul ... can only be a conspiration of individuals."

PIERRE TEILHARD de CHARDIN, *Human Energy*

"One person can make an extraordinary difference. The great task is to nourish and uplift this vision of empowerment and human transformation throughout the world."

SASHA WHITE

"The smallest effort is not lost,
Each wavelet on the ocean tost
Aids in the ebb-tide or the flow;
Each rain-drop makes some floweret blow;
Each struggle lessens human woe."

CHARLES MACKAY

"Households, cities, countries, and nations have enjoyed great happiness when a single individual has taken heed of the Good and Beautiful. . . . Such men not only liberate themselves; they fill those they meet with a free mind."

PHILO

"One man may hit the mark, another blunder; but heed not these distinctions. Only from the alliance of the one, working with and through the other, are great things born."

ANTOINE DE SAINT EXUPERY

"Nonviolence, in its dynamic condition, means conscious suffering. It does not mean submission to the will of the tyrant, but it means the pitting of one's whole soul against the will of the tyrant. Working under this law of our being, this 'soul-force,' it is possible for a single individual to defy the whole might of an unjust empire."

MOHANDAS   K.   (MAHATMA) GANDHI

"The character of a whole society is the cumulative result of countless small actions, day in and day out, of millions of persons. . . . Who we are, as a society, is the synergistic accumulation of who we are as individuals. . . . Small changes that seem insignificant in isolation can be great contributions when they are simultaneously undertaken by many others."

> DUANE ELGIN, *Voluntary Simplicity*

> "Have you not heard of the saying of Vivekananda, that if one but thinks a noble, selfless thought even in a cave, it sets up vibrations throughout the world and does what has to be done -- what can be done?"
>
> RAMANA MAHARSHI

"You have certainly heard of the 'butterfly effect.' It is a belief that everything in the world is so mysteriously and comprehensively interconnected that a slight, seemingly insignificant wave of a butterfly's wing in a single spot on this planet can unleash a typhoon thousands of miles away. I think we must believe in this effect in politics. We cannot assume that our microscopic, yet truly unique everyday actions are of no consequence simply because they apparently cannot resolve the immense problems of today. This is an a priori nihilistic assertion, and it is an expression of the arrogant, modern rationality that believes it knows how the world works."

> VACLAV HAVEL, *Address to World Economic Forum (February 4, 1992)*

"I have not the shadow of a doubt that any man or woman can achieve what I have, if he or she would make the same effort and cultivate the same hope and faith."

> MOHANDAS K. (MAHATMA) GANDHI

ii. Individual Worth

"[The wind speaks not more sweetly to the giant oaks than to the least of all the blades of grass;

And he alone is great who turns the voice of the wind into a song made sweeter by his own loving."

KAHLIL GIBRAN, *The Prophet*

"The high, the generous, the self-devoted sect will always instruct and command mankind. Never was a sincere word utterly lost. Never a magnanimity fell to the ground but there is some heart to greet and accept it unexpectedly. A man passes for what he is worth. What he is engraves itself on his face, on his form, on his fortunes, in letters of light."

RALPH WALDO EMERSON, *Essays*

"Each of us is a fragment of divinity, a diamond in the making, each a fragment of the same precious jewel to be cut and polished until we shine like stars."

WESLEY LA VIOLETTE, *The Creative Light*

"Every man is more than just himself; he also represents the unique, the very special and always significant and remarkable point at which the world's phenomena intersect, only once in this way and never again. That is why every man's story is important, eternal, sacred; that is why every man, as long as he lives and fulfills the will of nature, is wondrous and worthy of every consideration."

           HERMANN HESSE

"We must think away from our puny selves and narrow environments and the little gods we have set up in our hearts and homes."

           KATHERINE TINGLEY, *The Gods Await*

"Every man should know that since creation no other man ever was like him. Had there been such another, there would be no need for him to be. . . . Each is called to perfect his unique qualities."

           BAAL SHEM TOV

"Most of the shadows of this life are caused by standing in one's own sunshine."

           RALPH WALDO EMERSON

"We carry in our innermost treasury vast stores of wealth which plainly have an outside origin; but first, last, and all the time, i.e., in our sanity, we possess an integral self-identical self, which knows what it knows and does what it does. It is, or at least can become, a highly complex spiritual reality, with a sphere and range of its own. We are in large measure the makers of ourselves; but fortunately we start with a precious impartation, or birth-gift, which is big with its potentiality of spirit. . . . And that self of ours, whatever its ultimate destiny may be, is utterly unique."

           RUFUS JONES, *Spirit in Man*

iii. Vision

"Whoever becomes imbued with a noble idea kindles a flame from which other torches are lit, and influences those with whom he comes in contact, be they few or many."

HENRY GEORGE, *Progress and Poverty*

"To know is not to prove, nor to explain. It is to accede to vision. But if we are to have vision, we must learn to participate in the object of vision. The apprenticeship is hard."

ANTOINE DE SAINT EXUPERY, *Flight to Arras*

"Not failure, but low aim, is crime."

JAMES RUSSELL LOWELL, "*For an Autograph,*" *The Writings of James Russell Lowell*

"[T]he 'way' is not marked out by clear, definite guide-posts or finger pointers. Like all spiritual ventures it involves risk and danger; it calls for great vision and for creative, road-making work."

RUFUS JONES, "*An Interpretation of Quakerism*"

"I think the man of science makes the mistake, and the mass of mankind along with him, to suppose that you should give your chief attention to the phenomenon which excites you, as something independent of you, and not as it is related to you. The important fact is its effect on me. The man of science thinks I have no business to see anything else but just what he defines the rainbow to be, but I care not whether my vision is a wakening thought or dream remembered, whether it is seen in the light or in the dark. It is the subject of the vision, the truth alone that concerns me. The philosopher for whom rainbows . . . can be explained away never saw them."

HENRY   DAVID   THOREAU,
Autumn

"*Life* is too short to be little."

BENJAMIN DISRAELI

"*Where* there is no vision, people perish."

PROVERBS 29:18

"*If* the world has ever changed, it is only when people go into action. For directed actions we need leaders of vision, commitment, purpose and integrity. Ultimately, the real test of leadership in the future will be in the way people in every corner of the world will be mobilized to become part of a long global journey of reconstruction for healing all that is destroyed and caring for all that is sacred. We are called upon to create through enduring labor a world of human possibilities and not a utopia. It will be a world which respects all life and honors the sacredness of the Earth."

RASHMI MAYUR

"*The* only limits are, as always, those of vision."

JAMES BROUGHTON

"Faith is a deep-seated capacity in man to forecast possibilities, a preperception of the way forward, a leap of vision which carries one beyond the verifiable courses of action."

RUFUS JONES, *A Call to What is Vital*

"I might have been born in a hovel, but I determined to travel with the wind and stars."

JACQUELINE   COCHRAN, *The Stars at Noon*

"We must take life as we find it and improve it as we can. We can improve it only if we have a vision of things worth working for."
LLOYD GARRISON

iv. Faith

"Truly, I say to you, if you have faith and never doubt . . . if you say to this mountain 'Be taken up and cast into the sea,' it will be done. And whatever you ask in prayer, you will receive if you have faith."
MATTHEW 21:21

"The Enlightened One has told you in never-to-be-forgotten words that this little span of life is but a passing shadow, a fleeting thing, and if you realize the nothingness of all that appears before your eyes, the nothingness of this material case that we see before us ever changing, then indeed there are treasures for you up above, and there is peace for you down here, peace which passeth all understanding, and happiness to which we are utter strangers. It requires an amazing faith, a divine faith and surrender of all that we see before us."

MOHANDAS K. (MATHAMA) GANDHI

"Faith consists in believing when it is beyond the power of reason to believe. It is not enough that a thing be possible for it to be believed."

PATRIE VOLTAIRE

"Come to the edge
He said. They said:
We are afraid.
Come to the edge
He said. They came.
He pushed them, and
they flew . . ."

GUILLAUME APOLLINAIRE

"Without faith a man can do nothing; with it all things are possible."

SIR WILLIAM OSLER

"And Jesus said unto them, Because of your unbelief: for verily I say unto you, If ye have faith as a grain of mustard seed, ye shall say unto this mountain, Remove hence to yonder place; and it shall remove; and nothing shall be impossible unto you."

MATTHEW 17:20

"[W]e have the knowledge and the power to mold the very face of things
. . . what we need is the will and the faith. . . . Faith is the most potent
weapon ever devised. Faith in action is the wellspring of . . . great
strength, the source of . . . great power and achievement. Do not lose faith
in mankind, and in the purposes of the Creator. Do not lose faith in the
future. Much is being done to promote brotherhood, understanding, and
peace. . . ."

DAVID E. LILIENTHAL

"What we do not understand is that we already have all the faith we could
possibly need, but we must learn how to use it. Faith is a light of living
intelligence and power within the soul . . . it is a thinking entity within your
consciousness now . . . and if it is not functioning properly, it is because
you have not trained it to do your bidding. This you must do, for Faith is
the power that can unite all the other powers of man in a perfect pattern of
mastery and dominion. Faith can dissolve the cords that bind the will of
man, and when the spiritual center of Will is free, the Power of Authority
is also released and 'man has but to speak and it is done.'"

JOHN   RANDOLPH   PRICE,   The
Super Beings

"You must not be frightened . . . when a sadness arises within you of such
magnitude as you have never experienced, or when a restlessness
overshadows all you do, like light and the shadow of clouds gliding over
your hand. You must believe that something is happening to you, that life
has not forgotten you, that it holds you in its hand. It shall not let you
fall."

RAINER MARIA RILKE, Letters To
A Young Poet

"One result of the unbelief of our day is the tragedy of trying to live a maximum life on a minimum faith. What we need is not faith in more things, but more faith in a few profound things."

RUFUS JONES, *The Testimony of the Soul*

"'To have faith -- not to hesitate.' Also: not to doubt. 'Faith is the marriage of God and the Soul.' In that case, certainty of God's omnipotence <u>through</u> the soul: with God all things are possible, <u>because</u> faith can move mountains."

DAG HAMMARSKJOLD, *Markings*

"Faith is the substance of things hoped for, the evidence of things not seen."

HEBREWS 11:1

"Once there lived a village of creatures along the bottom of a great crystal river. . . . Each creature in its own manner clung tightly to the twigs and rocks of the river bottom, for clinging was their way of life, and resisting the current was what each had learned from birth. But one creature said at last, 'I am tired of clinging. Though I cannot see it with my eyes, I trust that the current knows where it is going. I shall let go, and let it take me where it will.'

"The other creatures laughed and said, 'Fool. . . . Let go and that current you worship will throw you tumbled and smashed across the rocks.'

Yet in time, as the creature refused to cling again, the current lifted him free from the bottom, and he was bruised and hurt no more."

RICHARD BACH, *Illusions*

"Ask, and it shall be given you; seek, and ye shall find; knock, and it shall be opened unto you. For every one that asketh, receiveth; and he that seeketh, findeth; and to him that knocketh it shall be opened."
MATTHEW 7:7, 8

v. Hope

"Our problems are man-made, therefore they may be solved by man. And man can be as big as he wants. No problem of human destiny is beyond human beings."

JOHN F. KENNEDY, *Speech at the American University, Washington, D.C. (June 10, 1963)*

"We judge of a man's wisdom by his hope, knowing that the perception of the inexhaustibleness of nature is an immortal youth."

RALPH WALDO EMERSON, <u>*Essays*</u>

"Let there be many windows in your soul
That all the glory of the universe
May beautify it. Not the narrow pane
Of one poor creed can catch the radiant rays
That shine from countless sources. Tear away
The blinds of superstition; let the light
Pour through fair windows broad as truth itself
And high as Heaven.
Why should the spirit peer
Through some priest-curtained orifice, and grope
Along dim corridors of doubt, when all
The splendour from unfathomed seas of space

Might bathe it with their golden seas of love?
Sweep up the debris of decaying faiths,
Sweep down the cobwebs of worn-out beliefs,
And throw your soul wide open to the light
Of reason and of knowledge. Tune your ear
To all the wordless music of the stars,
And to the voice of nature, and your heart
Shall turn to truth and goodness, as the plant
Turns to the sun. A thousand unseen hands
Reach down to help you from their peace-crowned heights,
And all the forces of the firmament
Shall fortify your strength. Be not afraid
To thrust aside half-truths and grasp the whole."

> RALPH WALDO TRINE, *In Tune with the Infinite*

"With just a micromeasure of hope, the task of attempting understanding becomes a joyous endeavor."

> HAROLD J. MOROWITZ, *"Biology as a Cosmological Science," Nature, Man, and Society: Main Currents in Modern Thought*

"... [A]s the springs return - regardless of time or man - so is HOPE! Sometimes but a tiny bud that has to push up through the hard shell of circumstance to reach the light of accomplishment. Do not give up HOPE!"

> DOROTHY MILLER COLE

"*L*oving means to love that which is unlovable or it is no virtue at all. Forgiving means to pardon the unpardonable. Faith means believing the unbelievable; and hoping means to hope when things are hopeless."

G. K. CHESTERTON

"*A*ll things are possible once enough human beings realize that the whole of the human future is at stake."

NORMAN COUSINS

"*F*aith has to do with things that are not seen, and hope with things that are not in hand."

SAINT THOMAS AQUINAS, *Summa Theologica*

"*H*ope is a memory of the future."

GABRIEL MARCEL

"*W*e must accept finite disappointment, but we must never lose infinite hope."

MARTIN LUTHER KING, JR.

"*H*ope is the thing with
  feathers
That perches in the soul,
And sings the tune without
  the words,
And never stops at all."

EMILY DICKINSON

"If you do not hope, you will not find what is beyond your hopes."
ST. CLEMENT OF ALEXANDRIA

"[There are no impossibilities to force us into a negation of hope."
RUFUS JONES, *Spirit in Man*

vi. Belief

~~~

"Hold onto dreams
For if dreams die,
Life is a broken winged bird
And cannot fly."
LANGSTON HUGHES

"If you have a strong dream, even if it seems an impossible one, something will happen -- signs, occasions, coincidences -- and help will come your way which will make your dream possible."
ROBERT MULLER, *A Planet of Hope*

"In this age of wonders no one will say that a thing or an idea is worthless because it is new. To say it is impossible because it is difficult, is again not in consonance with the spirit of the age. Things undreamt of are daily being seen, the impossible is ever becoming possible."
MOHANDAS K. (MAHATMA) GANDHI

"*W*ho dream the dream which all men always declare futile. Who dream the hour which is not yet on earth -- and lo! it strikes."

EDWARD CARPENTER

"*W*hat things soever ye desire, when ye pray, believe that ye receive them, and ye shall have them."

MARK 11:24

"*K*eep your face to the sunshine and you cannot see the shadow."

HELEN KELLER

"*I*n order to model a happy and beautiful world, we must believe in it, we must work at it, we must be in love with it."

ROBERT MULLER

"*A* miracle cannot prove what is impossible; it is useful only to confirm what is possible."

MAIMONIDES, *Guide of the Perplexed*

vii. Knowledge

> "A fool sees not the same tree that a wise man sees.
> He whose face gives no light, shall never become a star."
>
> WILLIAM BLAKE, *The Marriage
> of Heaven and Hell*

"Cosmically acceptable and effective decisions of humanity . . . will not be made by leaders single or plural, political or religious, military or mystic, by coercion or mob psychology.

The effective decisions can only be made by the independently thinking and adequately informed human individuals and their telepathically intercommunicated wisdom -- the wisdom of the majority of all such human individuals -- qualifying for continuance in the Universe as local cosmic problem-solvers -- in love with the truth and in individually spontaneous self-commitment to absolute faith in the wisdom, integrity, and love of God, who seems to wish Earthian humans to survive."

R.   BUCKMINSTER   FULLER,
Critical Path

"These days people seek knowledge, not wisdom. Knowledge is of the past; wisdom is of the future."

VERNON   COOPER   *(Lumbee
Indian)*

C. FIRE IN THE BELLY

i. Action

"Life is a romantic business. It is painting a picture, not doing a sum -- but you have to make the romance, and it will come to the question how much fire you have in your belly."

OLIVER WENDELL HOLMES, *Letter to Oswald Ryan (March 8, 1911)*

"No one, having put his hand to the plow, and looking back, is fit for the kingdom of God."

LUKE 9:62

"Knowledge will forever govern ignorance; and a people who mean to be their own governors, must arm themselves with the power which knowledge gives."

JAMES MADISON

"Live your beliefs and you can turn the world around."

HENRY DAVID THOREAU, *Walden*

"*What* is faith worth if it is not translated into action."
                    MOHANDAS K. (MAHATMA) GANDHI

"*People* have never fully used the powers they possess to advance the good in life because they have waited upon some power external to themselves to do the work they are responsible for doing."
                    JOHN DEWEY

"*All* Love is Divine. . . . Even when Love takes an object, It is holy, for Love is Love, and It is uncompromising in Its commitment to Its own purpose. As the first two leaves of a flower, which will later drop away, help the stem rise out of the soil, conditional Love is a herald of the unlimited Love to come. With Love we learn forgiveness, and with forgiveness, compassion. We come to understand that Love remains constant through the evolution of Its expression."
                    ALAN COHEN, *The Dragon*
                    Doesn't Live Here Anymore

"*Manhood* begins when we have in any way made truce with Necessity; begins even when we have surrendered to Necessity, as the most part only do; but begins joyfully and hopefully only when we have reconciled ourselves to Necessity; and thus, in reality, triumphed over it, and felt that in Necessity we are free."
                    THOMAS   CARLYLE,   "Burns,"
                    Critical and Miscellaneous Essays

"*I* don't want to be saved, I want to be spent."
                    FREDERICK S. PERLS

"*W*hen you are completely caught up in something, you become oblivious to things around you, or to the passage of time. It is this absorption in what you are doing that frees your unconscious and releases your creative imagination."

ROLLO MAY, *The Courage to Create*

"*O*ur life should be so active and progressive as to be a journey."

HENRY   DAVID   THOREAU, *Journals*

"*T*hings won are done, joy's soul lies in the doing."

WILLIAM SHAKESPEARE, *Troilus and Cressida*

"*L*et no one think that the birth of humanity is to be felt without terror. The transformations that await us cost everything in the way of courage and sacrifice. Let no one be deluded that a knowledge of the path can substitute for putting one foot in front of the other."

M. C. RICHARDS, *Centering*

"*M*any are called
but most are frozen
in corporate or
collective cold,
these are the stalled
who choose not to be chosen
except to be bought and sold."

LEE CARROLL PIEPER

"[*D*]o not wait for great strength before setting out, for immobility will weaken you further. Do not wait to see very clearly before starting: One has to walk toward the light. Have you strength enough to take this first step?"

PHILIPPE VERNIER

"*Only* life avails, not the having lived. Power ceases in the instant of repose; it resides in the moment of transition from a past to a new state, in the shooting of the gulf, in the darting to an aim."

RALPH WALDO EMERSON, *Essays*

"[*B*]y their fruits ye shall know them."

MATTHEW 7:20

"*Let* the beauty we love be what we do."

Jalal-ud-Din RUMI

"*N*ever measure the height of a mountain until you have reached the top. Then you will see how low it was."

DAG HAMMARSKJOLD

"*The* great end of life is not knowledge but action."

THOMAS HENRY HUXLEY

"*Do* the thing and you will have the power."

RALPH WALDO EMERSON

"*The* great aim of education is not knowledge but action."

HERBERT SPENCER

"God appears to you not in person but in action."

MOHANDAS   K.   (MAHATMA)
GANDHI

"Until you try, you don't know what you can't do."

HENRY JAMES

"Working at the edge of the development of human society is to work on the brink of the unknown. Much of what is done will one day prove to have been of little avail. That is no excuse for the failure to act in accordance with our best understanding, in recognition of its limits but with faith in the ultimate result of the creative evolution in which it is our privilege to cooperate."

DAG HAMMARSKJOLD

"However many holy words you read, however many you speak, what good will they do you if you do not act upon them?"

THE DHAMMAPADA

"You will decide on a matter, and it will be established for you, and light will shine on your ways."

JOB 22:28

"Love seeks no cause beyond itself and no fruit; it is its own fruit, its own enjoyment. I love because I love; I love in order that I may love."

SAINT BERNARD

"It is precisely the soul that is the traveler; it is of the soul and of the soul alone that we can say with supreme truth that 'being' necessarily means 'being on the way' (en route)."

GABRIEL MARCEL, *Homo Viator*

"*Never* look down to test the ground before taking your next step: only he who keeps his eye fixed on the far horizon will find his right road."

DAG HAMMARSKJOLD, *Markings*

"*Live* as though the day were here."

NIETZSCHE

"*Stamp* out hesitation before it grows into fear."

PAUL WILLIAMS, *Das Energi*

"*Waste* no more time talking about great souls and how they should be. Become one yourself!"

MARCUS AURELIUS, *Meditations*

"*For* a small reward a man will hurry away on a long journey, while for eternal life many will hardly take a single step."

THOMAS A. KEMPIS

"*Every* act leaves the world with a deeper or a fainter impress of God."

ALFRED NORTH WHITEHEAD, *Religion in the Making*

"*In* our era, the road to holiness necessarily passes through the world of action."

DAG HAMMARSKJOLD, *Markings*

"Science may have found a cure for most evils, but it has found no remedy for the worst of them all -- the apathy of human beings."

HELEN KELLER, *My Religion*

"Wisdom without action hath its seat in the mouth; but by means of action, it becometh fixed in the heart."

SHEKEL HAKODESH

"My writings should be cremated with my body. What I have done will endure, not what I have said and written."

MOHANDAS   K.   (MAHATMA) GANDHI

"'The Uncarved Block' -- remain at the Center, which is yours and that of all humanity. For those goals which it gives to your life, do the utmost which, at each moment, is possible for you. Also, act without thinking of the consequences, or seeking anything for yourself."

DAG HAMMARSKJOLD, *Markings*

"Don't say things. What you are stands over you the while, and thunders so that I cannot hear what you say to the contrary."

RALPH WALDO EMERSON, "*Social Aims*," *Letters and Social Aims*

"What happens to a dream deferred?
Does it dry up
like a raisin in the sun?
Or fester like a sore --
And then run?
Does it stink like rotten meat?
Or crust and sugar over --
like a syrupy sweet?

Maybe it just sags
like a heavy lead.

Or does it explode?"

LANGSTON HUGHES, "Harlem," *Selected Poems of Langston Hughes*

"The ultimate validation of belief is action."

ISRAEL GOLDSTEIN, *The Courage of Conviction*

ii. Purpose and Principle

"We may make mistakes -- but they must never be mistakes which result from faintness of heart or abandonment of moral principle."

FRANKLIN D. ROOSEVELT, *Fourth Inaugural Address (January 20, 1945)*

"*I* know that there are some rare spirits who find the inspiration of every moment, the aim of every act, in holiness. I am enough of a Puritan, I think, to conceive the exalted joy of those who look upon themselves only as instruments in the hand of a higher power to work out its designs. But I think that most men do and must reach the same result under the illusion of self-seeking. If the love of honor is a form of that illusion, it is no ignoble one. If it does not lift a man on wings to the sky, at least it carries him above the earth and teaches him those high and secret pathways across the branches of the forest the travellers on which are only less than winged."

> OLIVER WENDELL HOLMES, *Yale University Commencement Speech (June 30, 1886)*

"*W*ithout the transcendent and transpersonal, we get sick . . . or else hopeless and apathetic. We need something 'bigger than we are' to be awed by and to commit ourselves to . . ."

> ABRAHAM MASLOW, *Toward a Psychology of Being*

"*L*et us raise a standard to which the wise and honest can repair."
> GEORGE WASHINGTON

"*S*ocrates: 'Take no thought for your persons and your properties, but first and chiefly care about the great improvement of the soul.'"
> PLATO, *Apology*

"*T*is the business of little minds to shrink; but he whose heart is firm, and whose conscience approves his conduct, will pursue his principles unto death."

> THOMAS PAINE

"There are some men who lift the age they inhabit, till all men walk on higher ground in that lifetime."

MAXWELL ANDERSON, *Valley Forge*

"In matters of style, swim with the current; in matters of principle, stand like a rock."

THOMAS JEFFERSON

"Hold yourself responsible for a higher standard than anyone else expects of you. Never excuse yourself."

HENRY WARD BEECHER

"Set your hearts on his Kingdom realm first, and on his righteousness, and all those other things will be given to you as well."

MATTHEW 6:33

"You are here in order to enable the world to live more amply, with greater vision, with a finer spirit of hope and achievement. You are here to enrich the world, and you impoverish yourself if you forget the errand."

WOODROW WILSON

"The problem is to maintain . . . [a] cosmic standpoint in the face of an immediate earthly pain or joy. The taste of the fruit of the temporal draws the concentration of the spirit away from the center of the eon to the peripheral crisis of the moment. The balance of perfection is lost, the spirit falters, and the hero falls."

JOSEPH CAMPBELL, *The Hero with a Thousand Faces*

"Men of character are the conscience of the society to which they belong."

RALPH WALDO EMERSON, *Essays*

"Strong lives are motivated by dynamic purposes."
KENNETH HILDEBRAND

"When you are inspired by some great purpose, some extraordinary project, all your thoughts break their bonds; your mind transcends limitations, your consciousness expands in every direction, and you find yourself in a new, great and wonderful world. Dormant forces, faculties, talents become alive, and you discover yourself to be a greater person by far than you ever dreamed yourself to be."
PATANJALI

"The spiritual life . . . [is] no longer a matter for the monk or priest, but an urgent and vital requirement for all men as the fulfillment of their real nature . . ."

U. A. ASRANI, *"A Modern Approach to Mystical Experience," Nature, Man, and Society: Main Currents in Modern Thought*

"[The] . . . feature of a beyond within us, this capacity of before and after, this power to see our deed in the light of an ideal forecast, furnishes us with a fundamental form of distinction between what was, or is, and what might have been -- between a good and a possible better. . . . [W]e slowly roll up and accumulate through life-experience with others a concrete or dispositional conscience, which becomes, or may become, a perennial nucleus of inward moral wisdom and guidance. This becomes, or may become, to us the deep self which we really <u>are</u>, the self we propose to <u>be</u>, the self which we would even die to preserve. This deep-lying nuclear moral guardian in us is one of the most amazing features of a rightly fashioned life, . . ."

RUFUS JONES, *Spirit in Man*

"This is the true joy in life: the being used for a purpose recognized by yourself as a mighty one, the being thoroughly worn out before you're thrown on the scrap heap; the being a force of nature instead of a feverish little clod of ailments and grievances complaining that the world will not devote itself to making you happy."

GEORGE BERNARD SHAW

"A man is measured by the expanse of the moral horizon he chooses to inhabit."

SANDOR MCNAB

"We think our civilization near its meridian, but we are yet only at the cock-crowing and the morning star. In our barbarous society the influence of character is in its infancy. As a political power, as the rightful lord who is to tumble all rulers from their chairs, its presence is hardly yet suspected."

RALPH WALDO EMERSON, *Essays*

"Two things fill the mind with ever new and increasing admiration and awe: the starry heavens above me and the moral law within me."

IMMANUEL KANT

> "The most exalted type of heroism involves feelings that one has lived to some purpose that transcends one."
> ERNEST BECKER

"I think that we should be men first, and subjects afterward. It is not desirable to cultivate a respect for the law, so much as for the right."
HENRY DAVID THOREAU, *Civil Disobedience*

"I inherited a belief that no life was more satisfactory than one of selfless service to your country or humanity. This service required a sacrifice of all personal interests, but likewise the courage to stand up unflinchingly for your convictions concerning what was right and good for the community, whatever were the views in fashion."
DAG HAMMARSKJOLD

"Love, truth, and the courage to do what is right should be our own guideposts on this lifelong journey."
CORETTA SCOTT KING, *The Words of Martin Luther King, Jr.*

"Every person has his or her insight into the whole and I see that as a bonding. We all need each other to see the wholeness of the Great Spirit. All these separate visions and people receiving wholly and becoming holy make the world holy . . . We've got to make good manifest. By doing I don't necessarily mean activity, but simply by being real and eschewing anything that's off-centre, anything that is less than real, less than the whole, less than the dignity of being human."
MEINRAD CRAIGHEAD

"The most august thing in the world is the moral imperative of <u>ought</u> in us, the consciousness in a crisis that 'I cannot do otherwise' or, again, on occasion, that 'I <u>must</u> do this.' This impulsion of <u>must</u> gives us an unparalleled dignity. You do not become Adam -- the man -- until something of that order of <u>must</u> appears. The moral elevation of mind and character varies in degree from individual to individual, and scales so low in some that it appears from the outside observation to be almost absent. On the other hand, it rises in moral geniuses to a height of sublimity and seems like a divine commitment in the soul."

RUFUS JONES, *Spirit in Man*

"I have spent my days stringing and unstringing my instrument while the song I came to sing remains unsung."

RABINDRANATH TAGORE

"The purpose of life is a life of purpose."

ROBERT BYRNE

"Work that produces unnecessary consumer junk or weapons of war is wrong and wasteful. Work that is built upon false needs of unbecoming appetites is wrong and wasteful. Work that deceives or manipulates, that exploits or degrades is wrong and wasteful. Work that wounds the environment or makes the world ugly is wrong and wasteful. There is no way to redeem such work by enriching it or restructuring it, by specializing it or nationalizing it, by making it 'small' or decentralized or democratic."

THEODORE ROSZAK, *Person/Planet*

"Nothing is more powerful than an individual acting out of conscience, thus helping to bring the collective conscience to life."

NORMAN COUSINS

"It is easier to fight for one's principles than to live up to them."

ALFRED ADLER

"Conscience is . . . the surest moral authority within our reach -- a voice to be implicitly obeyed in the crisis of an action. It is our highest guide. No command on earth can take precedence over it."

RUFUS JONES, *The Nature and Authority of Conscience*

"The purpose of existence is that we human beings, all nations and the whole of humanity, should constantly progress toward perfection. We must search for these conditions and hold fast to these ideals. If we do this, our finite spirit will be in harmony with the infinite."

ALBERT SCHWEITZER, *Reverence for Life*

"[L]ike life itself, spiritual value will be determined largely by personal faith, qualities of character, dedication of spirit, sensitiveness to guidance and willingness to pay the cost of excellence."

RUFUS JONES, "*An Interpretation of Quakerism*"

iii. Truth

"Sometimes we are said to love another, that is, to stand in a true relation to our friend, so that we give the best to, and receive the best from, him. Between whom there is hearty truth, there is love, and in proportion to our truthfulness and confidence in one another, our lives are divine and miraculous, and answer to our ideal."

HENRY DAVID THOREAU, *A Week on the Concord and Merrimack Rivers*

"It is natural to man to indulge in the illusions of hope. We are apt to shut our eyes against a painful truth -- and listen to the song of that syren, till she transforms us into beasts. Is this the part of wise men, engaged in a great and arduous struggle for liberty? Are we disposed to be of the number of those, who having eyes, see not, and having ears, hear not, the things which so nearly concern their temporal salvation? For my part, whatever anguish of spirit it might cost, I am willing to know the whole truth; to know the worst, to provide for it."

PATRICK HENRY

"Character is a natural power, like light and heat, and all nature cooperates with it. The reason why we feel one man's presence, and do not feel another's, is as simple as gravity. Truth is the summit of being: justice is the application of it to affairs."

RALPH WALDO EMERSON, *Essays*

"Ye shall know the truth and the truth shall make you free."
JOHN 8:32

"Only a little of the first fruits of wisdom, only a few fragments of the boundless heights, breadths, and depths of truth, have I been able to gather."
MARTIN LUTHER

"There is little hope for us until we become tough-minded enough to break loose from the shackles of prejudice, half-truths and downright ignorance."
MARTIN LUTHER KING, JR.

"The moment you follow someone, you cease to follow Truth."
J. K. KRISHNAMURTI

"Seek truth and beauty together; you will never find them apart."
FRANCIS M. CORNFORD, "The Harmony of the Spheres"

"[P]lunge into the truth, find out who the teacher is, Believe in the great sound!"
KABIR

"Truth is completely spontaneous. Lies have to be taught."
R. BUCKMINSTER FULLER

iv. Sacrifice and Service

"When you cease to make a contribution, you begin to die."

ELEANOR ROOSEVELT, *Letters: The Years Alone*

"I don't know what your destiny will be, but one thing I know: the only ones among you who will be truly happy are those who will have sought and found how to serve."

ALBERT SCHWEITZER, *The Philosophy of Civilization*

"An individual has not started living until he can rise above the narrow confines of individualistic concerns to the broader concerns of all humanity."

MARTIN LUTHER KING, JR., *Words of M. L. King, Jr.*

"There is a growing awareness of people's responsibilities to each other and to the planet we share. Even though so much suffering continues to be inflicted upon individuals and peoples in the name of ideology, religion, history or development, a new hope is emerging for the downtrodden. People everywhere are displaying a willingness to sacrifice their own well-being and, at times, their lives for the rights and freedoms of their fellow human beings. The recent success of struggles for human rights and democracy in a number of Asian countries and elsewhere could not have taken place without the sympathy, support and concern of people . . . who feel a responsibility to help others."

> TENZIN GYATSO, 14TH DALAI LAMA OF TIBET, *Universal Responsibilities and Human Rights*

"There is no cause half so sacred as the cause of a people. There is no idea so uplifting as the idea of the service of humanity."

> WOODROW WILSON

"Until one learns to lose one's self he cannot find himself. No one can multiply himself by himself. He must first divide himself and give himself to the service of all, thus displacing himself within all others through acts of thoughtfulness and service."

> WALTER RUSSELL

"Do all the good you can,
By all the means you can,
In all the ways you can,
In all the places you can,
At all the times you can,
To all the people you can,
As long as ever you can."

> JOHN WESLEY, "Rule of Conduct," *Letters of John Wesley*

"Through this toilsome world, alas!
Once and only once I pass;
If a kindness I may show,
If a good deed I may do
To a suffering fellow man,
Let me do it while I can.
No delay, for it is plain
I shall not pass this way again."

AUTHOR UNKNOWN, "*I Shall Not Pass This Way Again,*" *The Best Loved Poems of the American People*

"There is no experience better for the heart than reaching down and lifting people up."

JOHN ANDREW HOLMER

"You will find as you look back upon your life that the moments when you have really lived are the moments when you have done things in the spirit of love."

HENRY DRUMMOND

"Then the virtuous will say to him in reply, 'Lord, when did we see you hungry and feed you; or thirsty and give you drink? When did we see you a stranger and make you welcome; naked and clothe you; sick or in prison and go to see you?' And the King will answer, 'I tell you solemnly, in so far as you did this to one of the least of these brothers of mine, you did it to me."

MATTHEW 25:37-41

"Though I speak with the tongues of men and of angels, and have not charity, I am become as sounding brass, or a tinkling cymbal.

And though I have the gift of prophecy, and understand all mysteries, and all knowledge; and though I have all faith, so that I could remove mountains, and have not charity, I am nothing.

And though I bestow all my goods to feed the poor, and though I give my body to be burned, and have not charity, it profiteth me nothing.

Charity suffereth long, and it is kind; charity envieth not; charity vaunteth not itself, is not puffed up.

Doth not behave itself unseemly, seeketh not her own, is not easily provoked, thinketh no evil;

Rejoiceth not in iniquity, but rejoiceth in the truth;

Beareth all things, believeth all things, hopeth all things, endureth all things.

Charity never faileth . . ."

I CORINTHIANS 13:1-8

"It makes us fearful to think of death.
But if one thinks of one's life as a service,
as a contribution to human ascent and evolution,
as a part of the flow of the mysterious universe,
then death is only a transformation,
a change of being."

ROBERT MULLER, A Planet of
Hope

"*We* are formed and molded by our thoughts. Those whose minds are shaped by selfless thoughts give joy when they speak or act. Joy follows them like a shadow that never leaves them."

> GUATAMA SIDDHARTHA (THE BUDDHA)

"*You* asked me to give you a motto. Here it is: Service. Let this word accompany each of you throughout your life. Let it be before you as you seek your way and your duty in the world. May it be recalled to your minds if ever you are tempted to forget it or set it aside. It will not always be a comfortable companion, but it will always be a faithful one. And it will be able to lead you to happiness."

> ALBERT SCHWEITZER

"*Human* progress is neither automatic nor inevitable. Even a superficial look at history reveals that no social advance rolls in on the wheels of inevitability. Every step toward the goal of justice requires sacrifice, suffering and struggle; the tireless exertions and passionate concern of dedicated individuals. Without persistent effort, time itself becomes an ally of the insurgent and primitive forces of irrational emotionalism and social destruction. This is no time for apathy and complacency. This is a time for vigorous and positive action."

> MARTIN LUTHER KING, JR.

"*The* Strait Road -- to live for others in order to save one's soul. The Broad -- to live for others in order to save one's self-esteem."

> DAG HAMMARSKJOLD, *Markings*

"I slept and dreamt that life
 was joy.
I awoke and saw that life was
 service.
I acted and behold, service
 was joy."

RABINDRANATH TAGORE

"The desire to serve others is the highest impulse of the human heart and the rewards of such service are beyond measure. If you wish to taste this joy, then just do it. Just take one step . . . You will see that the tyranny of self-concern, worry, and trivial pursuits can be released from your life with that single step. It doesn't really matter what you do, it only matters that you do it."

GANGA STONE

"We are free, not because we have freedom, but because we serve freedom."

CHRISTIAN   A.   HERTER,
Proclamation of Civil Rights
Week (December, 1955)

v. Struggle

"A man who has nothing which he is willing to fight for, nothing which he cares more about than he does about his personal safety, is a miserable creature who has no chance of being free, unless made and kept so by the exertions of better men than himself."

> JOHN STUART MILL, "*The Contest in America,*" *Fraser's Magazine (February 1862)*

"The struggle is my life."

> NELSON MANDELA

"[I]s he honest who resists his genius or conscience only for the sake of present ease or gratification?"

> WILLIAM BLAKE, *The Marriage of Heaven and Hell*

"When good people in any country cease their vigilance and struggle, then evil men prevail."

> PEARL S. BUCK, *Advice to Unborn Novelists*

"Man is a star bound to a body until in the end he is freed through his strife. Only by struggling and toiling thy utmost shall the star within thee bloom out in new life. He who knows the commencement of all things, free is his star from the realms of night."

> THE EMERALD TABLETS OF THOTH, Tablet III

"A man's life is interesting primarily when he has failed -- I well know. For it's a sign that he tried to surpass himself."

> GEORGES CLEMENCEAU, *Clemenceau, The Events of His Life as Told by Himself to His Former Secretary, Jean Martet*

"Strength does not come from physical capacity. It comes from an indomitable will."

> MOHANDAS   K.   (MAHATMA) GANDHI

"The heights by great men reached and kept
Were not attained by sudden flight,
But they, while their companions slept,
Were toiling upward in the night."

> HENRY   WADSWORTH LONGFELLOW

"Be strong!
We are not here to play, to dream, to drift;
We have hard work to do and loads to lift;
Shun not the struggle -- face it;
'tis God's gift."

> MALTBIE D. BABCOCK

> "*L*et him who seeks not cease from seeking
> until he finds;
> and when he finds,
> he will be disturbed;
> and when he is disturbed,
> he will marvel,
> and he shall reign over the All."
> THE GOSPEL OF THOMAS 2

"*O* joy of suffering!
To struggle against great odds! to meet enemies undaunted!
To be entirely alone with them! to find how much one can
    stand!
To love strife, torture, prison, popular odium, death, face
    to face!
To mount the scaffold! to advance to the muzzles of guns
    with perfect nonchalance!
To be indeed a God!"
WALT WHITMAN

"*The* block of granite which was an obstacle in the pathway of the weak,
became a stepping-stone in the pathway of the strong."
THOMAS CARLYLE

"One may not reach the dawn save by the path of the night."
KAHLIL GIBRAN, *Sand and Foam*

"*U*nrest of spirit is a mark of life."
KARL MENNINGER

"How hard the battle goes, the day how long
Faint not -- fight on! Tomorrow comes the song."
                                    MALTBIE D. BABCOCK

"Suffering is the ancient law of love; there is no quest without pain; there is no lover who is not also a martyr."
                                    HEINRICH SUSO

"People have, with the help of so many conventions, resolved everything the easy way, on the easiest side of easy. But it is clear that we must embrace struggle. Every living thing conforms to it. Everything in nature grows and struggles in its own way, establishing its own identity, insisting on it at all cost, against all resistance. We can be sure of very little, but the need to court struggle is a surety that will not leave us. . . . The fact that something is difficult must be one more reason to do it."

                        RAINER MARIA RILKE, *Letters To*
                        A Young Poet

"Who in this mortal life would see
The Light that is beyond all light,
Beholds it best by going forth,
Into the darkness of the Night."

                        ANGELUS SILESIUS, *The Cherubic*
                        Wanderer

"The highest reward for a person's toil is not what they get for it, but what they become by it."
                                    JOHN RUSKIN

"The ultimate measure of a man is not where he stands in moments of comfort and convenience, but where he stands at times of challenge and controversy. . . . In dangerous valleys and hazardous pathways, he will lift some bruised and beaten brother to a higher and more noble life."
MARTIN LUTHER KING, JR.

"Walls have been built against us, but we are always fighting to tear them down, and in the fighting, we grow, we find new strength, new scope."
ESLANDA GOODE ROBESON

"Opportunities to find deeper powers within ourselves come when life seems most challenging."
JOSEPH CAMPBELL

"Ultimately there is no way to avoid the hero's quest. It comes and finds us if we do not move out bravely to meet it. And while we may strive to avoid the pain, hardship and struggle it inevitably brings, life takes us eventually to the promised land, where we can be genuinely prosperous, loving, and happy. The only way out is through."
CAROL PEARSON, *The Hero Within: Six Archetypes We Live By*

"To be in circumstances that work in us, that place us before great aspects of nature from time to time, that is all we need."
RAINER MARIA RILKE, *Letters To A Young Poet*

"A clay pot sitting in the sun will always be a clay pot. It has to go through the white heat of the furnace to become porcelain."
MILDRED W. STOUVEN

"Nothing in this world can take the place of persistence. Talent will not; nothing is more common than unsuccessful men with great talent. Genius will not; unrewarded genius is almost a proverb. Education will not; the world is full of educated derelicts. Persistence, determination alone are omnipotent."

RAY KROC

"To fight out a war, you must believe something and want something with all your might. So must you do to carry anything else to an end worth reaching. More than that, you must be willing to commit yourself to a course, perhaps a long and hard one, without being able to foresee exactly where you will come out."

OLIVER WENDELL HOLMES, *Memorial Day Address (May 30, 1884)*

"Even as a teething child feels an aching and pain in its gums when a tooth has just come through, so does the soul of him who is beginning to grow his wings feel a ferment and painful irritation."

PLATO

"We choose to go to the moon in this decade, and do the other things, not because they are easy but because they are hard; because that goal will serve to organize and measure the best of our energies and skills."

JOHN F. KENNEDY, *Speech at Rice University (September 1962)*

vi. Fervor for Life

"The riders in a race do not stop short when they reach the goal. There is a little finishing cantor before coming to a standstill. There is time to hear the kind voice of friends and to say to one's self 'The work is done.' But just as one says that, the answer comes: 'The race is over, but the work never is done while the power to work remains.' The cantor that brings you to a standstill need not be only coming to rest. It cannot be while you are still alive. For to live is to function. That is all there is in living. And so I end with a line from a Latin poet who uttered the message more than fifteen hundred years ago. 'Death plucks my ears and says, Live -- I am coming.'"

OLIVER   WENDELL   HOLMES,
Radio Address on his 90th
Birthday (March 8, 1931)

"The addictive system is largely unaware of potential, gifts, excitement, aliveness, or the extravagance that surrounds us and in which we may take joy. The kind of extravagance I am talking about does not cost a great deal of money. . . . Simply, being alive is extravagant!"

ANNE   WILSON   SCHAEF, *The Addictive Organization*

"To be free, to be able to stand up and leave everything behind -- without looking back. To say 'Yes' . . ."

DAG HAMMARSKJOLD

"I want to be thoroughly used up when I die, for the harder I work, the more I live. I rejoice in life for its own sake. Life is no 'brief candle' to me. It is a sort of splendid torch which I have got hold of for a moment, and I want to make it burn as brightly as possible before handing it on to future generations."

GEORGE BERNARD SHAW

"Without work, all life goes rotten -- but when work is soulless, life stifles and dies."

ALBERT CAMUS

"It costs so much to be a full human being that there are very few who have the enlightenment, or the courage, to pay the price. . . . One has to abandon altogether the search for security, and reach out to the risk of living with both arms. One has to embrace the world like a lover, and yet demand no easy return of love. One has to accept pain as a condition of existence. One has to court doubt and darkness as the cost of knowing. One needs a will stubborn in conflict, but apt always to the total acceptance of every consequence of living and dying."

MORRIS L. WEST, The Shoes of the Fisherman

"Every great and commanding moment in the annals of the world is the triumph of some enthusiasm."

RALPH WALDO EMERSON, Nature Addresses and Lectures

"Goals and contingencies exist in the future and the past, beyond the pale of the sensory realm. Practice, the path of mastery, exists only in the present. You can see it, hear it, smell it, feel it. To love the plateau is to love the eternal now, to enjoy the inevitable spurts of progress and the fruits of accomplishment, then serenely to accept the new plateau that waits just beyond them. To love the plateau is to love what is most essential and enduring in your life."

GEORGE LEONARD, *Mastery: The Keys to Long-Term Success and Fulfillment*

"To him whose elastic and vigorous thought keeps pace with the sun, the day is a perpetual morning."

HENRY DAVID THOREAU, *Walden*

"Without belittling the courage with which men have died, we should not forget those acts of courage with which men . . . have <u>lived</u>. The courage of life is often a less dramatic spectacle than the courage of a final moment; but it is no less a magnificent mixture of triumph and tragedy. A man does what he must -- in spite of personal consequences, in spite of obstacles and dangers and pressures -- and that is the basis of all human morality. . . . In whatever arena of life one may meet the challenge of courage, whatever may be the sacrifices he faces if he follows his conscience -- the loss of his friends, his fortune, his contentment, even the esteem of his fellow men -- each man must decide for himself the course he will follow. The stories of past courage can define that ingredient -- they can teach, they can offer hope, they can provide inspiration. They cannot supply courage itself. For this each man must look into his own soul."

JOHN F. KENNEDY, *Profiles in Courage*

"When you were born, you cried and the world rejoiced. Live your life in such a manner that when you die the world cries and you rejoice."
OLD INDIAN SAYING

"If the people lived their lives
As if it were a song!
For singing out the light
Provides the music for the stars
To be dancing circles in the night."
RUSSIAN FOLKSONG

". . . If the day and night are such that you greet them with joy, and life emits a fragrance like flowers and sweet-scented herbs, is more elastic, more starry, more immortal -- that is your success. . . . The true harvest of my daily life is somewhat as intangible and indescribable as the tints of morning or evening. It is a little stardust caught, a segment of the rainbow which I have clutched. . . ."
HENRY DAVID THOREAU, *Walden*

"To finish the moment, to find the journey's end in every step of the road, to live the greatest number of good hours, is wisdom."
RALPH WALDO EMERSON, *Essays*

"We are not here just to survive and live long. . . . We are here to live and know life in its multi-dimensions -- to know life in its richness, in all its variety. And when a man lives multi-dimensionally, explores all possibilities available, never shrinks back from any challenge, Goes, rushes to it, welcomes it, rises to the occasion -- then life becomes a flame, life blooms."
BHAGWAN SHREE RAJNEESH

"*The* divinest things - religion, love, truth, beauty, justice -- seem to lose their meaning and value when we sink into lassitude and indifference. . . . It is a signal that we should quit meditation and books and go out into the open air, into the presence of nature, into the company of flocks and children, where we may drink new health and vigour from the clear and full-flowing fountains of life, afar from the arid wastes of theory and speculation; where we may learn again that it is not by intellectual questionings, but by believing, hoping, loving, and doing that man finds joy and peace."

JOHN LANCASTER SPALDING

"[*B*]ring your inner and outer life into harmony. . . . [F]ind enough patience within yourself to endure, and enough innocence to have faith. . . . [G]ain more and more trust in whatever is difficult for you. . . . Allow life to happen to you. . . . [L]ife is right in all cases."

RAINER MARIA RILKE, *Letters To A Young Poet*

"*People* say that what we're all seeking is a meaning for life. I don't think that's what we're really seeking. I think that what we're seeking is an experience of being alive, so that our life experiences on the purely physical plane will have resonances within our innermost being and reality, so that we actually feel the rapture of being alive."

JOSEPH CAMPBELL

"To laugh often and love much, to win the respect of intelligent persons and the affection of children; to earn the approbation of honest critics and to endure the betrayal of false friends; to appreciate beauty; to find the best in others; to give one's self; to leave the world a bit better, whether by a healthy child, a garden patch or a redeemed social condition; to have played and laughed with enthusiasm and sung with exaltation; to know even one life has breathed easier because you have lived, this is to have succeeded."

RALPH WALDO EMERSON, *Works of Ralph Waldo Emerson*

"What I cry out for, like every being, with my whole life and earthly passion, is something very different from an equal to cherish: it is a God to adore. To adore: that means to lose oneself in the unfathomable, to plunge into the inexhaustible, to find peace in the incorruptible, to be absorbed in immensity, to offer oneself to the fire and the transparency."

PIERRE TEILHARD de CHARDIN, *The Divine Milieu*

"There are men whose idea of life is static. . . . They forget that the true meaning of living is outliving, it is ever growing out of itself."

RABINDRANATH TAGORE, *Sadhana*

vii. Courage

"[The victory to be won in the twentieth century, this portal to the Golden Age, mocks the pretensions of individual acumen and ingenuity. For it is a citadel guarded by thick walls of ignorance and of mistrust which do not fall before the trumpets' blast or the politicians' imprecations or even a general's baton. They are, my friends, walls that must be directly stormed by the hosts of courage, of morality and of vision, standing shoulder to shoulder, unafraid of ugly truth, contemptuous of lies, half truths, circuses and demagoguery. . . ."

ADLAI E. STEVENSON, *Address to the Democratic National Convention (1952)*

"These are the times that try men's souls. The summer soldier and the sunshine patriot will, in this crisis, shrink from the service of their country; but he that stands it <u>now</u>, deserves the love and thanks of man and woman."

THOMAS PAINE, *The Writings of Thomas Paine*

"Our answer is the world's hope; it is to rely on youth. The cruelties and obstacles of this swiftly changing planet will not yield to obsolete dogmas and outworn slogans. It cannot be moved by those who cling to a present which is already dying, who prefer the illusion of security to the excitement of danger. It demands the qualities of youth: not a time of life but a state of mind, a temper of the will, a quality of the imagination, a predominance of courage over timidity, of the appetite for adventure over the love of ease."

ROBERT F. KENNEDY, "Day of Affirmation" (quoting Samuel Ullman)

"I decline to accept the end of man. It is easy enough to say that man is immortal simply because he will endure: that when the last ding-dong of doom has clanged and faded from the last worthless rock hanging tideless in the last red and dying evening, that even then there will still be one more sound: that of his puny and inexhaustible voice, still talking. I refuse to accept this. I believe that man will not merely endure: he will prevail. He is immortal, not because he alone among creatures has an inexhaustible voice, but because he has a soul, a spirit capable of passion and sacrifice and endurance. The poet's, the writer's, duty is to write about these things. It is his privilege to help man endure by lifting his heart, by reminding him of the courage and honor and hope and pride and compassion and pity and sacrifice which have been the glory of his past. The poet's voice need not merely be the record of man, it can be one of the props, the pillars to help him endure and prevail."

WILLIAM FAULKNER

"Those who won our independence by revolution were not cowards. They did not fear political change. They did not exalt order at the cost of liberty."

LOUIS D. BRANDEIS, Whitney v. California, 274 U.S. 357 (1927) (concurring opinion)

"Not gold but only men can make
A people great and strong;
Men who for truth and honor's sake
Stand fast and suffer long.

Brave men who work while others sleep,
Who dare while others fly --
They build a nation's pillars deep
And lift them to the sky."

RALPH WALDO EMERSON, "A Nation's Strength," *Masterpieces of Religious Verse*

"Behold the turtle. He makes progress only when he sticks his neck out."
JAMES V. CONANT

"It is impossible, I think, taking our nature into consideration, that anyone who fails to realize that he or she is favored by God should have the courage necessary for doing great things."
ST. TERESA OF AVILA, *Autobiography of St. Teresa of Avila*

"The Christ has chosen your hands to reach the lonely, your eyes to see innocence in the guilty, and your lips to utter words of comfort to the wounded. Let pain be no more! You have wandered in dark dreams for too long; now you must step into the light and stand for what you know is true. The world has suffered not from evil, but from the fear of the acknowledgment of good. That fear must be ended now, forever, and it is within your power to do so."

ALAN COHEN, *Lifestyles of the Rich in Spirit*

"God will not make himself manifest to cowards."

RALPH WALDO EMERSON, *Essays*

"[C]hanges cause many to lose perspective. . . . [A]s with the man on the pinnacle of the mountain, unusual imaginings emerge and strange sensations arise that seem to grow beyond everything endurable. . . . [I]t is necessary that we experience that also. We must accept our existence to the greatest extent possible; everything, the unprecedented also, needs to be accepted. That is basically the only case of courage required of us: to be courageous in the face of strangeness, the most . . . unexplainable thing that we could encounter.

The fact that people have been cowards in that regard has caused infinite harm to life."

RAINER MARIA RILKE, *Letters To A Young Poet*

"With courage you will dare to take risks, have the strength to be compassionate and the wisdom to be humble. Courage is the foundation of integrity."

KESHAVAN   NAIR,   *Beyond Winning*

"Often the difference between a successful man and a failure is not one's better abilities or ideas, but the courage that one has to bet on his ideas, to take a calculated risk -- and to act."

M A X W E L L   M A L T Z ,   *Psycho-Cybernetics*

"Far better is to dare mighty things, to win glorious triumphs even though checkered by failure, than to rank with those poor spirits who neither enjoy nor suffer much because they live in the gray twilight that know neither victory nor defeat."

THEODORE ROOSEVELT

"There are always risks in freedom. The only risk in bondage is that of breaking free."

GITA BELLIN

"How wonderful is the way in which, with quite ordinary folk, power leaps to our aid in any time of emergency. We lead timid lives, shrinking from difficult tasks till perhaps we are forced into them or ourselves determine on them, and immediately we seem to unlock the unseen forces. When we have to face danger, then courage comes, when trial puts a long-continued strain upon us, we find ourselves possessed by the power to endure; if when disaster ultimately brings the fall which we so long dreaded, we feel underneath us the strength as of the everlasting arms. Common experience teaches that, when great demands are made upon us, if only we fearlessly accept the challenge and confidently expend our strength, every danger or difficulty brings its own strength -- 'As thy days so shall thy strength be.'"

> J. A. HADFIELD, *The Psychology of Power*

> "We can easily forgive a child who is afraid of the dark; the real tragedy of life is when adults are afraid of the light."
> PLATO

"[T]he man who can most truly be counted brave is he who best knows the meaning of what is sweet in life and what is terrible, and then goes out undeterred to meet what is to come."
PERICLES

> "The exemplary man, the hero, is excited by the unknown. He hears the call and responds, not knowing where the journey will take him or what obstacles he will meet along the way. Cautious men will say that it is foolhardy to begin without a . . . report from a committee of experts and a promise of cooperation from appropriate governmental agencies. But official sanction for radical departures is seldom given. [H]eroes seldom ask permission from the authorities. In their foolishness they do not know the limits of the possible, so they screw up their courage, shoulder their doubts, and start down the path."

> SAM KEEN, *Fire in the Belly: On Being a Man*

"*How* could we be capable of forgetting the old myths that stand at the threshold of all mankind, myths of dragons transforming themselves at the last moment into princesses? Perhaps all dragons in our lives are really princesses just waiting to see us just once being beautiful and courageous. Perhaps everything fearful is basically helplessness that seeks our help."

RAINER MARIA RILKE, *Letters To A Young Poet*

"*Those* whose souls are weak settle for comfort or for violence."

ERICH FROMM, *The Sane Society*

"*We* must constantly build dykes of courage to hold back the flood of fear."

MARTIN LUTHER KING, JR.

"*When* the morning's freshness has been replaced by the weariness of midday, when the leg muscles quiver under the strain, the climb seems endless, and, suddenly, nothing will go quite as you wish -- it is then that you must not hesitate."

DAG HAMMARSKJOLD, *Markings*

"*As* long as you move from a place of fear and desire, you are self-excluded from immortality."

JOSEPH CAMPBELL

"*The* Master said, 'To see what is right and not to do it is want of courage.'"

CONFUCIUS, *Analects*

"Merely the simple, quiet, truthful carrying on of what you consider good and needful, quite independently of government and of whether it likes it or not. In other words: standing up for your rights, not as a member of the Literature Committee, not as a deputy, not as a landowner, not as a merchant, not even as a member of Parliament; but standing up for your rights as a rational and free man, and defending them, not as the rights of local boards or committees are defended, with concessions and compromises, but without any concessions and compromises, is the only way in which moral and human dignity can be defended."

LEO TOLSTOY, *The Kingdom of God Is Within You*

viii. Commitment

"There is something better, if possible, that a man can give than his life. That is his living spirit to a service that is not easy, to resist councils that are hard to resist, to stand against purposes that are difficult to stand against."

WOODROW WILSON, *Speech (May 30, 1919)*

>"*What* we now need to discover in the social realm is the moral equivalent of war; something heroic that will speak to man as universally as war does, and yet will be as compatible with their spiritual selves as war has proved to be incompatible."
>
> WILLIAM JAMES, *The Varieties Of Religious Experience*

"*Every* now and then I think about my own death, and I think about my own funeral. . . . I don't want a long funeral. And if you get somebody to deliver the eulogy, tell them not to talk too long. . . . Tell them not to mention that I have a Nobel peace prize. Tell them not to mention that I have three or four hundred other awards. I'd like somebody to mention that day that Martin Luther King Jr. tried to give his life to serving others. I'd like for somebody to say that day that Martin Luther King Jr. tried to love somebody.

Say that I was a drum major for justice. Say that I was a drum major for peace. That I was a drum major for righteousness. And all of the other shallow things will not matter. I won't have any money to leave behind. I won't have the fine and luxurious things of life to leave behind. But I just want to leave a committed life behind."

MARTIN LUTHER KING JR.

"*It's* not life that counts but the fortitude you bring in to it."

JOHN GALSWORTHY

"*Our* present way of life is characterized by lack of sensitivity and inventiveness, by a lack of freedom, by hypnotization by the profit motive. We need men and women who can think and invent with a mind filled with compassion, charged with the kind of creativity that finds a place for the smallest songbird and the largest elephant. We need people with the artistry to live in simplicity as the hummingbird does, enjoying the nectar without bruising the flower. We need men and women who delight in working together for a common goal."

EKNATH EASWARAN, *The Compassionate Universe: The Power of the Individual to Heal the Environment*

"Full effort is full victory. . . ."

MOHANDAS   K.   (MAHATMA) GANDHI

"Purity of heart is to will one thing."

SOREN KIERKEGAARD

"Put your heart, mind, intellect and soul even to your smallest acts. This is the secret of success."

S W A M I   S I V A N A N D A, *Karma-Yoga*

"Indifference is the invincible giant of the world."

OUIDA

"[The] emancipation of the self requires commitment."

REINHOLD NIEBUHR, *Religion and Freedom of Thought*

"The answer to helplessness is not so very complicated. A man can do something for peace without having to jump into politics. Each man has inside him a basic decency and goodness. If he listens to it and acts on it, he is giving a great deal of what it is the world needs most. It is not complicated but it takes courage. It takes courage for a man to listen to his own goodness and act on it. Do we dare to be ourselves? This is the question that counts."

PABLO CASALS

"Until one is committed, there is hesitancy, the chance to draw back, always ineffectiveness. Concerning all acts of initiative (and creation) there is one elementary truth the ignorance of which kills countless ideas and splendid plans: That the moment one definitely commits oneself then providence moves too.

All sorts of wonderful things occur to help one, that would never otherwise have occurred. A whole stream of events issues from the decision, raising in one's favor all manner of unforeseen incidents and meetings and material assistance which no one could have dreamed would come their way."

JOHANN   WOLFGANG   VON
GOETHE

ix. Boldness

"Prudence is a rich ugly old maid courted by Incapacity. He who desires but asks not, breeds pestilence."

WILLIAM BLAKE, *The Marriage of Heaven and Hell*

"If we would be guided by the light of reason, we must let our minds be bold."

LOUIS D. BRANDEIS

"To dare is to lose one's footing momentarily. To not dare is to lose oneself."

SOREN KIERKEGAARD

"Only those who risk going too far can possibly find out how far one can go."

T. S. ELIOT

"It is not because things are difficult that we do not dare; it is because we do not dare that they are difficult."

LUCIUS ANNAEUS SENECA

"Are you in earnest? Then seize
   this very minute.
What you can do, or dream you can,
   begin it;
Boldness has genius, power and magic in
   it;
only engage and then the mind
   grows heated;
Begin, and then the work will be
   completed."

JOHANN WOLFGANG VON GOETHE

"Tell me not, in mournful numbers,
　Life is but an empty dream! --
For the soul is dead that slumbers,
　And things are not what they seem.

Life is real! Life is earnest!
　And the grave is not its goal;
Dust though art, to dust returnest,
　Was not spoken of the soul.

Not enjoyment, and not sorrow,
　Is our destined end or way;
But to act, that each tomorrow
　Find us farther than today.

Art is long, and Time is fleeting,
　And our hearts, though stout and brave,
Still, like muffled drums, are beating
　Funeral marches to the grave.

In the world's broad field of battle,
　In the bivouac of Life,
Be not like dumb, driven cattle!
　Be a hero in the strife!

Trust no Future, howe'er pleasant!
　Let the dead Past bury its dead!
Act, -- act in the living Present!
　Heart within, and God o'erhead!

Lives of great men all remind us
　We can make our lives sublime,
And, departing, leave behind us
　Footprints on the sand of time;

Footprints, that perhaps another,
  Sailing o'er life's solemn main,
A forlorn and shipwrecked brother,
  Seeing, shall take heart again.

Let us, then, be up and doing,
  With a heart for any fate;
Still achieving, still pursuing,
  Learn to labor and to wait."

> HENRY   WADSWORTH
> LONGFELLOW, "*A Psalm of Life*"

"The solution to our environmental crisis lies in the fullness of our lives as individuals, in our compassion, daring, and artistry."

> EKNATH EASWARAN, *The Compassionate Universe: The Power of the Individual to Heal the Environment*

"Great spirits have always encountered violent opposition from mediocre minds."

> ALBERT EINSTEIN

"It is only in adventure that some people succeed in knowing themselves -- in finding themselves."

> ANDRE GIDE

"A decent boldness ever meets with friends."

> HOMER

"Only he who can expect anything, who does not exclude even the mysterious, will have a relationship to life greater than just being alive; he will exhaust his own wellspring of being. If we liken the existence of the individual to a room of a larger or smaller size, it is evident that most people are familiar with only a corner of their room, perhaps a window seat or a place where they pace to and fro. In that way they have a certain security. Yet every uncertainty fraught with danger is so much more human."

RAINER MARIA RILKE, *Letters To A Young Poet*

"Be a Columbus to whole new continents and worlds within you, opening new channels, not of trade, but of thought."

HENRY DAVID THOREAU, *Walden*

"Life is either an adventure, or it is nothing."

HELEN KELLER

"You must learn to make every act count, since you are going to be here for only a short while, in fact, too short for witnessing all the marvels of it. . . . Let each of your acts be your last battle on earth. Only under those conditions will your acts have rightful power. Otherwise, they will be . . . the acts of a timid man."

CARLOS CASTANEDA, *Journey to Ixtlan* (Don Juan)

"You pervade the universe and the universe exists in you. You are by nature Pure Consciousness. Do not be small-minded!"

ASHTAVAKRA SAMHITA 1.16

"He who hesitates on the brink of the dangerous waters of . . . knowledge, wishing for assurance of his safety before plunging, will never achieve inner certainty. One cannot learn to swim without swallowing much water."

SRI KRISHNA PREM, *Man, the Measure of All Things*

x. Passion

"I think that, as life is action and passion, it is required of a man that he should share the passion and action of his time at peril of being judged as not to have lived."

OLIVER WENDELL HOLMES, *Memorial Day Speech (May 30, 1884)*

"Your reason and your passion are the rudder and the sails of your seafaring soul.

If either your sails or your rudder be broken, you can but toss and drift, or else be held at a standstill in mid-seas.

For reason, ruling alone, is a force confining; and passion, unattended, is a flame that burns to its own destruction.

Therefore, let your soul exalt your reason to the height of passion, that it may sing;

And let it direct your passion with reason, that your passion may live through its own daily resurrection, and like the phoenix rise above its own ashes."

KAHLIL GIBRAN, *The Prophet*

"For it is not light that is needed, but fire; it is not the gentle shower, but thunder. We need the storm, the whirlwind, and the earthquake. The feeling of the nation must be quickened; the consciousness of the nation must be roused; the propriety of the nation must be startled; the hypocrisy of the nation must be exposed; and its crimes against God and man must be proclaimed and denounced."

FREDERICK DOUGLASS, "*What to the Slave Is the Fourth of July?*"

"The mother's battle for her child -- with sickness, with poverty, with war, with all the forces of exploitation and callousness that cheapen human life -- needs to become a common human battle, waged in love and in the passion for survival."

ADRIENNE RICH

"Complacency is a far more dangerous attitude than outrage."

NAOMI LITTLEBEAR, *The Dark of the Moon*

"What is required is a deed that a man does with his whole being."

MARTIN BUBER, *I and Thou*

xi. Crime of Silence

"To sin by silence, when we should protest,
Makes cowards out of men. The human race
Has climbed on protest. Had no voice been raised
Against injustice, ignorance, and lust,
The inquisition yet would serve the law,
And guillotines decide our least disputes.
The few who dare, must speak and speak again
To right the wrong of many. Speech, thank God,
Not vested power in this great day and land
Can gag or throttle. Press and voice may cry
Loud disapproval of existing ills;
May criticize oppression and condemn
The lawlessness of wealth-protecting laws,
That let the children and childbearers toil
To purchase ease for idle millionaires.

Therefore, I do protest against the boast
Of independence in this mighty land.
Call no chain strong, which holds one rusted link.
Call no land free, that holds one fettered slave.
Until the manacled slim wrists of babes
Are loosed to toss in childish sport and glee,
Until the mother bears no burden, save
The precious one beneath her heart, until
God's soil is rescued from the clutch of greed
And given back to labor, let no man
Call this the land of freedom."

ELLA   WHEELER   WILCOX,
"Protest," Poems of Problems

"*We* must never permit the voice of humanity within us to be silenced. It is man's symphony with all creatures that first makes him truly a man."

ALBERT   SCHWEITZER, *The Animal World of Albert Schweitzer*

"*The* worst sin towards our fellow-creatures is not to hate them but to be indifferent to them; that's the essence of inhumanity."

GEORGE BERNARD SHAW

"*The* only thing necessary for the triumph of evil is for good men to do nothing."

EDMUND BURKE

"*How* many years can a mountain exist
Before it's washed to the sea?
Yes,'n' how many years can some people exist
Before they're allowed to be free?
Yes, 'n' how many times can a man turn his head,
Pretending he just doesn't see?
The answer, my friend, is blowin' in the wind,
The answer is blowin' in the wind."

BOB   DYLAN, *"Blowin' in the Wind"*

"Peace has to be created in order to be maintained.
It is the product of Faith, Strength, Energy,
Will, Sympathy, Justice, Imagination, and the
triumph of principle. It will never be achieved
by passivity and quietism. Passivity and quietism
are invitations to war."

DOROTHY THOMPSON

"Mourn not the dead ...
But rather mourn the apathetic
  Throng --
The cowed and meek
Who see the world's great anguish
  And its wrong,
And dare not speak.

RALPH CHAPLIN, Mourn Not
The Dead

xii. Spiritual Warrior

"To abandon the struggle for private happiness, to expel all eagerness of temporary desire, to burn with passion for eternal things -- this is emancipation, and this is the free man's worship. And this liberation is effected by a contemplation of Fate; for Fate itself is subdued by the mind which leaves nothing to be purged by the purifying fire of Time."

BERTRAND A. RUSSELL, The Free
Man's Worship, Philosophical
Essays

"Of men can be found who revolt against the spirit of thoughtlessness, and who are personalities sound enough and profound enough to let the ideals of ethical progress radiate from them as a force, there will start an activity of the spirit which will be strong enough to evoke a new mental and spiritual disposition in mankind."

ALBERT SCHWEITZER, *Out of My Life and Thought*

"Hold firm, soldiers of Truth, to that which you cherish as dear. You may be tested and scorned, but the angel of the Valor protects you in your campaign. She looks over your shoulder in gentle support of your decision for God. Bear your loneliness bravely, and comrades of like purpose shall join you when you most need them."

ALAN COHEN, *The Dragon Doesn't Live Here Anymore*

"A spirituality that preaches resignation under official brutalities, servile acquiescence in frustration and sterility, and total submission to organized injustice is one which has lost interest in holiness and remains concerned only with a spurious notion of 'order.'"

THOMAS MERTON, *Conjectures of a Guilty Bystander*

"Life's fulfillment finds constant contradictions in its path; but those are necessary for the sake of its advance. The stream is saved from the sluggishness of its current by the perpetual opposition of the soil through which it must cut its way. It is the soil which form its banks. The Spirit of fight belongs to the genius of life."

RABINDRANATH TAGORE, *Glorious Thoughts of Tagore*

"To allow the spiritual warrior to emerge, there must be strong personal initiative and fire -- a vision-quest."

RON POLACK, *The Spiritual Warrior*

"The mission of the spiritual warrior is to bring into the world the full scope of divine light. The mission of the spiritual warrior is to drink passionately of the new wine of life."

MICHAEL EXETER, *The Spiritual Warrior*

D. BEAT OF DIFFERENT DRUMMER

i. Nonconformity

"Our dangers, as it seems to me, are not from the outrageous but from the conforming; not from those who rarely and under the lurid glare of obloquy upset our moral complaisance, or shock us with unaccustomed conduct, but from those, the mass of us, who take their virtues and their tastes, like their shirts and their furniture, from the limited patterns which the market offers."

LEARNED HAND, "The Preservation of Personality," Commencement Address at Bryn Mawr College, Bryn Mawr, Pennsylvania (June 2, 1927)

"If a man does not keep pace with his companion, perhaps it is because he hears a different drummer. Let him step to the music which he hears, however measured or far away."

HENRY DAVID THOREAU, *Walden*

"Conformity is the jailer of freedom and the enemy of growth."

JOHN F. KENNEDY, Speech to the United Nations General Assembly (September 25, 1961)

"Two roads diverged in a wood and I --
I took the one less traveled by,
And that has made all the difference."
　　　　　　　ROBERT FROST

"If you see in any given situation only what everybody else can see, you can be said to be so much a representative of your culture that you are a victim of it."
　　　　　　　S. I. HAYAKAWA

"Neutrality is at times a graver sin than belligerence."
　　　　　　　LOUIS D. BRANDEIS, *The Words of Justice Brandeis*

"The life-spirit and energy which contribute to the mastery of the creative process can never be fully engaged by a commitment to a compromise."
　　　　　　　ROBERT FRITZ, *The Path of Least Resistance*

"I find the great thing in this world is not so much where we stand, as in what direction we are moving: To reach the port of heaven, we must sail sometimes with the wind and sometimes against it -- but we must sail, and not drift, nor lie at anchor."
　　　　　　　OLIVER WENDELL HOLMES, *The Autocrat of the Breakfast-Table*

"*K*nowledge is not the conformity of the mind to the given, but an immersion in the process of transformation and construction of a new world."

GUSTAVO GUTIERREZ, *The Witness*

"*W*hoso would be a man must be a nonconformist."

RALPH WALDO EMERSON, *Essays*

"*A*nd be not conformed to this world: but be ye transformed by the renewing of your mind."

ROMANS 12:2

"*T*here are many who are living far below their possibilities because they are continually handing over their individualities to others. Do you want to be a power in the world? Then be yourself. Be true to the highest within your soul and then allow yourself to be governed by no customs or conventionalities or arbitrary man-made rules that are not founded on principle."

RALPH WALDO TRINE, *Two By Ralph Waldo Trine, In Tune With The Infinite*

"The way you activate the seeds of your creation is by making choices about the results you want to create. When you make a choice, you mobilize vast human energies and resources which otherwise go untapped. All too often people fail to focus their choices upon results and therefore their choices are ineffective. If you limit your choices only to what seems possible or reasonable, you disconnect yourself from what you truly want, and all that is left is a compromise."

ROBERT FRITZ, The Path of Least Resistance

"True satisfaction lies in swimming against the current of conditioned self-interest. It is dangerous, of course, but that is why it makes you glow with vitality. It is strenuous, but that is what makes your will and determination and dedication grow strong, your senses clear, your mind secure, and your heart overflowing with love and the desire to give and serve."

EKNATH EASWARAN, The Compassionate Universe: The Power of the Individual to Heal the Environment

"In every society . . . there are extraordinary men and women who, for a variety of reasons, stand outside the social consensus, shatter the norms, and challenge the status quo. These iconoclasts -- prophets, rebels, revolutionaries, reformers, shamans, visionaries, mystics, artists, madmen, geniuses, schizophrenics -- trouble the waters and disturb the majority but bring new creative energies into a society. As the pathfinders of new ways of being and seeing, they pay a high personal price. They are often painfully self-conscious and lonely, and are both stranger and stronger than average folk."

SAM KEEN, *Fire in the Belly: On Being a Man*

"I feel that what we must say to one another is based on encouraging each of us to be true to herself: 'Now that we are equal, let us dare to be different!'"

MARIA DE LOURDES PINTASILGO, *Sisterhood is Global*

"By conforming to spiritual ideals imposed from the outside through the force of tradition, people often channel themselves into models of behavior that violate their inner essence."

BRUGH JOY

"[The great creations of history, the creations that have their foundations upon the faith in the infinite in man, have not their origin in the common sense of practical men."

RABINDRANATH TAGORE, *Sadhana*

"Each one of us, as long as life stirs in him, may play a part in extricating himself from the power system by asserting his primacy as a person in quiet acts of mental or physical withdrawal -- in gestures of non-conformity, in abstentions, restrictions, inhibitions, which will liberate him from the domination of the pentagon of power."

LEWIS MUMFORD

"We must not allow other people's limited perceptions to define us."

VIRGINIA SATIR

"The only way the new kind of world will eventually come will be through the persistence, the patience and the unyielding faith of those who will not surrender, nor compromise, nor mistake expediency for truth."

RUFUS JONES, *The Faith and Practice of the Quakers*

"Never say: 'Let well enough alone.' . . . Be discontented. Be dissatisfied. 'Sweat and grunt' under present conditions. Be as restless as the tempestuous billow on the boundless sea. Let your discontent break mountain-high against the wall of prejudice, and swamp it to the very foundation. Then we shall not have to plead for justice nor on bended knee crave mercy; for we shall be men."

RIDGELY TORRENCE, *The Story of John Hope*

ii. Inner Guide

"There are moments in your life when you must act, even though you cannot carry your best friends with you. The 'still small voice' within you must always be the final arbiter where there is a conflict of duty."

MOHANDAS   K.   (MAHATMA) GANDHI

"No bird soars too high if he soars with his own wings."

WILLIAM BLAKE, *The Marriage of Heaven and Hell*

"Believe nothing, Oh monks, merely because you have been told it . . . or because it is traditional, or because you yourselves have imagined it. Do not believe what your teacher tells you merely out of respect for the teacher. But whatsoever, after due examination and analysis, you find to be conducive to the good, the benefit, the welfare of all beings -- that doctrine believe and cling to, and take it as your guide."

GUATAMA   SIDDHARTHA   (THE BUDDHA)

"If you do not express your own original ideas, if you do not listen to your own being, you will have betrayed yourself."

ROLLO MAY, *The Courage to Create*

"Love yourself. . . . And listen to what self says, what it needs to feel, and then pursue it, heartily, until you're bored with it. Boredom is a sign from our soul that you have learned all there is to learn from an experience, and that it is time to go on to another adventure. When you listen only to the feelings within you, then you are free to become in this moment whatever you choose to become."

RAMTHA

"There is a time in every man's education when he arrives at the conviction that envy is ignorance; that imitation is suicide; that he must take himself for better, for worse, as is his portion. . . . Trust thyself: every heart vibrates to that iron string. Accept the place the divine Providence has found for you: the society of your contemporaries, the connection of events."

RALPH WALDO EMERSON, *Essays*

"No one can ever set his foot upon the Path, can turn toward the Light within himself, and ever be the same again. If he stumbles on the way, if he grows confused, always there is heard the inner voice of distant memory to draw him back, to remind him of his deathless destiny. Always there are fitful gleams to remind him that his soul is never lost upon its Path. . . ."

WESLEY LA VIOLETTE, *The Creative Light*

"If ye know these things, happy are ye if ye do them."

JOHN 13:17

"[W]isdom comes only when you stop looking for it and start truly living the life the Creator intended for you."

LEILA FISHER *(Hoh Indian)*

"*We* need compassion; we need wisdom. In perplexity, when temptation turns us away from either or both, we need reliance on a guide who will remind us of their relevance to our lives, of their importance to ourselves as individuals, and because of our unique role in the history of our time, to the world which is emerging about us."

EARL WARREN, "*The Law Beyond the Law*," *Nature, Man, and Society: Main Currents in Modern Thought*

"[*B*]eneath the surface level of conditioned thinking in every one of us there is a single living spirit. The still small voice whispering to me in the depths of my consciousness is saying exactly the same thing as the voice whispering to you in your consciousness. 'I want an earth that is healthy, a world at peace, and a heart filled with love.' It doesn't matter if your skin is brown or white or black, or whether you speak English, Japanese, or Malayalam -- the voice, says the Gita, is the same in every creature, and it comes from your true self."

EKNATH EASWARAN, *The Compassionate Universe: The Power of the Individual to Heal the Environment*

"*Until* you can understand that nothing can happen to you, nothing can ever come to you or be kept from you, except in accord with your state of consciousness, you do not have the key to life."

PAUL TWITCHELL, *The Flute of God*

"*Be* a lamp to yourself. Be your own confidence. Hold to the truth within yourself, as to the only truth."

GUATAMA SIDDHARTHA (THE BUDDHA)

"When visions are deeply infused into the mind/body, supported by knowledge and charged with the power of emotion, do they begin to take the shape of reality. No other principle is really necessary. When people begin to experience, to understand, to believe -- and believe deeply -- about their true meaning and purpose, action will take place automatically . . . . "

EDGAR D. MITCHELL

"What a man does, that he has. What has he to do with hope or fear? In himself is his might. Let him regard no good as solid but that which is in his nature, and which must grow out of him as long as he exists. The goods of fortune may come and go like summer leaves; let him scatter them on every wind as the momentary signs of his infinite productiveness."

RALPH WALDO EMERSON, Essays

"[R]eflect on the world that you carry within yourself. And name this thinking what you wish. . . . [O]bserve carefully what wells up within you and place that above everything that you notice around you. Your innermost happening is worth all your love."

RAINER MARIA RILKE, Letters To
A Young Poet

"Until we learn to act from inner awareness instead of reacting to outside stimulus, we are only flotsam and jetsam on the sea of life."

DONNA H. LLOYD, The View from
Olympus: A New Gnostic Gospel

"The road to self-knowledge does not pass through faith. But only through the self-knowledge we gain by pursuing the fleeting light in the depth of our being do we reach the point where we can grasp what faith is."

DAG HAMMARSKJOLD, *Markings*

"There is only one Duty. It is to realize the divinity within. . . . It is our most sacred life purpose, the most honored ground of [our] existence, and everything else must be made to subserve it."

PAUL BRUNTON

"Do little things in an extraordinary way; be the best one in your line. You must not let your life run in the ordinary way; do something that nobody else has done, something that will dazzle the world. Show that God's creative principle works in you. Never mind the past. Though your errors be as deep as the ocean, the soul itself cannot be swallowed up by them. Have the unflinching determination to move on your path unhampered by limiting thoughts of past errors."

PARAMAHANSA YOGANANDA

"All paths lead to the same goal: to convey to others what we are. And we must pass through solitude and difficulty, isolation and silence, in order to reach forth to the enchanted place where we can dance our clumsy dance and sing our sorrowful song -- but in this dance or in this song there are fulfilled the most ancient rites of our conscience in the awareness of being human and in believing in a common destiny."

PABLO NERUDA

"Discovering the ways in which you are exceptional, the particular path you are meant to follow, is your business on this earth, whether you are afflicted or not. It's just that the search takes on a special urgency when you realize that you are mortal."

BERNIE SIEGEL, *Love, Medicine and Miracles*

"The artist within must fight the battle for Meaning with pen on paper, or brush on canvas, or chisel and wood and stone. But his Way, as that of Everyman, leads from ignorance, delusion, folly, self-inflation and phoniness to truth and authenticity. . . . The point of practicing an art is less to discover who you are than to become your truth, to be able to shed all sham, imposture and bluff in relation to yourself and others. True art is not in indulgence of the little self, but a manifestation of the Self."

FREDERICK FRANCK, *Art as a Way*

"I went down into my inmost self, to the deepest abyss where I feel dimly that my power of action emanates. But as I moved further and further away from the conventional certainties by which social life is superficially illuminated, I became aware that I was losing contact with myself. At each step of the descent a new person was disclosed within me of whose name I was no longer sure, and who no longer obeyed me. And when I had to stop my exploration because the path faded from beneath my steps, I found a bottomless abyss at my feet, and out of it comes -- arising I know not from where -- the current which I dare to call MY life."

PIERRE TEILHARD de CHARDIN

"If a plant cannot live according to its nature, it dies; and so a man."

HENRY DAVID THOREAU, *The Duty of Civil Disobedience*

"There is a force within that gives you life --
  seek that.
In your body there lies a priceless jewel --
  seek that.
Oh, wandering Sufi,
  if you are in search of the greatest treasure,
  don't look outside,
Look within, and seek that."

Jalal-ud-Din RUMI, *Diwan-i Shams-i Tabriz*

"All things consist of carrying to term and then giving birth. To allow the completion of every impression, every germ of a feeling deep within, in darkness, beyond words, in the realm of instinct unattainable by logic, to await humbly and patiently the hour of the descent of a new clarity: that alone is to live one's art, in the realm of understanding as in that of creativity."

RAINER MARIA RILKE, *Letters To A Young Poet*

iii. Follow Bliss

"All paths are the same: they lead nowhere . . . There are paths going through the bush, or in the bush. In my own life I could say I have traversed long, long paths, but I am not anywhere. My benefactor's question has meaning now. Does this path have a heart? If it does, the path is good; if it doesn't, it is of no use. Both paths lead nowhere; but one has a heart, the other doesn't. One makes for a joyful journey; as long as you follow it, you are one with it. The other will make you curse your life. One makes you strong; the other weakens you."

CARLOS   CASTANEDA,   *The Teachings of Don Juan*

"Do not lay up for yourselves treasures upon earth where moth and rust destroy and where thieves break through and steal. But lay up for yourselves treasures in heaven where neither moth nor rust destroys and where thieves do not break through and steal; for where your treasure is, there will your heart be also."

MATTHEW 6:19-21

"If the search for riches were sure to be successful, though I should become a groom with whip in hand to get them, I will do so. As the search may not be successful, I will follow after that which I love."

CONFUCIUS

"To believe your own thought, to believe that what is true for you in your private heart is true for all men -- that is genius. . . .

A man should learn to detect and watch that gleam of light which flashes across his mind from within, more than the luster of the firmament of bards and sages."

RALPH WALDO EMERSON, *Essays*

"[O]ur whole life consists primarily in our remaining faithful to the decisions which we have once made in the invisible and in full freedom. What is felt as renunciation represents itself merely as a transposition from the visible into the invisible. As a decision arrived at in the past it became valid for our present life; and that constellation in which this happened is at the same time our innermost core which rests in our deepest being and is thus our constant companion."

JEAN GEBSER, *Der unsichtbare Ursprung [The Invisible Origin]*

"Let us try to see, no longer with the eyes of the intellect alone, which grasps only the already made and which looks from the outside, but with the spirit, I mean with that faculty of seeing which is immanent in the faculty of acting and which springs up, somehow, by the twisting of the will on itself, when action is turned into knowledge, like heat, so to say, into light."

HENRI BERGSON, *Creative Evolution*

"The greater the joy within one's inner consciousness, the greater the force ... within one; .... The ecstatic man is the most dynamic, the most silent and the most undemonstrative of all men.

* * *

By ecstasy I mean inner joyousness, and by inner joyousness I mean those inspirational fires which burn within the consciousness of great geniuses, fires which give them an inconquerable vitality of spirit which breaks down all barriers as wheat bends before the wind.

He who cultivates that quiet, unobtrusive ecstasy of inner joyousness can scale any heights .... He who never finds it must be content to follow in the footsteps of those who do. ...."

WALTER RUSSELL, *The Man Who Tapped the Secrets of the Universe*

"You are what your deep, driving desire is."

BRIHADARANYAKA UPANISHAD

"If thou follows thy star, thou canst not fail of glorious heaven."

DANTE ALIGHIERI

"We hear with our hearts, or not at all, and not unless we are willing to be enchanted, inspirited, encouraged, and engaged."

SAM KEEN, *Fire in the Belly: On Being a Man*

"I know of no other advice than this: Go within and scale the depths of your being from which your very life springs forth."

RAINER MARIA RILKE, *Letters To A Young Poet*

"To find your own way is to follow your own bliss. This involves analysis, watching yourself and seeing where the real deep bliss is -- not quick little excitement, but the real, deep, life-filling bliss."

JOSEPH CAMPBELL

"To become free and responsible. For this alone was man created, and he who fails to take the Way which could have been his shall be lost eternally."

DAG HAMMARSKJOLD, *Markings*

"Let yourself be silently drawn
by the stronger pull of what you really love."

Jalal-ud-Din RUMI, *"An Empty Garlic"*

"Follow what you love! . . . Don't deign to ask what 'they' are looking for out there. Ask what you have inside. Follow not your interests, which change, but what you are and what you love, which will and should not change."

GEORGIE ANNE GEYER

"The road your Self must journey on lies in polishing the mirror of your heart. It is not by rebellion and discord that the heart's mirror is polished free of the rust of hypocrisy and unbelief; Your mirror is polished by your certitude by the unalloyed purity of your faith.

Break free from the chains you have forged upon yourself for you will be free when you are free of clay. The body is dark -- the heart is shining bright; the body is mere compost -- the heart a blooming garden."

HAKIM SANAI, *The Hadiqua --
The Walled Garden of Truth*

"Dance, . . . wherever you may be,
I am the Lord of the Dance, said he,
And I'll lead you all, wherever you may be,
And I'll lead you all in the dance, said he."

SYDNEY CARTER, "*'Tis a Gift to be
Simple*" a/k/a "*Lord of the Dance*"

"You must rediscover the moving power of your life. Tension, a lack of honesty, and a sense of unreality come from following the wrong force in your life."

JOSEPH CAMPBELL

iv. *H*eroes' Path

"*We* will not be driven by fear into an age of unreason if we . . . remember that we are not descended from fearful men, not from men who feared to write, to speak, to associate and to defend causes which were, for the moment, unpopular."

> EDWARD R. MURROW, "*See It Now*," *Television Broadcast (March 7, 1954)*

"*E*ach man's necessary path, though as obscure and apparently uneventful as that of a beetle in the grass, is the way to the deepest joys he is susceptible of. Though he converses only with moles and fungi, and disgraces his relatives, it does not matter, if he knows what is steel to his flint."

> HENRY   DAVID   THOREAU, *Autumn*

"*A* man's genius, the quality that differences him from every other, the susceptibility to one class of influences, the selection of what is fit for him, the rejection of what is unfit, determines for him the character of the universe. A man is a method, a progressive arrangement; a selecting principle, gathering his like to him, wherever he goes. He takes only his own, out of the multiplicity that sweeps and circles round him. . . .

* * *

. . . A few anecdotes, a few traits of character, manners, face, a few incidents, have an emphasis in your memory out of all proportion to their apparent significance, if you measure them by the ordinary standards. They relate to your gift. Let them have their weight, and do not reject them, and cast about for illustration and facts more usual in literature. Respect them, for they have their origin in deepest nature. What your heart thinks great is great. The soul's emphasis is always right."

RALPH WALDO EMERSON, Essays

"A clay pot sitting in the sun will always be a clay pot. It has to go through the white heat of the furnace to become porcelain."

· MILDRED WITTE STOUVEN

"We . . . have known . . . fully human individuals as 'heroes,' 'saints,' and 'sages.' The hero is the man of action who has served his fellow men in various notable ways, always involving a sustained self-sacrifice. The saint is known for a selfless love of God and His creatures, usually expressed in acts of devoted service. The sage is the man of wisdom whose knowledge is effectively directed to the attainment and maintenance of human welfare. These individuals have all displayed what are clearly supernormal powers of action, of devotion, and of knowledge . . . In terms of full humanity, they have actualized their individual human potential by means of singleness of purpose, self-discipline, and hard, sustained labor."

DAVID WHITE, "Toward Education for Full Humanity," Nature, Man, and Society: Main Currents in Modern Thought

"*N*ever be afraid to tread the path alone. Know which is your path and follow it wherever it may lead; do not feel you have to follow in someone else's footsteps."

EILEEN CADDY, *Footprints on the Path*

"*In* untroubled times, only extraordinary men and women radically question the consensus reality. However, in troubled times, the number of people thrown into psychological turmoil and radical questioning increases. And that, of course, is our present condition. . . . The hero's path is becoming crowded with individuals looking for a way into a more hopeful future."

SAM KEEN, *Fire in the Belly: On Being a Man*

"*The* characteristic of heroism is its persistency. All men have wandering impulses, fits and starts of generosity. But when you have chosen your part, abide by it, and do not weakly try to reconcile yourself with the world. The heroic cannot be the common, nor the common the heroic. Yet we have the weakness to expect the sympathy of people in those actions whose excellence is that they outrun sympathy, and appeal to a tardy justice."

RALPH WALDO EMERSON, *Essays*

"*The* hero must venture forth from the world of commonsense consciousness into a region of supernatural wonder."

JOSEPH CAMPBELL

"*In* the course of meeting a challenge that disrupts an initial state of innocence, the hero is initiated into a realm where he or she is faced with grave danger of some sort. With the assistance of allies, the hero breaks out of that world, to successfully meet the challenge and return home with a gift of a treasure or wisdom. The hero's return is celebrated and life is resumed -- somehow transformed by the Hero's Journey."

> LORNA CATFORD AND MICHAEL RAY, *The Path of the Everyday Hero*

"However close we sometimes seem to that dark and final abyss, let no man of peace and freedom despair. For he does not stand alone. . . ."

> JOHN F. KENNEDY, *Speech to the United Nations General Assembly (September 25, 1961)*

"[B]ecoming fully human means becoming an individual who works with unique effectiveness in one or more of three ways: by engaging in action for the welfare of his fellow creatures, by manifesting a selflessly loving devotion to God and man, or by showing extraordinary acuity in the application of knowledge to human good. . . . [I]n other words, . . . becoming a hero, a saint, or a sage."

> DAVID WHITE, *"Toward Education for Full Humanity," Nature, Man, and Society: Main Currents in Modern Thought*

E. CREATIVE BEING

i. Imagination

"Men are not prisoners of fate, but only prisoners of their own minds."
FRANKLIN D. ROOSEVELT, *Pan American Day Address (April 15, 1939)*

"Courage is the sine qua non of the virtues, for with it anything can happen, but without it only puny things occur. An increase in imagination often results in an increase in courage, for we get stuck when we see no way out of the fear, shame, or self-hatred that imprison us. Awakening the imagination awakens the heart and stretches it."
MATTHEW FOX, *Creation Spirituality: Liberating Gifts for the Peoples of the Earth*

"The Eternal Body of Man is The IMAGINATION."
WILLIAM BLAKE, *The Laocoon*

"Imagination is more important than knowledge."
ALBERT EINSTEIN

"The exhilarating quest for discovery, the search to find what magic lies beyond the stars and inside the atom, is at once wonderfully insatiable and wonderfully satisfying. We cannot find happiness in contemplating ourselves; but we can find it in contemplating infinity. Reaching out, with our imaginations, toward its majesty, it will in turn embrace us and inspire us."

JACQUES COUSTEAU, *The Cousteau Almanac*

"Every totalitarian regime is frightened of the artist. It is the vocation of the prophet to keep alive the ministry of imagination, to keep on conjuring and proposing alternative futures to the single one the king wants to urge as the only thinkable one."

WALTER BRUEGGEMANN, *The Prophetic Imagination*

"Every good idea and all creative work are the offspring of the imagination, and have their source in what one is pleased to call infantile fantasy. Not the artist alone but every creative individual owes all that is greatest in his or her life to fantasy. . . . Without this playing with fantasy no creative work has ever yet come to birth."

C. G. JUNG

"One of the most important things to remember is to use your imagination to the hilt. This is your intuitive force telling you to soar, and the more you use it the higher you will go with it. . . . Be an individual; think with your imagination."

GURU RHH

"I know of no other Christianity and of no other Gospel than the liberty both of body & mind to exercise the Divine Arts of Imagination."

WILLIAM BLAKE, *Jerusalem*

"[I]magination is the medium of the process of infinitizing . . . it is the faculty for all faculties. What feeling, knowledge, or will a man has depends in the last resort upon what imagination he has."

SOREN KIERKEGAARD, *Sickness Unto Death*

"Man's mind, once stretched by a new idea, never regains its original dimension."

OLIVER WENDELL HOLMES

"Within each of us is a capacity . . . to make break-throughs in our minds, to go beyond habit, to create and innovate, to imagine and to bring into our world not only a repetition of what has been, but an emergence of what could be."

DAVID SPANGLER

"The mightiest lever known to the moral world, Imagination."

WILLIAM WORDSWORTH

"Unite your imagination with the imagination of Nature and nothing will ever be impossible for you."

P. D. OUSPENSKY

"If our imagination is strong enough to accept the vision of ourselves as parts inseparable from the rest, and to extend our final interest beyond the boundary of our skins, it justifies even the sacrifice of our lives for ends outside of ourselves. The motive, to be sure, is the common wants and ideals that we find in man. Philosophy does not furnish motives, but it shows men they are not fools for doing what they already want to do. It opens to the forlorn hopes on which we throw ourselves away, the vista of the farthest stretch of human thought, the chord of a harmony that breathes from the unknown."

OLIVER   WENDELL   HOLMES,
Holmes Pollock Letters

"The primary IMAGINATION I hold to be the living Power and prime Agent of all human Perception, and as a repetition in the finite mind of the eternal act of creation in the infinite I AM."

SAMUEL   TAYLOR   COLERIDGE,
Biographia Literaria

ii. Idealism

"It is not a question of whether or not we are idealistic or realistic. All of us have some of each. The question is whether we see things as they are all around us today, or whether in the breadth of understanding and vision we see things as we think they ought to be. Too easily we become defeatists when all that we can see confronting us is chaos, upheaval and defeat. But those . . . who sound the battle-cry for the things that ought to be, and are willing to struggle, fight and if need be die to have them so; those who refuse to accept defeat, and turn the rout and tide of dark despair and deep defeat into a victory; they are the men who are the true realists. Always they have seen no image in their hearts save that of triumph, have seen no cross save that of victory. They labor now to realize the dreams of the future. They are the architects of all tomorrows."

WESLEY LA VIOLETTE, *The Creative Light*

"You see things; and you say, 'Why?' But I dream things that never were; and I say, "Why not?'"

GEORGE BERNARD SHAW, *Back to Methuselah*

"The idealists and visionaries, foolish enough to throw caution to the winds and express their ardor and faith in some supreme deed, have advanced mankind and have enriched the world."

EMMA GOLDMAN, *My Further Disillusion*

"No man has earned the right to intellectual ambition until he has learned to lay his course by a star which he has never seen -- to dig by the divining rod for springs which he may never reach. . . . For I say to you in all sadness of conviction, that to think great thoughts you must be heroes as well as idealists. Only when you have worked alone -- when you have felt around you a black gulf of solitude more isolating than that which surrounds the dying man, and in hope and in despair have trusted to your own unshaken will -- then only will you have achieved. Thus only can you gain the secret isolated joy of the thinker, who knows that, a hundred years after he is dead and forgotten, men who never heard of him will be moving to the measure of his thought -- subtle rapture of a postponed power, which the world knows not because it has no external trappings, but which to his prophetic vision is more real than that which commands an army. And if this joy should not be yours, still it is only thus that you can know that you have done what it lay in you to do -- can you say that you have lived, and be ready for the end."

OLIVER   WENDELL   HOLMES,
Lecture   Delivered   to
Undergraduates   of   Harvard
University (February 17, 1886)

"Every thing possible to be believ'd is an image of truth."

WILLIAM BLAKE, The Marriage
of Heaven and Hell

"Ah, but a man's reach should exceed his grasp,
Or what's a heaven for?"

ROBERT BROWNING, Andrea Del
Sarto

"With monotonous regularity, apparently competent men have laid down the law about what is technically possible or impossible -- and have been proved utterly wrong, sometimes while the ink was scarcely dry from their pens."

ARTHUR C. CLARKE, *Profiles of the Future*

"To dream the impossible dream,
To fight the unbeatable foe,
To bear the unbearable sorrow,
To run where the brave dare not go.

To right the unrightable wrong,
To love pure and chaste from afar,
To try when your arms are too weary,
To reach the unreachable star!"

JOE DARION, "The Impossible Dream (The Quest)," *Man of La Mancha*

"If you have built castles in the air . . . put the foundations under them."

HENRY DAVID THOREAU, *Walden*

"Life would soon lose its charm for most of us . . . if we could no longer pursue the unattainable."

BRADFORD TORREY, *Birds in the Bush*

"One can never consent to creep when one feels an impulse to soar."
HELEN KELLER

"The future belongs to those who believe in the beauty of their dreams."
ELEANOR ROOSEVELT

"The only reason someone is a genius, and knows things you do not know, is because he has opened his mind to contemplate the what-ifs, the outrageous thoughts, the thoughts of brilliance that go beyond the limited thinking of man. He has allowed himself to entertain and reason with these thoughts, whereas you have rejected them.

If any one thing can be conceived or pondered, it exists; for whatever is dreamed or imagined is already in the realm of existence. That is how all of creation came into existence."
RAMTHA

"If one advances confidently in the direction of his dreams, and endeavors to live the life which he has imagined, he will meet with a success unexpected in common hours. He will put something behind, will pass an invisible boundary; new, universal, and more liberal laws will begin to establish themselves around and within him, and the old laws will be expanded and interpreted in his favor in a more liberal sense; and he will live with the license of higher order of beings."
HENRY DAVID THOREAU

"A soul without a high aim is like a ship without a rudder."
EILEEN CADDY, *The Dawn of Change*

"The person who says it cannot be done should not interrupt the person doing it."

CHINESE PROVERB

"History is simply man's desperate effort to give body to his most clairvoyant dreams."

ALBERT CAMUS, *Neither Victims Nor Executioners*

"Not a few men who cherish lofty and noble ideals hide them under a bushel for fear of being called different."

MARTIN LUTHER KING, JR.

"As human beings we are made to surpass ourselves and are truly ourselves only when transcending ourselves."

HUSTON SMITH

"Reality can destroy the dream; why shouldn't the dream destroy reality?"

GEORGE MOORE

"Dreams are real while they last. Can we say more of life?"

HAVELOCK ELLIS

"Not merely to save the world, but primarily to save our own souls, there should again be dreamers, planners and fighters, in the midst of our nations, who would take upon themselves the important social function in democracy of raising our sights -- so far ahead that their proponents again form a definite minority in their nations and avoid the unbearable discomfort for reformers of a climate of substantial agreement."

GUNNAR   MYRDAL,   *An International Economy*

"Great ideals are the glory of man alone. No other creature can have them. Only man can get a vision and an inspiration that will lift him above the level of himself and send him forth against all opposition or any discouragement to do and to dare and to accomplish wonderful and great things for the world and for humanity."

MATTHEW A. HENSON

"To believe only possibilities is not faith, but mere philosophy."

SIR   THOMAS   BROWNE,   *Religio Medici*

"An <u>immanent</u> ideal, operating in all our life aims, is essential to our nature as persons. There is always a 'more yet' which carries our minds over and beyond the margins of any given situation. . . . It is this principle which gives us our 'imaginative dominion' over all of our human experiences and which makes it possible for us to see in given situations what ought to be, and to have an inward victory, which after all is the victory that overcomes the world."

RUFUS JONES, *Spirit in Man*

iii. Co-Creators

"*Possunt quia posse videntur*. (They can because they think they can.)"
VIRGIL, *Aeneid*

> "Even your body knows its heritage and its rightful need and will not be deceived.
>
> And your body is the harp of your soul,
>
> And it is yours to bring forth sweet music from it or confused   sounds."
> KAHLIL GIBRAN, *The Prophet*

"Each of us literally chooses by his way of attending to things what sort of universe he shall appear to himself to inhabit."
WILLIAM JAMES, *Principles of Psychology*

"The greatest formal talent is worthless if it does not serve a creativity which is capable of shaping a cosmos."
ALBERT EINSTEIN

"*H*umankind, full of all creative possibilities, is God's work. Humankind alone is called to assist God. Humankind is called to co-create. With nature's help, humankind can set into creation all that is necessary and life-sustaining."

HILDEGARDE OF BINGEN

"*Th*ere lives a creative being inside all of us and we must get out of its way for it will give us no peace unless we do."

M. C. RICHARDS, *Centering*

"*Th*ere is no value in life except what you choose to place upon it, and no happiness in any place except what you bring to it yourself."

LIN YUTANG, *On the Wisdom of America*

"*W*e are not creatures of circumstance; we are creators of circumstance."

BENJAMIN DISRAELI

"[*H*]ere, today, we weave a seamless garment of eternity."

WESLEY LA VIOLETTE, *The Creative Light*

". . . [*H*]e allowed himself to be swayed by his conviction that human beings are not born once and for all on the day their mothers give birth to them, but that life obliges them over and over again to give birth to themselves."

GABRIEL GARCIA MARQUES

"*Th*ere is no greater work of art for man to create than himself."

ALBERT CAMUS

" . . . '[*B*]eing' is nothing other than the total aspect of becoming."

LAMA ANAGARIKA GOVINDA, "*The Problem of Past and Future*," *Nature, Man, and Society: Main Currents in Modern Thought*

"[*F*]or a conscious being, to exist is to change, to change is to mature, to mature is to go on creating oneself endlessly."

HENRI BERGSON, *Creative Evolution*

"*The* desire to be a creator, to give birth, to guide the growth process, is nothing without its constant materialization in the world, nothing without the thousandfold consent of things and animals. Its enjoyment is so indescribably beautiful and rich only because it is filled with inherited memories of millions of instances of procreations and births. In one thought of procreation a thousand forgotten nights of love are resurrected and that thought is fulfilled in grandeur and sublimity."

RAINER MARIA RILKE, *Letters To A Young Poet*

"*God* so created all things that he nevertheless always creates in the present. The act of creation does not fade into the past but is always in the beginning and in process and new."

MEISTER ECKHART

"*This* is a universe of entelechy and purposiveness, but with an enormous amount of freedom. We can choose to co-create with the mystery or not."

JEAN HOUSTON, "*The Promise of The New Millennium*"

"I'm the opposite of a reformer; I am what I call a new former."
                                    BUCKMINSTER FULLER

"Every culture has a story about creation. A goddess lays the cosmic egg, or a god speaks the magic words, creating light. The archetype of the Magician teaches us about creation, about our capacity to bring into being what never was there before, about claiming our role as co-creators of the universe. . . .

The Magician is not other, we discover, but ourselves. At this point [we] come to believe that the universe is not a static thing. It is in the process of being created all the time. All of us are involved in that creation, and thus all of us are Magicians.

We cannot not be the Magicians. We cannot live without ordering and arranging life. . . .

To experience fully the Magician's power . . . requires us to give our lives fearlessly to the universe. . . .

The Magician learns that we are not life's victims; we are part of the unfolding of God."
                        CAROL S. PEARSON, *The Hero Within*

"Don't be satisfied with stories, how things have gone with others. Unfold your own myth."
                                    Jalal-ud-Din RUMI

"When I came to understand that there are mythic patterns in all our lives, I knew that all of us, often unbeknownst to ourselves, are engaged in a drama of soul which we were told was reserved for gods, heroes, and saints."
                    DEENA METZGER, "*Miracles At Canyon De Chelly*"

"The past is only the present become invisible and mute; and because it is invisible and mute, its memoried glances and its murmurs are infinitely precious. We are tomorrow's past."

MARY WEBB, *Precious Bane*

"We are co-creators with God, not puppets on a string waiting for something to happen. We make things happen; we create the difference, not in our old dysfunctional pattern of isolated control, but in choosing a partnership with our Higher Power. Then, by appreciating that we are powerful human beings, we ourselves become the 'somebody' who can fix us. This healing gives birth to a healthy spirituality and a rewarding relationship with God."

FATHER LEO BOOTH, *When God Becomes a Drug*

"In the last analysis, the essential thing is the life of the individual. This alone makes history, here alone do the great transformations just take place, and the whole future, the whole history of the world, ultimately spring as a gigantic summation from these hidden sources in individuals. In our most private and most subjective lives we are not only the passive witnesses of our age, and its sufferers, but also its makers. We make our own epoch."

C. G. JUNG, "*The Meaning of Psychology for Modern Man*"

iv. Inner Power

"He who knows that power is inborn, that he is weak because he has looked for good outside of himself and elsewhere, and so perceiving, throws himself unhesitatingly on his thought, instantly rights himself, stands in the erect position, commands his limbs, works miracles . . ."

RALPH WALDO EMERSON, *Essays*

"We sometimes fall into the delusion that power is elsewhere, that we are unable to find access to it. Nothing could be further from the truth. The universe oozes with power, waiting for anyone who wishes to embrace it. Because the powers of cosmic dynamics are invisible, we need to remind ourselves of their universal presence. Who reminds us? The rivers, plains, galaxies, hurricanes, lightning branches, and all our living companions."

BRIAN SWIMME, *The Universe Is
a Green Dragon*

"Who looks outside dreams; who looks inside wakes."
C. G. JUNG, *Memories, Dreams, Reflections*

"Dig within. Within is the wellspring of Good; and it is always ready to bubble up, if you just dig."

MARCUS AURELIUS, *Meditations*

"What lies behind us, and what lies before us are tiny matters, compared to what lies within us."

RALPH WALDO EMERSON, *Works
of Ralph Waldo Emerson*

"*W*ithin each one of us, here, this moment, in our lives, there lies the innate power of mind always waiting to emancipate us from . . . bondage."

WESLEY LA VIOLETTE, *The Creative Light*

v. *L*imitless Potentiality

"*F*or all sad words of tongues or pen
The saddest are these: It might have been."

JOHN GREENLEAF WHITTIER

"*Y*ou who perceive yourself as weak and frail
with futile hopes and devastated dreams,
born but to die, to weep and suffer pain,
hear this:
All power is given unto you in earth and Heaven.
There is nothing that you cannot do."

A COURSE IN MIRACLES

"*W*ell-being is possible only to the degree to which one has overcome one's narcissism; to the degree to which one is open, responsive, sensitive, awake, empty. Well-being means to be fully related to man and nature effectively, to overcome separateness and alienation, to arrive at the experience of oneness with all that exists. . . . Well-being means to be fully born, to become what one potentially is."

ERICH FROMM, *The Art of Loving*

"All things are possible to him that believeth."
MARK 9:23

"[T]here are inexhaustible resources of divine grace for those who are resolved to rise above the fog and mist, the sleet and snow of dreary inward weather."

RUFUS JONES, "*Present Day Papers*"

"The only way to discover the limits of the possible is to go beyond them, to the impossible."
ARTHUR C. CLARKE

"It is necessary; therefore, it is possible."
G. A. BORGESE

"Those who succeed and do not push on to greater failure are the spiritual middle classers. Their stopping at success is the proof of their compromising insignificance. How pretty their dreams must have been! ... Only through the unattainable does man achieve a hope worth living and dying for -- and so attain himself."
EUGENE O'NEILL

"No limits are set to the ascent of man, and to each and every one the highest stands open. Here it is only your personal choice that decides."
HASIDIC SAYING

"If civilization has conquered the last geographical frontiers, there are still spiritual frontiers, eternal vistas spreading illimitably for those who have the imagination and the will to see; for those who seek the Diety living in their own heart."

WESLEY LA VIOLETTE, *The Creative Light*

"*N*othing we ever imagined is beyond our powers, only beyond our present self-knowledge."

THEODORE ROSZAK

"*W*ho could ever have supposed that a new individual, bringing with him the hereditary traits of the generations behind him, could ever come over the infinitesimal bridge of a cell of protoplasm? . . . There is nothing more staggering with impossibilities than that original event which actually happens. After that nothing need amaze us. What could be more unlikely, again, than the emergence of the mutations that have successively raised the level of the march of life through its long processes of evolution and made it possible for us to head the procession! What impossibility is so sheerly impossible as that leap from a molecular process in the cortex of the brain to the consciousness that I ought to live, and under conditions, to die, for an impalpable Truth!"

RUFUS JONES, *Spirit in Man*

F. CHILD WITHIN

i. Through the Eyes of Children

"Truly, I say to you, unless you are converted and become like children, you shall not enter the kingdom of heaven."
                              MATTHEW 18:3

"The wolf shall dwell with the lamb, and the leopard shall lie down with the goat; and the calf and the young lion and the fatling together; and a little child shall lead them."
                              ISAIAH 11:6

"A childlike adult is not one whose development has been arrested; on the contrary, he is an adult who has given himself a chance of continuing to develop long after most people have muffled themselves in the cocoon of middle age habit and convention."

                    ALDOUS   HUXLEY, *Music at Night*

"The law of love could be best understood and learned through little children."

                    MOHANDAS   K.   (MAHATMA) GANDHI

"I can imagine that someday we will regard our children not as creatures to manipulate or to change but rather as messengers from a world we once deeply knew, but which we have long since forgotten, who can reveal to us more about the true secrets of life, than our parents were ever able to."
ALICE MILLER

"When we lose our innocence -- when we start feeling the weight of the atmosphere and learn that there's death in the pot -- we take leave of our senses. Only children can hear the song of the malehouse mouse. Only children keep their eyes open. The only thing they <u>have</u> got is sense; they have highly developed 'input systems,' admitting all data indiscriminately. . . ."

ANNIE DILLARD, *Pilgrim at Tinker Creek*

"The artist is like a child in so far as he sees things for the first time. But no child remains for long in a state of wonder. Children are realists, not artists, and soon weary of the latest wonderment. To carry on the feelings of childhood into the powers of manhood: to combine the child's sense of wonder and novelty with the appearances, which every day for perhaps forty years had rendered familiar . . . this is the character of genius."

HOLBROOK JACKSON, *The Reading of Books*

"The great man is he who does not lose his child's heart."
MENCIUS

"May God bless and keep you always,
May your wishes all come true,
May you always do for others,
And let others do for you.
May you build a ladder to the stars,
And climb on every rung,
May you stay forever young,
Forever young, forever young,
May you stay forever young.

May you grow up to be righteous,
May you grow up to be true,
May you always know the truth,
And see delights surrounding you.
May you always be courageous,
And upright and be strong,
May you stay forever young,
Forever young, forever young,
May you stay forever young.

May your hands always be busy,
May your feet always be swift,
May you have a strong foundation,
When the winds of changes shift.
May your heart always be joyful,
May your song always be sung,
May you stay forever young,
Forever young, forever young,
May you stay forever young."

BOB DYLAN, *"Forever Young"*

"It is never too late to recover the prayerfulness which is as natural to us as breathing. . . . The child within us stays alive. And the child within us never loses the talent to look with the eyes of the heart, to combine concentration with wonderment. . . . The more we allow the child within us to come into its own, the more mature we become. . . . This is surely one meaning of the saying that we must 'become like children.'"

DAVID STEINDL-RAST,
Gratefulness, the Heart of Prayer

"It is the Child that sees the primordial secret in Nature and it is the child of ourselves that we return to. The child within us is simple and daring enough to live the Secret."

LAO TZU

"Mother Earth is in jeopardy, caused by the anthropocentrism of religion, education, and science during the past three centuries. A new beginning is required, centered on the <u>sacredness of the planet</u> . . . [but] worship that bores people is a sin. Worship is meant to <u>awaken</u>, to challenge, to delight and to empower. We believe all adults can touch the divine child that exists within us."

MATTHEW FOX, "*My Final Statement
Before Being Silenced by the Vatican*"

"So long as one does not become simple like a child, one does not get divine illumination. Forget all the worldly knowledge that thou hast acquired and become as ignorant as a child, and then wilt thou get the divine wisdom."

SRI RAMAKRISHNA

"Grown men may learn from very little children, for the hearts of little children are pure, and, therefore, the Great Spirit may show to them many things which older people miss."

BLACK ELK *(Oglala Sioux)*

"Zen is to have the heart and soul of a little child."
                              TAKUAN

"The Pupil must regain <u>the child state he hath lost</u> ere the first sound can fall upon his ears."
                              TIBETAN PRECEPT

"The universe is being reimagined at every second in the mind of God. . . . [W]hen you see with a child's mind, you see that everything is always eternally fresh, nothing is old, nothing is stale. You see the Unborn. You see the Timeless in time. When you enter that total freshness you see that the Divine Fire is giving birth to the universe every millisecond and that you are participating in this Divine birth at every millisecond. . . . [Y]ou are living from birth to birth."

                    ANDREW HARVEY, *The Way of Passion, a Celebration of Rumi*

ii. *W*onder and Mystery

"*A* child's world is fresh and new and beautiful, full of wonder and excitement. It is our misfortune that for most of us that clear-eyed vision, that true instinct for what is beautiful and awe-inspiring, is dimmed and even lost before we reach adulthood. If I had influence with the good fairy who is supposed to preside over the christening of all children I should ask that her gift to each child in the world be a sense of wonder so indestructible that it would last throughout life, as an unfailing antidote against the boredom and disenchantment of later years, the sterile preoccupation with things that are artificial, the alienation from the sources of our strength."

RACHEL CARSON, *A Sense of Wonder*

"*K*now you what it is to be a child? It is to be something very different from the man of to-day. It is to have a spirit yet streaming from the waters of baptism; it is to believe in love, to believe in loveliness, to believe in belief; it is to be so little that the elves can reach to whisper in your ear; it is to turn pumpkins into coaches, and mice into horses, lowness into loftiness, and nothing into everything, for each child has its fairy godmother in its own soul; it is to live in a nutshell and to count yourself the king of infinite space; it is

'To see a world in a grain of sand,
And a Heaven in a wild flower,
Hold infinity in the palm of your hand,
And eternity in an hour;'

it is to know not as yet that you are under sentence of life, nor petition that it be commuted into death."

> FRANCES THOMPSON, "Shelley,"
> The Works of Frances Thompson
> (quoting "Auguries of Innocence"
> by William Blake)

"The true mystics I have known have been people who never lost the sense of the child in wonder. The mystic, after all, is the divine child in us all wanting to play in the universe."

> MATTHEW   FOX,   Creation
> Spirituality: Liberating Gifts for
> the Peoples of the Earth

"The first function of mythology -- myths and mystical rituals, sacred songs and ceremonial dances -- is to awaken in the individual a sense of awe, wonder, and participation in the inscrutable mystery of being."

> JOSEPH CAMPBELL, The Power of
> Myth

"Youth is not a time of life -- it is a state of mind. It is not a matter of red cheeks, red lips and supple knees. It is a temper of the will; a quality of the imagination; a vigor of emotions; it is a freshness of the deep springs of life.   Youth means a temperamental predominance of courage over timidity, of the appetite for adventure over a life of ease. This often exists in a man of fifty, more than in a boy of twenty. Nobody grows old by merely living a number of years; people grow old by deserting their ideals.

Years may wrinkle the skin, but to give up enthusiasm wrinkles the soul. Worry, doubt, self-trust, fear and despair -- these are the long, long years that bow the head and turn the growing spirit back to dust.

Whether seventy or sixteen, there is in every being's heart a love of wonder; the sweet amazement at the stars and starlike things and thoughts; the undaunted challenge of events, the unfailing childlike appetite for what comes next, the joy in the game of life.

You are as young as your faith, as old as your doubt; as young as your self-confidence, as old as your fear, as young as your hope, as old as your despair.

In the central place of your heart there is a wireless station. So long as it receives messages of beauty, hope, cheer, grandeur, courage, and power from the earth, from men and from the Infinite -- so long are you young. When the wires are all down and the central places of your heart are covered with the snows of pessimism and the ice of cynicism, then are you grown old, indeed!"

SAMUEL ULLMAN, "Youth"

"All my life through, the new sights of nature made me rejoice like a child."

MARIE CURIE

"All children under nine or ten years of age are poets and philosophers. They pretend to live with the rest of us, and the rest of us imagine that we influence them so that their lives are only a reflection of our own. But, as a matter of fact they are as self-contained as cats and as continuously attentive to the magical charm of what they see inwardly. Their mental wealth is extraordinary; only the greatest artists or poets, whose resemblance to children is a banal certainty, can give us some idea of it. . . . Most intelligent children . . . have the philosopher's doubts about the existence of the world. You see them looking curiously at a stone; you think 'children are so funny' and all the time they are wondering if the stone may not be eternal. . . . Have I not heard a little girl of nine interrupt a conversation of professors who were talking about nothing to ask the astounding question: 'Father, what is beauty? What makes it?'"

ERNEST DIMNET, *The Art of Thinking*

"The higher goal of spiritual living is not to amass a wealth of information, but to face sacred moments. . . . Spiritual life begins to decay when we fail to sense the grandeur of what is eternal in time. . . ."

ABRAHAM JOSHUA HESCHEL, *The Earth Is the Lord's*

"The sense of wonder, that is our sixth sense."

D. H. LAWRENCE

"We have stripped all things of their mystery and numinosity; nothing is holy any longer."

C. G. JUNG, *Man and His Symbols*

"For after all the great religions have been preached and expounded, or have been revealed by brilliant scholars, or have been written in fine books and embellished in fine language with finer covers, man -- all man -- is still confronted with the Great Mystery."

CHIEF LUTHER STANDING BEAR
(Oglala Sioux)

"God does not die on the day when we cease to believe in a personal deity, but we die on the day when our lives cease to be illumined by the steady radiance, renewed daily, of a wonder, the source of which is beyond all reason."

DAG HAMMARSKJOLD, *Markings*

"I've read all the books but one
Only remains sacred: this
Volume of wonders, open
Always before my eyes."

KATHLEEN RAINE, *Collected Poems* 1935-80

"Awe enables us to perceive in the world intimations of the divine, to sense in small things the beginning of infinite significance, to sense the ultimate in the common and the simple; to feel in the rush of the passing the stillness of the eternal."

ABRAHAM JOSHUA HESCHEL

"As long as you have mystery you have health; when you destroy mystery you create morbidity. The ordinary man has always been sane because the ordinary man has always been mystic. He has permitted the twilight."

G. K. CHESTERTON, *Orthodoxy*

"If we can't meet the power of despair today with the power of awe and wonder and joy, then we are not going to have the energy or imagination to do something about overcoming the causes of despair."

MATTHEW FOX

iii. Miracles

"The invariable mark of wisdom is to see the miraculous in the common. . . . To the wise, therefore, a fact is true poetry, and the most beautiful of fables. . . ."

RALPH WALDO EMERSON, *From an Essay, "Prospects," Nature Addresses and Lectures*

"Everything is a miracle from somebody's point of view."

BRADFORD TORREY, *Birds in the Bush*

"I believe a leaf of grass is no less than
   the journey-work of the stars,
And the pismire is equally perfect, and
   a grain of sand, and the egg of the wren,
And the tree-toad is a chef-d'oeuvre for
   the highest,
And the running blackberry would
   adorn the parlors of heaven
And the narrowest hinge in my hand
   puts to scorn all machinery,
And the cow crunching with depress'd
   head surpasses any statue,
And a mouse is miracle enough to
   stagger sextillions of infidels."

WALT WHITMAN, *Song of Myself, Leaves of Grass*

"Miracles are natural. When they do not occur something has gone wrong."

A COURSE IN MIRACLES

"Decide to live joyfully,
exultantly, gratefully, openly,
and then miracles will begin to happen."

ROBERT MULLER, *A Planet of Hope*

"Abandon in God is the power that changes all things. This is the nuclear power we need if we are going to turn the world around in twenty years. This power is given only to the child, because only the child loves enough to hold this power totally for the Divine and never for himself or herself. Only the child is so much in love with love that he or she only wants to do what love wants, and so can be moved by love from miracle to miracle."

ANDREW HARVEY, *The Way of Passion, a Celebration of Rumi*

iv. Enchantment

"To live as a mature human being is the journey home, and our home is enchantment."

BRIAN SWIMME, *The Universe Is a Green Dragon*

"*L*et mystery have its place in you; do not be always turning up your whole ploughshare of self-examination, but leave a little fallow corner in your heart ready for any seed the wind may bring, and reserve a nook of shadow for the passing bird; keep a place in your heart for the unexpected guest, an alter for the unknown God."

HENRI FREDERIC AMIEL

"*W*e come as children of the dawn."

WESLEY LA VIOLETTE, *The Creative Light*

"*A*mazement is the beginning of philosophy."

SAINT THOMAS AQUINAS, *Summa Theologica*

v. *J*oy

"*J*oy & Woe are woven fine
A Clothing for the Soul Divine
Under every grief & pine
Runs a joy with silken twine."

WILLIAM BLAKE, *Auguries of Innocence*

"[I]nner ecstasy of the mind is the secret fountain of perpetual youth and strength in any man. He who finds it finds omnipotence and omniscience."
WALTER RUSSELL

"Joy is the one thing of which indisputably the healthy animal, and even the healthy plant, gives us an example. And we need them to remind us that beauty and joy can come of their own accord when we let them."
JOSEPH WOOD KRUTCH, *The Best of Two Worlds*

"All feelings that integrate and inspire are pure. . . . Everything that causes you to be more than you have been in your best hours is right. Every advancement is good if it pervades your whole bloodstream, when it is not due to intoxication, not due to being conditioned to sadness, but to transparent joy."
RAINER MARIA RILKE, *Letters To A Young Poet*

"Sheer joy is God's, and this demand's companionship."
SAINT THOMAS AQUINAS

"Every child is unique, and only the child is unique, because only the child is free to be completely itself. Being completely oneself means living inwardly beyond all conventions, beyond all guilt, beyond all religion and dogma, beyond all hierarchy, beyond all fantasy about heaven or earth, beyond all spiritual longing for spiritual achievement, beyond everything. Only the child is pure, naked and joyful in the present moment. . . . When you have become a child, the whole world radiates with the beauty of the Beloved."

ANDREW HARVEY, *The Way of Passion, a Celebration of Rumi*

G. SEAT OF CHANGE

i. Change Within

"A new insight must dawn on people: you do not solve world problems by applying technological fixes within a framework of narrowly self-centered values and short-sighted national institutions. Coping with mankind's current predicament calls for inner changes, for a human and humanistic revolution mobilizing new values and aspirations, backed by new levels of personal commitment and political will."

ERVIN LASZLO, *The Inner Limits of Mankind*

"Man alone is the architect of his destiny. The greatest revolution in our generation is that human beings, by changing the inner attitudes of their minds, can change the outer aspects of their lives."

WILLIAM JAMES

"Do you think that civilization advances because of things written in books? Not a bit of what is written in books ever got there until after the thought of it happened in man's mind. He first had to collect it from space, or recollect it from its electrical pattern to which he had attuned himself. The book is but a record of what has already happened. It is history only, to bring others up to date by informing them. It is a means of thought transference only, and not a creative process until you have made it so by transformation within you."

WALTER RUSSELL

"Change your awareness, and you live in a different world, you experience a different reality."

LAMA ANAGARIKA GOVINDA, *Creative Meditations and Multi-Dimensional Consciousness*

"Both Wordsworth and Thoreau knew that when the light of common day seemed no more than common it was because of something lacking in them, not because of something lacking in it, and what they asked for was eyes to see a universe they knew was worth seeing. For that reason theirs are the best of all attempts to describe what real awareness consists of . . . that the rare moment is not the moment when there is something worth looking at but the moment when we are capable of seeing it."

JOSEPH WOOD KRUTCH, *The Desert Years*

"As human beings, our greatness lies not so much in being able to remake the world -- that is the myth of the 'atomic age' -- as in being able to remake ourselves."

MOHANDAS   K.   (MAHATMA) GANDHI

"The most powerful thing you can do to change the world, is to change your own beliefs about the nature of life, people, reality to something more positive . . . and begin to act accordingly."

SHAKTI   GAWAIN, *Creative Visualization*

"The greatest discovery of my generation is that human beings can alter their lives by altering their attitudes of mind."

WILLIAM JAMES

"Things do not change; we change."

HENRY DAVID THOREAU, *Walden*

"We live at a peculiar moment in history. If we look at the reality of the world from the viewpoint of the industrial era, it is clear there is no hope. . . . But there is another way to look at our situation. We can discover the large number of people who have decided to change. . . . If we do this, it seems equally impossible that we shall fail to solve our problems."

ROBERT THEOBALD

"Something we were withholding made us weak
  Until we found it was ourselves."

ROBERT FROST

"[U]ltimately, our thinking, our languages, our attitudes, our values and our fundamental life-views must undergo profound transformation if we are to create a new age of global integrity. That is where everything begins."

RASHMI MAYUR

"If we change and extend our understanding of consciousness, we change and extend our understanding of human nature."

WILLIAM ANDERSON, *Ancient Futures: Learning from Ladakh*

"Genius . . . means little more than the faculty of perceiving in an inhabitual way."

WILLIAM JAMES

"[W]hat we call fate emerges from human beings; it does not enter into them from the outside."

RAINER MARIA RILKE, *Letters To A Young Poet*

"In order to transform others, you have first to transform yourself."

MOHANDAS K. (MAHATMA) GANDHI

"Human beings destroy the ecology at the same time as they destroy one another. . . . Healing our society goes hand in hand with healing our personal, elemental connection with the phenomenal world."

CHOGYAM TRUNGPA

"*A*lthough responsible use may be defined, advocated, and to some extent required by organizations, it cannot be implemented or enacted by them. It cannot be effectively enforced by them. The use of the world is finally a personal matter, and the world can be preserved in health only by the forbearance and care of a multitude of persons."

WENDELL BERRY, *The Unsettling of America*

"*R*evolution begins with the self, in the self."

TONI CADE BAMBARA, *The Black Woman*

"*T*hink of ideas as a beat. To change a mind is to change the world."

DEAN JOAN KONNER

"*I*f you are serious about the sufferings of mankind, you must perfect the only source of help you have -- yourself."

SRI NISARGADATTA

"*T*he most important act of the individual is to take good care of his own life. . . . You cannot expect the world to change before you change yourself."

ROBERT MULLER

"*L*ife is a series of collisions with the future; it is not a sum of what we have been, but what we yearn to be."

JOSE ORTEGA Y GASSET, *The Revolt of the Masses, Man and Crisis*

"Of all the creatures of earth, only human beings can change their patterns. Man alone is the architect of his destiny. . . . Human beings, by changing the inner attitudes of their minds, can change the outer aspects of their lives."

WILLIAM JAMES, *The Will To Believe*

"[W]e are not prisoners. There are no traps or snares set for us, and there is nothing that should frighten or torture us. We are placed into life, into the element best suited to it. . . . [T]hrough thousands of years of adaptation, we have acquired such a resemblance to this life, that we, if we stood still, would hardly be distinguishable from our surroundings. We have no reason to mistrust our world, for it is not against us. If it has terrors, they are our own terrors. If it has precipices, they belong to us. If dangers are present, we must try to love them. And if we fashion our life according to that principle, which advises us to embrace that which is difficult, then that which appears to us to be the very strangest will become the most worthy of our trust, and the truest."

RAINER MARIA RILKE, *Letters To A Young Poet*

"When I believed that my existence was such a further fact, I seemed imprisoned in myself. My life seemed like a glass tunnel, through which I was moving faster every year, and at the end of which there was darkness. When I changed my view, the walls of my glass tunnel disappeared. I now live in the open air."

DEREK PARFIT, *Reasons and Persons*

"A new world is only a new mind."

WILLIAM CARLOS WILLIAMS

ii. Start at Home

"My creed: -- To love justice, to long for the right, to love mercy, to pity the suffering, to assist the weak, to forget wrongs and remember benefits, to love the truth, to be sincere, to utter honest words, to love liberty, to wage relentless war against slavery in all its forms, to love wife and child and friend, to make a happy home, to love the beautiful in art, in nature, to cultivate the mind, the be familiar with the mighty thoughts that genius has expressed, the noble deeds of all the world; to cultivate courage and cheerfulness, to make others happy, to fill life with the splendor of generous acts, the warmth of loving words, to discard error, to destroy prejudice, to receive new truths with gladness, to cultivate hope, to see the calm beyond the storm, the dawn beyond the night, to do the best that can be done and then be resigned. . . . "

ROBERT G. INGERSOLL, *Liberty of Man, Woman and Child*

"The great lesson from the true mystics, from the Zen monks, and now also from the Humanistic and Transpersonal psychologists, is that the sacred is in the ordinary, that it is to be found in one's daily life . . . in one's own back yard."

ABRAHAM MASLOW, *The Further Reaches of Human Nature*

"*R*esponsibility does not only lie with the leaders of our countries or with those who have been appointed or elected to do a particular job. It lies with each of us individually. Peace, for example, starts within each one of us. When we have inner peace, we can be at peace with those around us. When our community is in a state of peace, it can share that peace with neighboring communities, and so on. When we feel love and kindness toward others, it not only makes others feel loved and cared for, but it helps us also to develop inner happiness and peace. And there are ways in which we can consciously work to develop feelings of love and kindness. For some of us, the most effective way to do so is through religious practice. For others, it may be non-religious practices. What is important is that we each make a sincere effort to take seriously our responsibility for each other and for the natural environment."

> TENZIN GYATSO, 14TH DALAI LAMA OF TIBET, *Nobel Peace Prize Lecture, Oslo, Norway (1989)*

"*It* does not matter what you do. What does matter is that you do it the best. If you are a street sweeper, then be the best street sweeper that there ever was. Do your work with pride, and do it with dignity, and in so doing it, you will be doing it with greatness!"

> MARTIN LUTHER KING, JR., *Speech entitled "Remaining Awake During a Great Revolution"*

"*We* shall not cease from exploration
And the end of all our exploring
Will be to arrive where we started
And know the place for the first time."

> T. S. ELIOT, *Four Quartets*

"If there be righteousness in the heart,
   there will be beauty in the character.
If there be beauty in the character,
   there will be harmony in the home.
If there be harmony in the home,
   there will be order in the nation.
If there be order in the nation,
   there will be peace in the world."

CONFUCIUS

"There is only one corner of the universe you can be certain of improving and that is your own self."

ALDOUS HUXLEY

"Perseverance is more prevailing than violence; and many things which cannot be overcome when they are together, yield themselves up when taken little by little."

PLUTARCH

"Almost all of the great teachers lived a saintly life -- not luxuriously like kings or emperors, but as simple human beings."

TENZIN GYATSO, 14TH DALAI
LAMA OF TIBET

"[The profound and the transcendental are to be found in the factory. It may not fill you with bliss to look at it, it may not sound as good as the spiritual experiences that we have read about, but somehow reality is to be found there, in the way in which we relate with everyday problems. If we relate to them in a simple, earthy way, we will work in a more balanced manner, and things will be dealt with properly."

CHOGYAM TRUNGPA

"In everything one does it is possible to foster and maintain a state of being which reflects our true destiny. When this possibility is actualized the ordinary day is no longer ordinary. It can even become an adventure of the spirit."

KARLFRIED GRAF VON DURCKHEIM, *Daily Life as Spiritual Exercise*

"The only aspect of time that is eternal is <u>now</u>."

A COURSE IN MIRACLES

"The center of human nature is rooted in ten thousand ordinary acts of kindness that define our days."

STEPHEN JAY GOULD

iii. Power in Moment

"Each of us has the opportunity today to decide when he will begin to walk in understanding. . . . Each of us is weaving colored threads into garments we shall wear now and hereafter. Every action, whether it is good or bad, is woven into the spiritual energy and character. Only as we see this . . . and understand it, can we alter intelligently the fate we decree for ourselves, the lives we weave upon the loom of Time."

WESLEY LA VIOLETTE, *The Creative Light*

"The surest way to create something is losing oneself in the present, being inspired by the surroundings, yielding to what is directly before oneself."

VINCENT VAN GOGH, *Letters*

"The creative person, in the inspirational phase of the creative furor, loses his past and his future and lives only in the moment. He is all there, totally immersed, fascinated and absorbed in the present."

ABRAHAM MASLOW, *The Further Reaches of Human Nature*

"There is only one courage and that is the courage to go on dying to the past, not to collect it, not to accumulate it, not to cling to it. We all cling to the past, and because we cling to the past we become unavailable to the present."

BHAGWAN SHREE RAJNEESH, *Walking in Zen, Sitting in Zen*

"The great man knew not that he was great. It took a century or two for that fact to appear. What he did, he did because he must; it was the most natural thing in the world, and grew out of the circumstances of the moment."

RALPH WALDO EMERSON, *Essays*

"If we are truly in the present moment, not being carried away by our thoughts and fantasies, then we are in a position to be free of fate and available to our destiny. When we are in the present moment, our work on Earth begins."

RESHAD FEILD

"To improve the golden moment of opportunity, and catch the good that is within our reach, is the great art of life."
WILLIAM JAMES

"Time is an invention. Now is a reality. So much creativity is happening for the simple reason that we have withdrawn ourselves from past and future. Our whole energy remains blocked either in the past or in the future. When you withdraw all your energy from past and future a tremendous explosion happens. That explosion is creativity."
BHAGWAN SHREE RAJNEESH

"[N]ow is the closest approximation of eternity that this world offers."
A COURSE IN MIRACLES

"In silence . . . man stands confronted once again by the original beginning of all things: everything can begin again, everything can be re-created. In every moment of time, man through silence can be with the origins of all things. . . . "
MAX PICARD, *The World of Silence*

"Without any shadow of doubt, amidst this vertigo of shows and politics, I settle myself ever the firmer in the creed that we should not postpone and refer and wish, but do broad justice where we are, by whomsoever we deal with, accepting our actual companions and circumstances, however humble or odious, as the mystic officials to whom the universe has delegated its whole pleasure for us."
RALPH WALDO EMERSON, *Essays*

"Above all, we cannot afford not to live in the present. He is blessed over all mortals who loses no moment of the passing life in remembering the past."

> HENRY   DAVID   THOREAU,
> *Walking*

"The challenge is to learn to respond immediately to whatever it is time for."

> SAINT BENEDICT

"God speaks to everyone through what is happening to them moment by moment."

> JEAN   PIERRE   de   CAUSSADE,
> *Abandonment   to   Divine*
> *Providence*

"To change one's life: Start immediately. Do it flamboyantly. No exceptions (no excuses)."

> WILLIAM JAMES

"Every moment and every event of every man's life plants something in his soul. For just as the wind carries thousands of winged seeds, so each moment brings with it germs of spiritual vitality that come to rest imperceptibly in the minds and wills of men. Most of these unnumbered seeds perish and are lost, because men are not prepared to receive them. For such seeds as these cannot spring up anywhere, except in the good soil of freedom, spontaneity, and love."

> THOMAS MERTON

"There is nowhere to be safe, except on the diamond point of this moment, where lunacy, ecstacy and sober purity coalesce. This is where you must learn how to dance. It is there on the diamond point that the Divine is always to be found, in eternity. It is on that absolutely minuscule atomic speck of *now* that you must dance, rising above both worlds, find the eternal, and enter immortality."

ANDREW HARVEY, *The Way of Passion, a Celebration of Rumi*

IX.

GATHERING OF LIGHT

"And God said, 'Let there be light,' and there was light."

GENESIS 1:3

A. BEING OF LIGHT

i. Boundless Self

"[D]espite the horrors and insanities of past and present human behavior, we are <u>not</u> sinners, doomed to failure; we are beings of light, kin to the immortals, capable of royal conquest of soul if we would but trust the whisperings of our god-selves and live accordingly."

GRACE F. KNOCHE

"The hidden well-spring of your soul must needs rise and run murmuring to the sea;

And the treasure of your infinite depths would be revealed to your eyes.

But let there be no scales to weigh your unknown treasure;

And seek not the depths of your knowledge with staff or sounding line.

For self is a sea boundless and measureless."

KAHLIL GIBRAN, *The Prophet*

"Man goes to great trouble to acquire knowledge of the material world. He learns all branches of mundane science. He explores the earth, and even travels to the moon. But he never tries to find out what exists within himself. Because he is unaware of the enormous power hidden within him, he looks for support in the outer world. Because he does not know the boundless happiness that lies inside his heart, he looks for satisfaction in mundane activities and pleasures. Because he does not experience the inner love, he looks for love from others.

The truth is that the inner Self of every human being is supremely great and supremely lovable. Everything is contained in the Self. The creative power of this entire universe lies inside every one of us. The divine principle that creates and sustains this world pulsates within us as our own Self. It scintillates in the heart and shines through all our senses. If, instead of pursuing knowledge of the outer world, we were to pursue inner knowledge, we would discover that effulgence very soon."

SWAMI MUKTANANDA, *I Am That*

"The heart that breaks open can contain the whole universe. . . . All is registered in the 'boundless heart' of the bodhisattva. Through our deepest and innermost responses to our world -- to hunger and torture and threat of annihilation -- we touch that boundless heart."

JOANNA MACY

"What bars our way? We still tremble before the Self like children before the falling dark. Yet once we have dared to make our passage inside the heart, we will find that we have entered into a world in which depth leads on to light, and there is no end to entrance."

GABRIEL SAUL HEILIG

"The Self is one. Unmoving, it moves faster than the mind. The senses lag, but Self runs ahead. Unmoving, it outruns pursuit. Out of Self comes the breath that is the life of all things.

Unmoving, it moves; is far away, yet near; within all, outside all.

* * *

The Self is everywhere, without a body, without a shape, whole, pure, wise, all knowing, far shining, self-depending, all transcending; in the eternal procession assigning to every period its proper duty."

THE UPANISHADS

"I do not think seventy years is the time of a man or woman, nor that seventy million of years is the time of man or woman, nor that years will ever stop the existence of me, or anyone else."

WALT WHITMAN, *Leaves of Grass*

"If you don't make yourself equal to God, you can't perceive God; for like is known by like. Leap free of everything that is physical, and grow as vast as that immeasurable vastness; step beyond all time and become eternal; then you will perceive God. Realize that nothing is impossible for you; recognize that you too are immortal and that you can embrace all things in your mind; find your home in the heart of every living creature; make yourself higher than all heights and lower than all depths; bring all opposites inside yourself and reconcile them; understand that you are everywhere, on the land, in the sea, in the sky; realize that you haven't yet been begotten, that you are still in the womb, that you are young, that you are old, that you are dead, that you are in the world beyond the grave; hold all this in your mind, all times and places, all substances and qualities and magnitudes; then you can perceive God."

HERMETIC WRITINGS

"[T]he soul walks upon all paths.

The soul walks not upon a line, neither does it grow like a reed.

The soul unfolds itself, like a lotus of countless petals."
                    KAHLIL GIBRAN, *The Prophet*

"Most people live, whether physically, intellectually or morally, in a very restricted circle of their potential being. They make use of a very small portion of their possible consciousness, and of their soul's resources in general, much like a man who, out of his whole bodily organism, should get into a habit of using and moving only his little finger."
                    WILLIAM JAMES

"The growing into maturity as a human is experienced as an ever widening sense of self, from identification with the individual bodymind, to self as family, self as circle of friends, as nation, as race, as human race, as all living things, and perhaps finally to self as all that is."
                    JEREMY HAYWARD, *"Ecology and*
                    the Experience of Sacredness"

"Only That which made us, meant us to be
  mightier by and by,
Set the sphere of all the boundless Heavens
  within the human eye,
Sent the shadow of Himself, the boundless,
  thro' the human soul;
Boundless inward, in the atom, boundless
  outward, in the whole."
                    ALFRED,   LORD   TENNYSON,
                    Locksley   Hall   Sixty   Years
                    After

"[T]he personal self pecks at the fruit of this world,
bewildered by suffering, always hungry for more.
But when he meets the True Self, the resplendent God,
the source of creation, all his cravings are stilled.
Perceiving Self in all creatures, he forgets himself,
in the service of all; good and evil both vanish;
delighting in Self, playing like a child with Self,
he does whatever is called for, whatever the result."

MUNDAKA UPANISHAD

"In the ocean are many bright strands
and many dark strands like veins that are seen
when a wing is lifted up.
Your hidden self is blood in those, those veins
that are lute strings that make ocean music,
not the sad edge of surf, but the sound of no shore."

Jalal-ud-Din RUMI, "*The Diver's Clothes Lying Empty*"

"[M]an himself is now the crucial mystery. Man is that alien presence with whom the forces of egoism must come to terms, through whom the ego is to be crucified and resurrected, and in whose image society is to be reformed. Man, understood however not as 'I' but as 'Thou': for the ideals and temporal institutions of no tribe, race, continent, social class, or century, can be the measure of the inexhaustible and multifariously wonderful divine existence that is the life in all of us."

JOSEPH CAMPBELL

"This infinite of which I speak is below. It is above. It is to the west, to the east, to the south, to the north. It is, in fact, this whole world. And accordingly, with respect to the notion of ego (ahamkaradesa): I also am below, above, to the west, to the east, to the south, and to the north. I, also, am this whole world.

Or again, with respect to the Self (atman): The Self (the Spirit) is below, above, to the west, to the east, to the south, and to the north. The Self (the Spirit), indeed, is the whole world.

Verily, the one who sees this way, thinks and understands this way, takes pleasure in the Self, delights in the Self, dwells with the Self and knows bliss in the Self; such a one is autonomous, moving through all the world at pleasure. Whereas those who think otherwise are ruled by others (anya-rajan), know but perishable pleasures, and are moved about the world against their will (akamacara)."

CHANDOGYA UPANISHAD

"The notion that man has a body distinct from his soul is to be expunged; this I shall do by . . . melting apparent surfaces away, and displaying the infinite which was hid."

WILLIAM BLAKE

"If . . . we view time as a moving image of eternity, then each generation of humanity stands poised between the present moment and the timeless immensity of the eternal. Rather than being a worthless speck meaninglessly situated in the infinite expanse of space, each person . . . is a microcosm, a complete image of the entire cosmos, with one foot located in the realm of eternal principles and the other foot rooted in a particular world of manifestations. Poised as he is between time and eternity, matter and spirit, man possesses an incredible freedom to learn, create and know, limited only by those principles on which creation is based.

From this vantage point, humanity is engaged in a never-ceasing dialectic between time and eternity, possessing the ability to incarnate eternal principles in time (and in this sense mirror the creative work of Nature), yet also possessing the ability to elevate the particular to the universal through conscious understanding.

[T]he creative endeavors of humanity . . . attain their peak of excellence precisely at that point when the intermediate nature of humanity is actively recognized. For with this recognition comes the realization that one must actively integrate the particular and universal aspects of being."

DAVID R. FIDELER, *The Pythagorean Sourcebook And Library (Introduction)*

"My bounty is as boundless as the sea,
My love as deep; the more I give to thee,
The more I have, for both are infinite."

SHAKESPEARE, *Romeo and Juliet*

"The Self is Brahma, the Self is Vishnu, the Self is Indra, the Self is Shiva; the Self is all this universe. Nothing exists except the Self."

SRI SANKARACHARYA

ii. *Rebirth*

> "*I* am the rest between two notes
> which, struck together, sound discordantly,
> because death's note would claim a higher key.
>
> But in the dark pause, trembling, the notes meet,
> harmonious.
>
> And the song continues sweet."
>
> RAINER MARIA RILKE, *The Book of Hours*

"*Like* the ocean is your god-self;
It remains forever undefiled.
And like the ether it lifts but the winged.
Even like the sun is your god-self;
It knows not the ways of the mole nor seeks it the holes of
  the serpent.
But your god-self dwells not alone in your being.
Much in you is still man, and much of you is not yet man,
But a shapeless pygmy that walks asleep in the mist search-
  ing for its own awakening."

KAHLIL GIBRAN, *The Prophet*

"Man's urge towards spirituality is the inner driving of the spirit within him towards emergence.

...

Spirituality is in its essence an awakening to the inner reality of our being, to a spirit, self, soul which is other than our mind, life and body, an inner aspiration to know, to feel, to be that, to enter into contact with the greater Reality beyond and pervading the universe which inhabits also our own being, to be in communion with It and union with It, and a turning, a conversion, a transformation of our whole being as a result of the aspiration, the contact, the union, a growth or waking into a new becoming or new being, a new self, a new nature."

SRI AUROBINDO GHOSE, *The Life Divine*

"'[T]he time' has come: you must wake up now: . . . The night is almost over, it will be daylight soon -- let us give up all the things we prefer to do under cover of the dark; let us arm ourselves and appear in the light."
ROMANS 13:11-13

"[T]hink of him [God] as the coming one, who has been at hand since eternity, the future one, the final fruit of the tree, with us as its leaves. What is keeping you from hurling his birth into evolving times and from living your life as though it were one painful beautiful day in the history of a great pregnancy? Don't you see that everything that happens becomes a beginning again and again? Could it not be His beginning, since a beginning in itself is always so beautiful? If . . . he is the most perfect one, would not what is less than perfect have to precede him, so that he can choose himself from great abundance? Would not He have to be the last one, in order to envelop everything within himself? And what sense would our existence make, if the one we longed for had already had his existence in the past?

By extracting the most possible sweetness out of everything, just as the bees gather honey, we . . . build Him. With any insignificant thing, even with the very smallest thing -- if only it is done out of love -- we begin, with work, with a time of rest following, with keeping silent or with a small lonely joy, with everything that we do alone, without participants or supporters, we begin Him: the one whom we shall not experience in this lifetime, even as our ancestors could not experience us. Yet they who belong to the distant past are in us, serving as impetus, as a burden to our fate, as blood that can be heard rushing, as a gesture rising out of the depths of time.

Is there anything now that can rob you of the hope of someday being in Him, who is the ultimate, in the infinite future . . .?

Celebrate . . . with this reverent feeling that He perhaps needs exactly this, your fear of life, in order to begin. Perhaps these very days of your transition are the times that He is touched by everything within you. Perhaps you are influencing him, just as you as a child with breathless effort left a mark on Him. Be patient and without rancor and believe that the least we can do is to make His evolving no more difficult than the earth does for spring, when it wishes to come."

RAINER MARIA RILKE, *Letters To A Young Poet*

"[S]oul alone among creatures is generative. . . . There is where the birth takes place; there is where the Son is born. This birth does not take place once a year or once a month or once a day but all the time, that is, beyond time in that space where there is neither here and now nor nature and thought."

MEISTER ECKHART

"A cover of darkness, separation, and confusion are necessary prerequisites for the eventual rebirth of a lost and wandering soul."

NOR HALL

"We are the mother of Christ when we carry him in our heart and body by love and a pure and sincere conscience. And we give birth to him through our holy works which ought to shine on others by our example."
                                        FRANCIS OF ASSISI

"[You have to become a womb."
                                        Jalal-ud-Din RUMI

iii. Infinite Being

"If the doors of perception were cleansed every thing would appear to man as it is: infinite.

For man has closed himself up, till he sees all things thro' narrow chinks of his cavern."

                                        WILLIAM BLAKE, _The Marriage of Heaven and Hell_

"Self is everywhere, shining forth from all beings,
vaster than the vast, subtler than the most subtle,
unreachable, yet nearer than breath, than heartbeat.
Eye cannot see it, ear cannot hear it nor tongue
utter it; only in deep absorption can the mind,
grown pure and silent, merge with the formless truth.
He who finds it is free; he has found himself;
he has solved the great riddle; his heart forever is at
   peace.
Whole, he enters the Whole. His personal self
returns to its radiant, intimate, deathless source."
                              MUNDAKA UPANISHAD

"Each of us is a universe. Life and death are equal halves of a single turn,
a whole sphere, alternating phases of the one abiding mystery."
                 MEINRAD   CRAIGHEAD,   *The*
                     Feminist Mystic

"Weapons cannot hurt the Self and fire can never burn him. Untouched
is he by drenching waters, untouched is he by parching winds. Beyond the
power of sword and fire, beyond the power of waters and winds, the Self
is everlasting. . . . never changing . . . ever One. Know that he is, and
cease from sorrow."
                     BHAGAVAD-GITA

"We shall not expect to be immortal until we discover something in us
which is infinitely precious and eternally worthy to be conserved in a realm
to which we inherently belong -- the Over-World of Spirit."
                     RUFUS JONES, *Spirit in Man*

"The soul is winged to fly only along the skyways of eternity. Beyond, or far into unmeasured space, above the torrents of the earth, unerringly it spreads its wings. As we fetter souls with thought alone, and we design our own, then we ourselves do choose the scope, immensity of flight that we shall reach while weighted here with all the obstacles of earth and earthly flesh, unless we will to walk in Light."

WESLEY LA VIOLETTE, *The Creative Light*

"Fractured and unfinished though he be, modern man need not despair. He can work actively towards healing the fracture and completing himself, which is self-evolution. . . . [I]n the immortal image of man's soul . . . man is like a charioteer drawn by two winged horses (his infinite and his finite selves . . .); if he can keep them abreast of one another, he may actually ascend to the realm of the gods."

ERLING SKORPEN, "The Whole Man," *Nature, Man, and Society: Main Currents in Modern Thought*

"When love has carried us above all things . . . we receive in peace the Incomprehensible Light, enfolding us and penetrating us. What is this Light, if it be not a contemplation of the Infinite, and an intuition of Eternity? We behold that which we are, and we are that which we behold; because our being, without losing anything of its own personality, is united with the Divine Truth."

RUYSBROECK, "*The Book of Truth*"

"When the Creation of God is finished, when the Child is formed in the light, and the life breathed into him, then God brings him forth into his holy Land."

ISAAC PENINGTON, *The Way of Life and Death. In Works*

"The human being is the microcosm reflecting the macrocosm; in essence a droplet of divinity and therefore immortal and imperishable. The essential being, the I, always was and always will be and cannot possibly die, since it is an attribute of God."

SIR GEORGE TREVELYAN,
Summons to a High Crusade

"Thine own consciousness, shining, void, and inseparable from the Great Body of Radiance, hath no birth, nor death, and is the Immutable Light ..."
Tibetan Book of the Dead

B. GOD WITHIN

i. Human Temple

"This is my simple religion. There is no need for temples; no need for complicated philosophy. Our own brain, our own heart is our temple; the philosophy is kindness."

TENZIN GYATSO, 14TH DALAI LAMA OF TIBET,
"Hope for the Future," The Path of Compassion: Writings on Socially Engaged Buddhism

"In the centuries dark with ignorance and superstition . . . it was necessary that men should have built temples of worship, cathedrals in which to come into the sacred Presence. . . . [A]s the light begins to dawn, men will find the temple is not made with hands. The new temple is within themselves."

WESLEY LA VIOLETTE, *The Creative Light*

"What one man can do is change the world
And make it new again."

JOHN DENVER

"[T]he soul in man is not an organ, but animates and exercises all the organs; is not a function, like the power of memory, of calculation, of comparison -- but uses these as hands and feet; is not a faculty, but a light; is not the intellect or the will, but the master of the intellect and the will; is the vast background of our being, in which they lie -- an immensity not possessed and that cannot be possessed. From within or from behind, a light shines through us upon things, and makes us aware that we are nothing, but the light is all. A man is the facade of a temple wherein all wisdom and all good abide."

RALPH WALDO EMERSON, *Essays*

"For man is a rainbow of miraculous para-normal powers and talents, yet an observer must be in the right relative position to be able to see its full spectrum of hues. A rainbow cannot be separated from the environment of the whole; it cannot be isolated from the prismatic water droplets, the clouds, the rain, the ocean and the transforming light of the sun. Consciousness is that rainbow on the seashore of time; it is a potential which is always there, only needing all the elements to come together to reveal itself to the wonder of the onlooker.

* * *

Man is a great temple of life, yet we seldom give ourselves more than a cursory glance and that only in a mirror to see if it matches the social norm of any peer group. The terrible suffering and senseless separation felt by this first 'global' generation, starts with the basic ignorance of who we really are and the universe in which we live."

YATRI, *Unknown Man: The Mysterious Birth of a New Species*

"Do not consider your body a mere lump of flesh made of seven components. It is a noble instrument. In it are situated all holy places, gods, mantras, and the source of all extraordinary powers in this world. . . . God dwells in the body. He is present as fully in you as in the highest heavens. Why are you exhausting yourself looking for Him in different places instead of in your own heart? You should live your normal life, but accord Him the chief place among your daily activities. Whatever may be your religion or philosophy, do not make yourself a foolish, weak, and trivial creature. Do not head towards decline and disaster by regarding this body as godless. Do not commit spiritual suicide by belittling yourself through defective understanding."

SWAMI MUKTANANDA

"Tell me, where is the soul's abode? -- Upon the pinions of the wind."

MEISTER ECKHART

ii. Indwelling Spirit

"And I will pray the Father, and He will give you another Helper, that He may abide with you forever -- the Spirit of truth, who the world cannot receive, because it neither sees Him nor knows Him; but you know Him, for He dwells with you and will be in you. I will not leave you orphans; I will come to you. A little while longer and the world will see Me no more, but you will see Me. Because I live, you will live also. At that day you will know that I am in my Father, and you in Me, and I in you."

JOHN 14:16-20

"We must bring the vision within and no longer see in the mode of separation. We need no longer look outside for our vision of the divine being; it is but the strength to see divinity within."

PLOTINUS, *On Intellectual Beauty*

"If anyone is bewildered, it is only because they do not see the creator, the holy Lord abiding within themselves."

MAITRAYANA-BRAHMANA
UPANISHAD

"Each has felt the brush of angels' wings as he has turned his face toward the light, has turned toward his better Self."

WESLEY LA VIOLETTE, *The Creative Light*

"The seed of God is in us. Pear seeds grow into pear trees, nut seeds into nut trees, and God seeds into God."

MEISTER ECKHART, *Sermons*

"The highest revelation is that God is in everyone."

RALPH WALDO EMERSON, *Journals*

"This coming age will mark an epochal advancement in man's evolution toward his goal of omniscience and omnipotence.

Man becomes a higher being with greater power as he acquires knowledge. In knowledge alone lies power. Only through knowledge can man become co-creator with God.

Knowledge can be obtained by man only through awareness of the spirit within him. Lack of that awareness is the tragedy of today's civilization."

WALTER RUSSELL, *The Secret of Light*

"There is a breath of God in every man, a force lying deeper than the stratum of will, which may be stirred to become an aspiration strong enough to give direction and even to run counter to all winds."

ABRAHAM JOSHUA HESCHEL, *The Wisdom of Heschel*

"[The universe lets great spiritual realities 'break through' as soon as our spirits are formed to be the organs of them."

RUFUS JONES, *Spirit in Man*

"With your whole heart and soul, seek to regain Reality, nay, seek for Reality within your own heart, for Reality, in truth, is hidden within you. The heart is the dwelling place of that which is the Essence of the universe, within the heart and soul is the very Essence of God. Like the saints, make a journey into your self; like the lovers of God, cast one glance within. As a lover now, in contemplation of the Beloved, be unveiled within and behold the Essence. Form is a veil to you and your heart is a veil. When the veil vanishes, you will become all light."

ATTAR

"It is as if one stood before a high mountain and cried God! Art thou there? The echo comes back Art thou there? If one cries out Come out, the echo comes back Come out!"
                                        MEISTER ECKHART

iii. Union

"The ultimate questions of our life transcend knowledge. One riddle after another surrounds us. But the final question of our being has but one concern, and it decides our fate. Again and again we are thrown back to it. What will become of our own will? How does it find itself in the will of God? The highest insight man can attain is the yearning for peace, for the union of his will with an infinite will, his human will with God's will. Such a will does not cut itself off and live in isolation like a puddle that is bound to dry up when the heat of summer comes. No, it is like a mountain stream, relentlessly splashing its way to the river, there to be swept on to the limitless ocean."
                        ALBERT SCHWEITZER, *Reverence for Life*

"Only those who see God in themselves find eternal peace."
                                        KATHA UPANISHAD

"God became a human being in order that human beings might become God."
                                        ST. IRENAEUS

"One day, you will sit on a plateau and the wind will blow through your hair, and you'll have a simple cloak on. And you will sit there and you will contemplate your life and you will realize the magnificent creature that you really are. And you will not have done one thing that would have ever harmed you or hurt you or would have disrespected you in any way, because, above all, it was your respect that you upheld and no one else's. That is when you can sleep and slumber at night and rejoice during the day and love what you are. Then you are a happy entity and, indeed, a happy God."

RAMTHA

"[W]ithin man is the soul of the whole; the wise silence; the universal beauty, to which every part and particle is equally related; the eternal ONE."

RALPH WALDO EMERSON, *Essays*

"Man is slowly perceiving that the inner self evolves and is found and fulfilled in the whole."

ERLING SKORPEN, "The Whole Man,"
*Nature, Man, and Society: Main
Currents in Modern Thought*

"God is light; there is no darkness in him at all.

* * *

[I]f we live our lives in the light,
as he is in the light,
we are in union with one another . . ."

I JOHN 1:5-7

"Heaven is under our feet as well as over our heads."

HENRY DAVID THOREAU, *Walden*

"[E]ach person and nation finds its own path back to the stream of evolution. It is not that we must perform the heroic task of saving nature. Nature is self-sustaining, once we cease to interfere. The same pulsation of life flows through the whole world, emanating from the gods of God. That unimaginable force created the galaxies and at the same time preserves the most fragile mountain flower. All around us life gushes forth and meets itself coming back, curving in joy onto itself and leaping in jubilation in its own infinite strength. We are part of this stream too. We issued from it, and our destiny continues to ride its crest."

DEEPAK CHOPRA, M.D., *"The Wishing Tree and The Science of Life"*

"We see the world piece by piece, as the sun, the moon, the animal, the tree; but the whole, of which these are the shining parts, is the soul."

RALPH WALDO EMERSON, *Essays*

"The seat of the soul is where the inner world and the outer world meet. Where they overlap, it is in every point of the overlap."

NOVALIS

"The Divine Love in every Person or Spirit lives not in it self as a part, but in the life or the whole, in the Divine, the Universal Spirit, the Spirit of Love, the Spirit of the whole. I live not, saith St. Paul, but Christ liveth in me. Again, if you live in the Spirit, walk in the Spirit. Thus, the Divine Love having its life in each person, in the life of the whole, the Universal Spirit, being one Spirit with that Spirit, which is the Unity of the whole, comprehendeth all things with strictest tenderest imbraces in it self, as one self with it self."

PETER STERRY

"[The great work in front of us requires that we unite as a collective whole. The new doorways cannot be opened or passed through by any of us still operating as individual units of consciousness. They are brought into manifestation through our Unified Presence, through our focused intent, through our total commitment to serving our Higher Purpose as One."

SOLARA, *11:11: Inside the Doorway*

"Wherever two or more of you are gathered in His name, there is love."

"Wedding Song (There is Love)"

Public Domain Foundation

"The only proper end of love is union."

EVELYN UNDERHILL, *Mysticism*

iv. Kingdom

"The Kingdom will not come by expectation. They will not say 'see here, see there.' The Kingdom of the Father is spread upon the earth, and men do not see it."

THE GOSPEL OF THOMAS 113

"The kingdom of God does not come with observation; nor will they say, 'See here!' or 'See there!' For indeed, the kingdom of God is within you."

LUKE 17:20-21

"Among the hills, when you sit in the cool shade of the white poplars, sharing the peace and serenity of distant fields and meadows -- then let your heart say in silence, 'God rests in reason.'

And when the storm comes, and the mighty wind shakes the forest, and thunder and lightening proclaim the majesty of the sky, -- then let your heart say in awe, 'God moves in passion.'

And since you are a breath in God's sphere, and a leaf in God's forest, you too should rest in reason and move in passion."

KAHLIL GIBRAN, *The Prophet*

"God is in your heart, yet you search for God in the wilderness."

THE GRANTH

"The Lord abides in the heart of all things."

BHAGAVAD-GITA

"The kingdom of the Father is not
going to come through expectation.

We bring it about in our own hearts.

The Kingdom is here."
                    JOSEPH CAMPBELL

"It is because we don't know who we are, because we are unaware that
the Kingdom of Heaven is within us, that we behave in the generally silly,
the often insane, the sometimes criminal ways that are so characteristically
human. We are saved, we are liberated and enlightened, by perceiving the
hitherto unperceived good that is already within us, by returning to our
eternal Ground and remaining where, without knowing it, we have always
been."
                    ALDOUS HUXLEY

"When you make the two one, and when you make the inner as the outer,
and the outer as the inner, and the above as the below . . . . then shall you
enter the Kingdom."
                    THE GOSPEL OF THOMAS 106

"When the mind returns into itself from the confusions of sense, as it does
when it reflects, it passes into another region than the sensuous one, the
region of that which is pure and everlasting, immortal and unchanging; and,
feeling itself kindred thereto, it dwells there under its own control and has
rest from its wanderings, and being in communion with the unchanging is
itself unchanging."
                    PLATO, *Phaedo*

"Man, enter into thyself. For this Philosophers' Stone is not to be found in foreign lands."

ANGELUS SILESIUS

"Reconciliation with God by opening to the Light in the depths brings us into unity with the depths of the totality of being, with the New Creation."

R. MELVIN KEISER, "Inward Light and The New Creation"

"[The Kingdom is inside of you, and it is outside of you. When you come to know yourselves, then you will be known, and you will realize that you are the sons of the living Father. But if you will not know yourselves, then you will dwell in poverty, and it is you who are that poverty."

THE GOSPEL OF THOMAS 3

v. Divine Image

"Creation does not merely take place only in the beginning, but also at every moment throughout the whole of time. . . . All of us created in the image of God are potentially able to become images of the Divine."

MARTIN BUBER, The Way of Response

"He who knows his own self knows God."

MUHAMMAD, The Hadith

"Every creature is a witness to God's power and omnipotence; and its beauty is a witness to the divine wisdom. . . . Every creature participates in some way in the likeness of the Divine Essence."

SAINT THOMAS AQUINAS

"If indeed thy heart were right, then would every creature be to thee a mirror of life, and a book of holy doctrine."

THOMAS A. KEMPIS, *Adaptive Coloration of Animals*

"For this alone I need; that you will hear the words I speak, and give them to the world. You are my voice, my eyes, my feet, my hands through which I save the world."

A COURSE IN MIRACLES

"Light is the shadow of God."

PLATO

"There is in all of us a higher man . . . a man more entirely of the celestial rank, almost a god, reproducing God. When the soul begins again to mount, it comes not to something alien but to its very self. The self thus lifted, we are in the likeness of the Supreme."

PLOTINUS

"The boundaries of man are the mansions of eternity."

DONALD HATCH ANDREWS, *"The New Dimensions of Nature and Man," Nature, Man, and Society: Main Currents In Modern Thought*

"If you go on working with the light available, you will meet your Master, as he himself will be seeking you."

RAMANA MAHARSHI

"Oh couldst thou only express . . . all that lives so full and warm in thyself, that it might become the mirror of thy soul, as thy soul is the mirror of the infinite God."

JOHANN WOLFGANG VON GOETHE, *Die Leiden des jungen Werthers*

"These sparks, human souls, which come directly from God, have no end: they are imprinted forever with the stamp of God's beauty."

DANTE ALIGHIERI

"I often feel as if my life were a lamp: a temporary container filled with light, a flow of energy, condensed and held together for a little while in a mysterious, marvelous living cosmos linked with the rest of the Earth and the heavens through material, touchable elements and immaterial, invisible elements. Someday the lamp will extinguish. The material elements will be reabsorbed by the Earth in its chains of life and energy. The immaterial elements will return to a universal soul to be reborn in other forms on this planet or elsewhere in the universe. We are cosmic matter come alive, partaking of the divine character of our Creator."

ROBERT MULLER, *A Planet of Hope*

"Christ has no body now on earth but yours,
  no hands but yours,
  no feet but yours,
Yours are the eyes through which is to look out
  Christ's compassion to the world;
Yours are the feet with which he is to go about
  doing good;
Yours are the hands with which he is to bless men now."

SAINT TERESA OF AVILA, *You Are Christ's Hands*

"Finding your Self, discovering who you really are, means to find God, for there is nothing outside Him. . . . When one finds one's Self, one has found God; and finding God, one has found one's Self."

ANANDAMAYI MA, *As the Flower Sheds its Fragrance*

"God expects but one thing of you, and that is that you should come out of yourself in so far as you are a created being and let God be God in you."

MEISTER ECKHART

"[We, with our unveiled faces reflecting like mirrors the brightness of the Lord, all grow brighter as we are turned into the image that we reflect. . . ."

2 CORINTHIANS 3:18

"The world is a mirror of infinite beauty, yet no man sees it. It is a Temple of Majesty, yet no man regards it. It is a region of Light and Peace, did not men disquiet it. It is the Paradise of God."

THOMAS TRAHERNE

"The lover is his mirror in which he is beholding his Self."
                    PLATO, *Phaedrus*

"Let him who desires to see God wipe his mirror and cleanse his heart."
                    RICHARD OF SAINT-VICTOR

"The eye by which I see God is the same eye by which God sees me."
                    MEISTER ECKHART

"The Divine Love is the sun of perfection, its Light is the command, and the creatures are its shadows."
                    Jalal-ud-Din RUMI

"When the mind is awakened to the presence of the Divine Light in all things, the eyes change, and into them comes the gaze that you see . . . and those who know that what they are looking at is not separate from them, but they are looking at reality itself with infinite awareness, infinite compassion, infinite joy, infinite intelligence and understanding."
                    ANDREW HARVEY, *The Way of Passion, a Celebration of Rumi*

vi. Child of God

"Though we are God's sons and daughters, we do not realize it yet."
                    MEISTER ECKHART

"*B*lessed are the poor in spirit: for theirs is the kingdom
of heaven.
Blessed are they that mourn: for they shall be comforted.
Blessed are the meek: for they shall inherit the earth.
Blessed are they which do hunger and thirst after righteous-
ness: for they shall be filled.
Blessed are the merciful: for they shall obtain mercy.
Blessed are the pure in heart: for they shall see God.
Blessed are the peacemakers: for they shall be called the
children of God.
Blessed are they which are persecuted for righteousness'
sake: for theirs is the kingdom of heaven.
Blessed are ye, when men shall revile you, and persecute
you, and shall say all manner of evil against you falsely,
for my sake.
Rejoice, and be exceeding glad: for great is your reward in
heaven, for so persecuted they the prophets which were
before you."

MATTHEW 5:3-12

"*F*rom Judaism, Christianity, and Islam to Hinduism, Buddhism, Taoism,
and Native American and Goddess religions, each offers images of the
sacred web into which we are woven. We are called children of one God
and 'members of one body;' we are seen as drops in the ocean of Brahman;
we are pictured as jewels in the Net of Indra. We interexist -- like
synapses in the mind of an all-encompassing being."

JOANNA MACY, *Despair*

"*I*f in your heart you make
a manger for his birth,
then God will once again
become a child on earth."

ANGELUS SILESIUS

"Men are children of the Gods, and sacred Nature all things hid reveals."

ANTOINE FABRE d'OLIVET, *Golden Verses, quoting Pythagoras*

"We are all of us by birth the offspring of God -- more nearly related to Him than we are to one another, for in Him we live, and move, and have our being."

WILLIAM LAW

"Everyone moved by the Spirit is a son of God. . . . The Spirit himself and our spirit bear united witness that we are children of God. And if we are children we are heirs as well: heirs of God and co-heirs with Christ, sharing his sufferings so as to share his glory. . . . The whole creation is eagerly waiting for God to reveal his sons. . . . From the beginning till now the entire creation, as we know, has been groaning in one great act of giving birth."

ROMANS 8:14, 16, 17, 19, 22

"When we transcend ourselves and become in our ascent towards God so simple that the bare supreme Love can lay hold of us, then we cease, and we and all our selfhood die in God. And in this death we become the hidden children of God, and find a new life within us."

RUYSBROECK, *"De Calculo"*

"*You* are a child of the Universe no less than the trees and the stars. You have a right to be here, and whether or not it is clear to you, no doubt the universe is unfolding as it should. Therefore, be at peace with God, whatever you conceive him to be. And whatever your labors and aspirations, in the noisy confusion of life, keep pace in your soul. With all its sham, drudgery and broken dreams, it is still a beautiful world."

MAX EHRMANN, *The Poems of Max Ehrmann (excerpt from "Desiderata")*

C. PATH OF LIGHT

i. Love

"*The* root of the matter is a very simple and old-fashioned thing, a thing so simple that I am almost ashamed to mention it, for fear of the derisive smile with which wise cynics will greet my words. The thing I mean -- please forgive me for mentioning it -- is love, Christian love, or compassion. If you feel this, you have a motive for existence, a guide for action, a reason for courage, an imperative necessity for intellectual honesty."

BERTRAND A. RUSSELL, *The Impact of Science on Society*

"*L*ove seeketh not itself to please, nor for itself hath any care, but for another gives its ease, and builds a Heaven in Hell's despair."

WILLIAM BLAKE, *The Clod and the Pebble*

"*L*ove and kindness are the very basis for society. If we lose these feelings, society will face tremendous difficulties; the survival of humanity will be endangered."

TENZIN GYATSO, 14TH DALAI LAMA OF TIBET

"[*T*]he timeless in you is aware of life's timelessness,

And knows that yesterday is but today's memory and tomorrow is today's dream.

And that that which sings and contemplates in you is still dwelling within the bounds of that first moment which scattered the stars into space.

Who among you does not feel that his power to love is boundless?

And yet who does not feel that very love, though boundless, encompassed within the centre of his being, and moving not from love thought to love thought, nor from love deed to other love deeds?

And is not time even as love is, undivided and spaceless?"

KAHLIL GIBRAN, *The Prophet*

"*L*ove is the magician, the enchanter, that changes worthless things to joy, and makes right royal kings and queens of common clay. It is the perfume of that wondrous flower, the heart, and without that sacred passion, that divine swoon, we are less than beasts; but with it, earth is heaven, and we are gods."

ROBERT   G.   INGERSOLL, "*Orthodoxy*"

"*The* day will come when, after harnessing the ether, the winds, the tides, gravitation, we shall harness for God the energies of love. And, on that day, for the second time in the history of the world, man will have discovered fire."

PIERRE TEILHARD de CHARDIN, "*The Evolution of Chastity*," *Toward the Future*

"*L*ove is the subtlest force in the world."

MOHANDAS   K.   (MAHATMA) GANDHI

"*There* is no difficulty that enough love will not conquer; no disease that enough love will not heal; no door that enough love will not open; no gulf that enough love will not bridge; no wall that enough love will not throw down; no sin that enough love will not redeem.

It makes no difference how deeply seated may be the trouble, how hopeless the outlook, how muddled the tangle, how great the mistake. A sufficient realization of love will dissolve it all. If only you could love you would be the happiest and most powerful being in the world."

EMMET FOX

"*We* all can build bridges of love each day
With our eyes, our smiles, our touch
With our will to find a way
There is no distance we cannot span
The vision is in our hearts
The power is in our hands

For now more than ever
What the world needs more of
Is to reach for each other
With bridges of love."

STEVEN LONGFELLOW FISKE AND
JAI MICHAEL JOSEPHS, "*Bridges of Love*"

"*The* pure, unadulterated love of one person can nullify the hatred of millions."

MOHANDAS   K.   (MAHATMA) GANDHI

"*You* have been told also that life is darkness, and in your weariness you echo what was said by the weary.

And I say that life is indeed darkness save when there is urge,

And all urge is blind save when there is knowledge,

And all knowledge is vain save when there is work,

And all work is empty save when there is love;

And when you work with love you bind yourself to yourself, and to one another, and to God."

KAHLIL GIBRAN, *The Prophet*

"*The* loving personality seeks not to control, but to nurture, not to dominate, but to empower. Love is the richness and fullness of your soul flowing through you.

Humbleness, forgiveness, clarity and love are the dynamics of freedom. They are the foundations of authentic power."

GARY ZUKAV, *The Seat of the Soul*

"*The* new earth exists only in the heart of man."

NIKOS KAZANTZAKIS, *Saviours of God*

"[*L*]ove and beauty are not chaos. They are the fulfillment, not the violation of Law."

F. L. KUNZ, *"The Reality of the Non-Material," Nature, Man, and Society: Main Currents in Modern Thought*

"[*W*]e . . . have great capacities that can be harnessed to restore the environment -- restorative powers as great as any found in nature. And we have them in abundant supply: intelligence, discrimination, will, judgment, and -- most important -- love. Do not underestimate the power of these resources. They too can do much to heal the earth, if we give them a chance."

EKNATH EASWARAN, *The Compassionate Universe: The Power of the Individual to Heal the Environment*

"*L*ove alone can unite living beings so as to complete and fulfill them . . . for it alone joins them by what is deepest in themselves. All we need is to imagine our ability to love developing until it embraces the totality of men and of the earth."

PIERRE TEILHARD de CHARDIN

"*L*ove to faults is always blind,
Always is to joy inclined,
Lawless, winged, and unconfined,
And breaks all chains from every mind."

WILLIAM BLAKE

"*You* have no idea of the tremendous release and deep peace that comes from meeting yourself and your brothers totally without judgment."
A COURSE IN MIRACLES

"*If* you will love what seems to be insignificant and will in an unassuming manner, as a servant, seek to win the confidence of what seems poor, then everything will become easier, more harmonious, and somehow more conciliatory, not for your intellect -- that will most likely remain behind, astonished -- but for your innermost consciousness, your awakeness, and your inner knowing."

RAINER MARIA RILKE, *Letters To A Young Poet*

"*By* using the power of our inner space, we can radiate our loving worldwide and thereby transform the planet."

BRIAN   O'LEARY,   "*Redefining Science*"

"*The* desire and pursuit of the whole is called love."
PLATO

"[*The* sorry mess that has developed on earth can no longer be left unresolved, and the longing for meaning and fulfillment must be addressed. However, it requires men and women who will let their lives be given passionately to the source of life. Then there is the means for which is unfolding to be stewarded wisely and with understanding. Our caring flows out to encompass whatever is occurring, and to provide for it in gentleness and love.

Central to this process of transformation is the creative interrelationship that develops between people when they love the creative process of life and are not afraid to acknowledge that love amongst themselves. .... As our passion is placed where it belongs -- and nothing will change without passion -- we discover that we are together, we are one. In this, we may allow a luminous power to be released which transforms the world."

MICHAEL EXETER, *Living at the Heart of Creation: Practical Wisdom for Extraordinary Times*

"He is forever free who has broken out
Of the ego-cage of I and mine
To be united with the Lord of Love.
This is the supreme state. Attain thou this
And pass from death to immortality."

BHAGAVAD-GITA, *The Illumined Man*

"To love is not a state: it is a direction."
SIMONE WEIL

"The soul is made of love, and must ever strive to return to love."
MECHTHILD OF MAGDEBURG

"The entire Universe is condensed in the body, and the entire body in the Heart. Thus the Heart is the nucleus of the whole Universe."
SRI RAMANA MAHARSHI

"Love desires to be aloft, and will not be kept back by anything low and mean."

THOMAS   A.   KEMPIS,   *The Imitation of Christ*

"The topic of unselfish love has been placed on the agenda of history and is about to become its main business."

PITIRIM SOROKIN

"Divine wisdom descends through mercy as far as the human intellect ascends through love."

MAXIMUS

"Wherever Beauty looks,
  Love is also there;
Wherever Beauty shows a rosy cheek
  Love lights Her fire from that flame.
When Beauty dwells in the dark folds of night
  Love comes and finds a heart
  entangled in her tresses.
Beauty and Love are as body and soul.
Beauty is the mine, Love is the diamond."

JAMI

"If you want to experience love, you have to start by loving yourself. First you have to love your body, then those who are related to your body, and then the master of the body, the inner Self. . . . The truth is that God has no physical body; the only body He has is the body of love. If the love you experience in your daily life -- the little love you feel for your friends, your relatives, your pets, and even your possessions -- could be turned toward the inner Self, that would be enough to bring you liberation."

SWAMI MUKTANANDA, *I Have Become Alive*

"You live that you may learn to love. You love that you may learn to live. No other lesson is required of Man."

MIRDAD

"Love lures the patterns of creation out of the void."

JEAN HOUSTON, *Godseed: The Journey of Christ*

"The sail (of the boat) is love, the Holy Spirit its mast."

JOHANNES TAULER

"A single atom of the love of God in a heart is worth more than a hundred thousand paradises."

BAYAZID al-BISTAMI

"Love feels no burden, thinks nothing of trouble, attempts what is above its strength, pleads no excuse of impossibility; for it thinks all things lawful for itself and all things possible."

THOMAS A. KEMPIS, *The Imitation of Christ*

"To merge into the heart is prayer."

SRI RAMANA MAHARSHI

"Love has to spring spontaneously from within. It is in no way amenable to any form of inner or outer force. Love and coercion can never go together; but though Love cannot be forced on anyone, It can be awakened in him through Love itself. Love is essentially self-communicative. Those who do not have It catch It from those who have It. True Love is unconquerable and irresistible; and It goes on gathering power and spreading Itself, until eventually It transforms everyone whom It touches."

MEHER BABA

"Love is man's natural endowment, but he doesn't know how to use it. He refuses to recognize the power of love because of his love of power."

DICK GREGORY

"Follow the thunder of our passing
into new lives,
dark, our shadow, long on the land;
green, the earth beneath us, drumming dance of swiftness,
gold, the light within our eyes, we see the sun before us;
we are one, unstoppable, untameable, untouchable,
and are yours, are yours, in the power of love."

WOLFE VAN BRUSSEL, "*The Horsewoman*"

"Know that it is the waves of Love that turns the wheels of Heaven."
Jalal-ud-Din RUMI

"Only Love and actions springing from Love can help us now."

ANDREW HARVEY, *The Way of Passion, a Celebration of Rumi*

ii. Compassion

"Whosoever on the night of the nativity of the young Jesus, in the great snows, shall fare forth bearing a succulent bone for the lost and lamenting hounds, a wisp of hay for the shivering horse, a cloak of warm raiment for the stranded wayfarer, a bundle of faggots for the twittering crone, a flagon of red wine for him whose marrow withers, a garland of bright red berries for one who has worn chains, a dish of crumbs with a song of love for all huddled birds who thought that song was dead, and divers lush sweetmeats for such babes' faces as peer from lonely windows, to him shall be proffered and returned gifts of such an astonishment as will rival the hues of the peacock and the harmonies of heaven, so that though he live to the great age when man goes stooping and querulous because of the nothing that is left of him, yet shall he walk upright in remembering, as one whose heart shines like a great star in his breast."

AUTHOR UNKNOWN

"Let us just be side by side -- helping, respecting, and understanding each other -- in a common effort to serve humankind. The aim of human society must be the compassionate betterment of human beings."

TENZIN GYATSO, 14TH DALAI LAMA OF TIBET

"Lao-Tse . . . wrote, 'From caring comes courage.' We might add that from it also comes wisdom. It's rather significant, we think, that those who have no compassion have no wisdom. Knowledge, yes; cleverness, maybe; wisdom, no. A clever mind is not a heart. Knowledge doesn't really care. Wisdom does. We also consider it significant that cor, the Latin word for 'heart,' is the basis for the word, courage."

BENJAMIN HOFF, The Tao of Pooh

"I myself have no power. . . . Real power comes only from the Creator. It's in His hands. . . . [I]f you're asking about strength, not power, then I say that the greatest strength is gentleness."

CHIEF LEON SHENANDOAH (Grand Council of the Six Nations Iroquois Confederacy)

"*What* faith in God needs to begin with is the fair and simple assumption that great good can come to be, if we follow the call of conscience toward the heights and reach out for all possible resources in the struggle for good."

WALTER MARSHALL HORTON,
The God We Trust

"*Our* hands are the tools we use to create whatever we want in the types of work we do. The fingers represent life, unity, equality for eternity. When we extend our hands to reach out, we touch in peace."

TWYLAH NITSCH *(Seneca)*

"*The* key to the Grail is compassion,
suffering with, feeling another's sorrow
as if it were your own.

The one who finds
the dynamo of compassion
is the one who's found the Grail."

JOSEPH CAMPBELL

"Compassion may be defined as 'emotion' without charge, 'thought' without attachment to the outcome, and 'feeling' without distortion.

...

Compassion allows the ability to view the events and actions of life for the purity of what they are as opposed to the judgments that your experienced fear placed upon them. In compassion, there can be no right, no wrong, no good, no bad. There simply 'is' and there is the consequences of choice."

> GREGG BRADEN, *Walking Between the Worlds, The Science of Compassion*

"Look deeply: I arrive in every second
to be a bud on a spring branch,
to be a tiny bird, with wings still fragile,
    learning to sing in my new nest,
to be a caterpillar in the heart of a flower,
to be a jewel hiding itself in a stone. . . .

Please call me by my true names,
    so I can wake up,
and so the door of my heart can be left open,
the door of compassion."

> THICH NHAT HANH

"As a mother at the risk of her life watches over her only child, so let everyone cultivate a boundlessly compassionate mind toward all beings."

> GUATAMA SIDDHARTHA (THE BUDDHA)

iv . Forgiveness

"What could you want
forgiveness cannot give?
Do you want peace? Forgiveness offers it.
Do you want happiness, a quiet mind,
a certainty of purpose,
and a sense of worth and beauty
that transcends the world?
Do you want care and safety,
and the warmth of sheer protection
    always?
Do you want a quietness that cannot be
    disturbed,
a gentleness that never can be hurt,
a deep, abiding comfort,
and a rest so perfect it can never be
    upset?
All this forgiveness offers you."

A COURSE IN MIRACLES

"Let the Forces of Light bring illumination to all mankind.
Let the Spirit of Peace be spread abroad.
May men of goodwill everywhere meet in a spirit of
    co-operation.
May forgiveness on the part of all men be the keynote at
    this time.
Let power attend the efforts of the Great Ones.
So let it be and help us to do our part."

ALICE A. BAILEY, <u>The</u>
<u>Externalisation of the Hierarchy</u>

"Forgiveness is this world's equivalent of Heaven's justice. It translates the world . . . into a simple world, where justice can be reflected from beyond the gate behind which total lack of limits lies. . . .

Forgiveness turns the world . . . into a world of glory, wonderful to see. . . . There is no sadness and there is no parting here, for everything is totally forgiven. And what has been forgiven must join, for nothing stands between to keep them separate and apart. . . ."

A COURSE IN MIRACLES

v. Gift of Self

"To be religious is to give your life so that the world may be more beautiful, more just, more at peace; it is to prevent egotistical and self-serving ends from disrupting this harmony of the whole."

ARTURO PAOLI, *Meditations on Saint Luke*

"All choices in the world depend on this; you choose between your brother and yourself, and you will gain as much as he will lose, and what you lose is what is given him. How utterly opposed to truth is this, when all the lesson's purpose is to teach that what your brother loses _you_ have lost, and what he gains is what is given _you_."

A COURSE IN MIRACLES

"It is within my power either to serve God, or not to serve Him. Serving Him, I add to my own good and the good of the whole world. Not serving Him, I forfeit my own good and deprive the world of that good, which was in my power to create."

LEO TOLSTOY

"Loving others is a quality of one's own heart. . . [C]ontentment is dependent on one's lovingness, upon creating a field of harmony inside one's own heart. That field of harmony, like a beautiful open field of flowers, has to contain love, emotional independence, contentment with oneself as one is, not the seeking of love or approval but rather the giving of approval and love."

AYYA KHEMA, *Be an Island unto Yourself*

"For a man to be called a man, he must live his life as an offering before God."

ISRAEL OF RIZHYN

"As Heaven's peace and joy intensify when you accept them as God's gift to you, so does the joy of your Creator grow when you accept His joy and peace as yours. True giving is creation. It extends the limitless to the unlimited, eternity to timelessness, and love unto itself. It adds to all that is complete already, not in simple terms of adding more, for that implies that it was less before. It adds by letting what cannot contain itself fulfill its aim of giving everything it has away, securing it forever for itself."

A COURSE IN MIRACLES

D. *L*IGHT OF THE WORLD

i. *S*ingle Candle

> "*L*et no man imagine that he has no influence. Whoever he may be, and wherever he may be placed, <u>man becomes a light and a power</u>."
>
> HENRY GEORGE, *Progress and Poverty*

"*I*t is better to light one small candle than curse the darkness."

CONFUCIUS, *Analects*

"*The* lightening spark of thought generated in the solitary mind awakens its likeness in another mind."

THOMAS CARLYLE, *Essays*

"*Those* who . . . kindle . . . fires of illumination within them are the ones who . . . give us a new kind of civilization; who . . . interpret invisible rhythms into visible ones; who . . . transpose their inner ecstasies to recognizable forms and symbols. . . ."

WALTER RUSSELL, *The Man Who Tapped the Secrets of the Universe*

"The thunderbolt falls on an inch of ground, but the light of it fills the horizon."

RALPH WALDO EMERSON

"Inside my empty bottle I was constructing a lighthouse while all the others were making ships."

C. S. LEWIS

"Give light, and the darkness will disappear of itself."

DESIDERIUS ERASMUS

"You can become light-bearers, knowing . . . that 'in that light you will see Light' -- and so will your fellowmen."

ALICE A. BAILEY, *Education in The New Age*

"Be original. Be inventive. Be strong. Be upright. Think with your own head. Be yourself. Do not lean on the crutches of others. All perfection and every divine virtue are hidden within you -- reveal them to the world. Wisdom too is already within you -- let it strike forth."

BABAJI

"Love's glory is not a small thing."

Jalal-ud-Din RUMI

ii. Light of Love

"You are the salt of the earth. But if salt becomes tasteless, what can make it salty again? It is good for nothing and can only be thrown out to be trampled underfoot.

You are the light of the world. A city built on a hill-top cannot be hidden. No one lights a lamp to put it under a tub; they put it on the lamp-stand where it shines for everyone in the house. In the same way your light must shine in the sight of men, so that, seeing your good works, they may give praise to your Father in heaven."

MATTHEW 5:13-16

"I am the light of the world."

JOHN 8:12; 9:5

"In this dwelling of Perfect Wisdom -- you shall become a saviour of the helpless, a defender of the defenseless . . . a light to the blind, and you shall guide to the path those who have lost it, and you shall become a support to those who are without support."

JOANNA MACY, *Perfection of Wisdom: Mother of All Buddhas*

"[The universal soul breathes through a man's intellect, it is genius; when it breathes through his will, it is virtue; when it flows through his affection, it is love."

RALPH WALDO EMERSON, *Essays*

"[O]n his sound and creative behavior man is motivated by sympathy, benevolence and unselfish love rather than by egotism, hate and cruelty. . . . [T]he energy of this love is indispensable for the generation, continuity and growth of living forms, for the survival and multiplication of the species, and . . . for the health of infants and their growth into mentally and morally sound citizens. . . . [L]ove . . . is the heart of a true freedom; . . ."

> PITIRIM A. SOROKIN, "*Three Basic Trends of Our Times,*" *Nature, Man, and Society: Main Currents in Modern Thought*

"[I]f men wish to draw near to God, they must seek him in the hearts of men. They should speak well of all men, whether present or absent, and if they themselves seek to be a light to guide others, then, like the sun, they must show the same face to all. To bring joy to a single heart is better than to build many shrines for worship, and to enslave one soul by kindness is worth more than setting free a thousand slaves."

> ABU SA'ID IBN ABI'L-KHAYR

"[A]nyone who loves his brother is living in the light."

> I JOHN 2:10

"God enjoys himself in all things. The sun casts its bright light upon all creatures. Whatever the sun casts its light upon draws the sun up into itself; yet as a result the sun does not lose any of its power of illumination."

> MEISTER ECKHART

"[W]hen your being is filled with light you can go into any dark place on the planet and that light will shine forth and the darkness cannot withstand the light. . . [T]his is something that each individual needs to do, to claim their Christ-light now. And know that they are <u>beacons</u> of light and that they can shine this light forth and this is the way more and more light can be created in the world."

EILEEN CADDY

"Look round our World; behold the chain of Love
Combining all below and all above."

ALEXANDER POPE, An Essay on Man

"Beloved, the fires of Love descend from heaven in many shapes and forms, but their impress on the world is one. The tiny flame that lights up the human heart is like a blazing torch that comes down from heaven to light up the paths of mankind."

KAHLIL GIBRAN, The Voice of The Master

"What makes you glitter like gold is the commitment to love, the experience of that love, and the unashamed display of that love. . . ."

Jalal-ud-Din RUMI

iii. Children of Light

> *"What* does the word 'soul' mean? ... No one can give a definition of the soul. But we know what it feels like. The soul is the sense of something higher than ourselves, something that stirs in us thoughts, hopes, and aspirations which go out to the world of goodness, truth and beauty. The soul is a burning desire to breathe in this world of light and never to lose it -- to remain children of light."
>
> ALBERT SCHWEITZER, *Reverence for Life*

"*Jesus* said, if they say to you, 'Where did you come from?', say to them, 'We came from the light, the place where the light came into being on its own accord and established itself and became manifest through their image.' If they say to you, 'Is it you?', say, 'We are its children,' ..."

THE GOSPEL OF THOMAS 50

"*The* Law was planted
to reward the Children of Light
with healing and abundant peace,
with long life,
with fruitful seed of everlasting blessings,
with eternal joy
in immortality of Eternal Light."

THE DEAD SEA SCROLLS, "*The Manual of Discipline*"

"*A* little while longer the light is with you. Walk while you have the light, lest darkness overtake you; he who walks in darkness does not know where he is going. While you have the light, believe in the light, that you may become sons of light."

JOHN 12:35-36

"*We* are immortal spirits winged with Light. And when we fetter those wings with the weight of earth and things, we only hinder and delay the day when we shall be released and wing our way toward the realm of perfect day, the realm of endless Light."

WESLEY LA VIOLETTE, *The Creative Light*

"*We* are evolving into a species of whole individuals, individuals who are aware of their nature as beings of Light, and who shape their Light consciously, wisely and with compassion. . . ."

GARY ZUKAV, *The Seat of the Soul*

"[*W*]e are children of the truth."

I JOHN 3:19

"*A* creature of light am I."

THE EGYPTIAN BOOK OF THE DEAD

"*A*ncestral sun, do you remember us,
Children of light, who behold you with living eyes?"

KATHLEEN RAINE

"*H*ave thy heart in heaven and thy hands upon the earth. Ascend in piety and descend in clarity. For this is the Nature of Light and the way of the children of it."

THOMAS VAUGHAN

"*It* is still one of the tragedies of human history that the 'children of darkness' are frequently more determined and zealous then the 'children of light.'"

MARTIN LUTHER KING, JR.

"*K*now thou are one with the cosmos, a flame and a child of the Light."

THE EMERALD TABLETS OF THOTH *Tablet* VII

"*B*ut you, children of space, you restless in rest, you shall not be trapped nor tamed.

Your house shall not be an anchor but a mast.

It shall not be a glistening film that covers a wound, but an eyelid that guards the eye.

You shall not fold your wings that you may pass through doors, nor bend your heads that they strike not against a ceiling, nor fear to breathe lest walls should crack and fall down.

You shall not dwell in tombs made by the dead for the living.

And though of magnificence and splendour, your house shall not hold your secret nor shelter your longing.

For that which is boundless in you abides in the mansion of the sky, whose door is the morning mist, and whose windows the songs and the silences of night."

KAHLIL GIBRAN, *The Prophet*

"*A*ll is light, then, light from light; and we are light, children of the light."

JOHN SCOTUS ERIUGENA

E. *N*ET OF INDRA

i. *O*ne and Many

"*I*n the heaven of Indra there is said to be a network of pearls, so arranged that if you look at one you see all the others reflected in it, and if you move into any part of it you set off the sound of bells that ring through every part of the network, through every part of reality.

In the same way, each person, each object in the world, is not merely itself, but involves every other person and object and, in fact, on one level is every other person and object."

ADATAMSKA SUTRA

"*A*wake! awake O sleeper of the land of shadows, wake! expand!
I am in you and you in me, mutual in love divine: . . .
I am not a God afar off, I am a brother and friend;
Within your bosoms I reside, and you reside in me:
Lo! We are One . . ."

WILLIAM BLAKE, *Jerusalem*

"The One becomes Many.
The Unity becomes Diversity.
The Identical becomes Variety.
Yet the Many remains One;
the Diversity remains Unity;
and the Variety remains Identical."

SECRET   DOCTRINE   OF   THE
ROSICRUCIANS

"All for one, one for all, that is our devise, is it not?"

ALEXANDRE DUMAS, *The Three*
Musketeers

"False imagination teaches such things as light and shade, long and short, black and white are different and are to be discriminated; but they are not independent of each other; they are only different aspects of the same thing, they are terms of relation, not of reality. Conditions of existence are not of a mutually exclusive character; in essence things are not two but one."

LANKAVATARA SUTRA

"When one sees Eternity in things that pass away and Infinity in finite things, then one has pure knowledge.

But if one merely sees the diversity of things, with their divisions and limitations, then one has impure knowledge.

And if one selfishly sees a thing as if it were everything, independent of the ONE and the many, then one is in the darkness of ignorance."

BHAGAVAD-GITA

"I give You thanks for what my brothers are. As each one elects to join with me, the song of thanks from earth to Heaven grows from tiny scattered threads of melody to one inclusive chorus from a world redeemed . . . giving thanks to You."

A COURSE IN MIRACLES

"Not until we see the Many-in-One can we know simplicity, serenity within the knowing Self that seeks to light the way for every weary traveler . . . "

WESLEY LA VIOLETTE, *The Creative Light*

"From all, one; and from one, all."

HERACLITUS

"[W]e are the body of Christ, and members in particular."

I CORINTHIANS 12:27

"Functioning in a context of love, trust and safety, small teams of people around the world join with one another for the betterment of all. Eventually, a sufficient unified field is built, which 'jumps' the entire system to a new level of consciousness. All humanity, all life on this planet and throughout the Universe shifts to an exalted level of love and awareness. Each particle finds its place in the whole and experiences the truth of the ancient wisdom: I am One, We are One, All is One."

CAROLYN ANDERSON, *"Co-Creating Heaven on Earth: Birthing New Structures for Empowerment"*

"Every cell of each one of us, children and mothers, fathers, brother cedar, uncle mountain stream, sister arroyo, aunt snowfield, cousin grizzly, grandmother night sky, grandfather dew, one inside the other inside the other, which is no other than ourselves."

PETER LEVITT, "*An Intimate View*"

"The ruler supreme, inner Self of all,
Multiples his oneness into many.
Eternal joy is theirs who see the Self
In their own hearts. To none else does it come!

Changeless amidst the things that pass away,
Pure consciousness in all who are conscious,
The One answers the prayers of many.
Eternal peace is theirs who see the Self
In their own hearts. To none else does it come!"

KATHA UPANISHAD

"The radiating balanced pattern of the sun
Is our bright symbol of life's many in the One.
Joyous redeeming structure of earth's Brotherhood
Built from the shining sustance of eternal Good."

RUTH HARWOOD, "*Sun Seal of the Light Templars*"

"What is the Kingdom:

It lies in our realization of the ubiquity
of the divine presence in our neighbors,
in our enemies, in all of us."

JOSEPH CAMPBELL

"The Tao produced One; One produced Two; Two produced Three; Three produced All things."

TAO TE CHING

"'As above, so below.' . . . The One and the many, time and eternity, are all One."

RESHAD FIELD, *Steps to Freedom*

"Separate yourself from all twoness. Be one on one, one with one, one from one."

MEISTER ECKHART

"A vast unseen web is said to link each of us. In its time-honored metaphor, we are all individual buds of being on the great Tree of Life, whose roots lie in heaven."

EDWARD HOFFMAN, *The Way of Splendor: Jewish Mysticism and Modern Psychology*

"[T]he ancients, who were superior to us and dwelt nearer to the Gods, have handed down a tradition that all things that are said to exist consist of a One and a Many and contain in themselves the connate principles of Limit and Unlimitedness."

PLATO, *Philebus*

"The One remains, the many change and pass, Heaven's light forever shines, earth's shadows fly. . . ."

P. B. SHELLEY, "*Adonais*"

"One of perfect prayer is he who,
   withdrawing from all mankind,
   is united with all mankind.
One of perfect prayer is he who
   regards himself as existing with all people
   and sees himself in every person."
                    THE PHILOKALIA

"[To touch human nature at one point is to touch the whole of humanity."

                    KATHERINE TINGLEY, *The Gods Await*

"With the intuition comes a special joy. . . . a sort of recognition, as though we were always two, a brother of the light who lives in the light and a brother of shadows, ourself, who lives down below and repeats gropingly, in the shadow, knocking himself about everywhere, the gestures of the brother of the light, the movement, the knowledge, the great adventure of the brother of light, but it is all paltry down below, scraggy, clumsy; then suddenly there is a coincidence . . . we are one. We are one in a point of light. For once there is no difference and this is joy.

And when we shall be one at all points, this will be the Life Divine."
                    SATPREM

"This universe . . . is both One and Many."
                    DIONYSIUS

"Everything is enveloped in the Unity of Knowledge, symbolized by the Point."
                    SHAYKH AHMAD-al-ALAWI

"All things have been derived from One."

THE EMERALD TABLET OF HERMES

"If you take away the One there will remain neither whole nor part nor anything else in the world; for all things are contained beforehand and embraced by the One as an Unity in Itself."

DIONYSIUS

"All this diversity is fundamentally and basically one single unity."

HENRY SUSO

"It is called, by <u>Philosophers</u>, one <u>Stone</u>, although it is extracted from many Bodies or Things."

GEBER

"In God's sight all men are one man, and one man is all men."

JULIAN OF NORWICH

"All are really one."

BLACK ELK *(Oglala Sioux)*

"All know that the drop merges into the ocean but few know that the ocean merges into the drop."

KABIR

"You are plurality transformed into Unity,
And Unity passing into plurality;
This mystery is understood when man
Leaves the part and merges in the Whole."

SHABISTARI

"All are but parts of one stupendous whole,
Whose body Nature is, and God the soul."
                    ALEXANDER POPE, *An Essay on
                    Man*

"Oh Hidden Life! vibrant in every atom;
Oh Hidden Light! shining in every creature;
Oh Hidden Love! embracing all in Oneness;
May each who feels himself as one with Thee,
Know he is also one with every other."
                    ANNIE BESANT

ii. Mirror

"The lamps are different,
But the Light is the same.
One matter, one energy, one Light, one Light-mind,
Endlessly emanating all things.
One turning and burning diamond.
One, one, one.
Ground yourself, strip yourself down,
To Blind loving silence.
Stay there, until you see
You are gazing at the Light
With its own ageless eyes."
                    Jalal-ud-Din RUMI

"[*B*]eauty is life when life unveils her holy face.
But you are life and you are the veil.
Beauty is eternity gazing at itself in a mirror.
But you are eternity and you are the mirror."

KAHLIL GIBRAN, *The Prophet*

"The Logos is the mirror reflecting Divine Mind, and the Universe is the mirror of the Logos."

HELENA P. BLAVATSKY,
The Secret Doctrine

"The consciousness of each of us is evolution looking at itself and reflecting upon itself."

PIERRE TEILHARD de CHARDIN

"The love of God, unutterable and perfect,
  flows into a pure soul the way that light
  rushes into a transparent object.
The more love that it finds, the more it gives
  itself, so that, as we grow clear and open,
  the more complete the joy of heaven is.
And the more souls who resonate together,
  the greater the intensity of their love,
  and, mirror-like, each soul reflects the other."

DANTE ALIGHIERI

"The Self is the light reflected by all."

KATHA UPANISHAD

"It is like an image reflected in a mirror, it is seen but it is not real; the one Mind is seen as a duality by the ignorant when it is reflected in the mirror constructed by our memory. . . . The existence of the entire universe is due to memory that has been accumulated since the beginningless past but wrongly interpreted."

LANKAVATARA SUTRA

"When the Void looks into the mirror
It sees us
When we look into the Void
we see the mirror
When we look in the mirror
We see the Void
When the mirror looks in the mirror . . .
It laughs."

YATRI, *Unknown Man: The Mysterious Birth of a New Species*

"[I]mprove your vision, and . . . you will understand that the world is God."

SWAMI MUKTANANDA, *I Have Become Alive*

"All existence is probed to its profoundest depths when we see Self as ever-luminous, as an inextinguishable part of the whole; when we see everything as eternal, somehow divining the earthly self as a mirror to the deathless spirit."

WESLEY LA VIOLETTE, *The Creative Light*

"In the Beatific Vision God manifests Himself to the elect in a general epiphany, which, nevertheless, assumes various forms according to the mental conceptions of God formed by the faithful on earth."

IBN ARABI

"The Universe is the mirror of God -- the mirror in which His majesty and perfection are reflected, the mirror in which He sees Himself -- and the heart of man is the mirror of the Universe; if the Traveler then would know God, he must look into his own heart."

AZIZ ibn MUHAMMAD al-NASAFI

"Man, if thou wishest to see God, there or here on earth, thy heart must first become a pure mirror."

ANGELUS SILESIUS

"Knowing the world to consist of consciousness, the mind of the wise man is rapt in the thought of his universality and roams free, seeing the cosmos as space in his own consciousness."

YOGA-VASISHTHA

"They who ponder on the pages of 'the living Book of Nature' . . . behold in full the beauty and the sublimity, which their own immortal spirits create, reflected back on them who are its authors."

HENRY   WORDSWORTH,   The Prelude

"The rays of the mirror of the soul make the world manifest."

Jalal-ud-Din RUMI

"[*W*]e are at once love, the lover, and the beloved; at once the mirror, the beauty and the eye that sees it. There is only one love and only one glory, reflected in a thousand million forms and situations. When you come into the presence of the glory, you realize that you are looking at the glory with the glory's own eyes; feeling the glory with the glory's own heart; loving the glory with the glory's own love; and dancing in the glory with the glory's own resplendence. That is what it means to be a mirror of the divinity."

ANDREW HARVEY, *The Way of Passion a Celebration of Rumi*

"*Man* is the eye of the world, and . . . . the world is the reflection of God, and . . . . God himself is the light of this eye. Man is the eye which looks in the mirror, and like the mirror reflects the face of the person who is looking into it, the reflection possessing itself an eye, and in the same time that the eye looks in the mirror, the reflection of this eye looks at it also. God, which is the eye of man, looks at himself through man."

LAHIJI

X.

ETERNAL FLAME

"The divine spark of creative power is still alive in us, and if we have the grace to kindle it into flame, then the stars in their courses cannot defeat our efforts to attain the goal of human endeavor."

ARNOLD J. TOYNBEE, *Study of History*

A. Spirit Within

"Peace comes when our souls realize that . . . at the center of the. Universe dwells the Great Spirit, and that the center is really everywhere, it is within each of us."

BLACK ELK *(Oglala Sioux)*

"Essence is in the world like gold in the rock. It is not the rock. It is in the rock."

A. H. ALMAAS

"The life force is in everything, the life force is manifested on all planes."

SEVENTH HERMETIC PRINCIPLE

"When the heart weeps for things that are lost, the spirit laughs for what it has found."

SUFI PROVERB

"There is the grain of the prophet in the recesses of every human existence."

ABRAHAM JOSHUA HESCHEL,
God in Search of Man

"The divine Providence . . . has shown the heaven and earth to every child and filled him with a desire for the whole; a desire raging, infinite; a hunger, as of space to be filled with planets; a cry of famine, as of devils for souls. Then, for the satisfaction, to each man is administered a single drop, a bead of dew of vital power, <u>per day</u> -- a cup as large as space, and one drop of the water of life in it."

RALPH WALDO EMERSON, *Essays*

"Use the cosmic energy in you. Attract it like a magnet for the benefit of all. Cosmic energy is seeking to build. If it feels that you are a builder, it will come to you. If you ignore it, it will flee you. We have not yet learned to use the cosmic, divine forces in and around us."

ROBERT MULLER, *A Planet of Hope*

"The spirit of man is the candle of the Lord."

PROVERBS 20:27

"It is foolhardy to say that the whole creation is inside us. The stars are there all right, and without their vast sparkling cataclysm, nothing would happen. But it's also clear -- imaginary or not -- that a spirit, a light, is inside us. From ceaseless angles of being, we look out to see it reflected back -- from the lake at dusk, from the streaks of clouds on the horizon, from the distant meadows on the mountainside, and from each other's faces. It is reflected through us, our memories, and the billions of flowers in the fields."

RICHARD   GROSSINGER, *The Night Sky*

"In it [the 'Spark of the Soul'] is hidden something like the original outbreak of all goodness, something like a brilliant·light which incessantly gleams, and something like a burning fire which burns incessantly. This fire is nothing other than the Holy Spirit."

                              MEISTER ECKHART

"There is a Soul, a Self, a God in the world and in man who works concealed and all is his self-concealing and gradual self-unfolding. His minister I have been, slowly to unseal your eyes, remove the thick integuments of your vision until there is only my own luminous veil between you and him. Remove that and make the soul of man one in fact and nature with this Divine; then you will know yourself, discover the highest and widest law of your being, become the possessors or at least the receivers and instruments of a higher will and knowledge than mine and lay hold at last on the true secret and the whole sense of a human and yet divine living."

              SRI AUROBINDO GHOSE, *The Human Cycle*

"[W]e are in fact creation itself, we are the life of the ever-living spirit which manifests itself in all the innumerable lives of the world."

                              KATHLEEN RAINE

"[T]here lies within each one of us a natural resource which has remained so far virtually untapped. We call that energy the spirit or soul."

                              DADI JANKI

"[The . . . distinction of an immortal spirit from the mortal soul . . . is . . . the fundamental doctrine of the Philosophia Perennis . . ."

              ANANDA K. COOMERASWAMY, *Hinduism and Buddhism*

"*The* journey of the spirit is unconditioned in respect of Time and Space: our body learned from the spirit how to journey."

Jalal-ud-Din RUMI

"[*The* matter of our lives is a spiritual incipience potent with Spirit."

R. MELVIN KEISER, "*Inward Light and The New Creation*"

B. *L*IGHT WITHIN

"*W*hich was Born in a Night to perish in a Night
When the Soul Slept in Beams of Light
God Appears & God is Light
To those poor souls who dwell in Night·
But does a Human Form Display
To those who Dwell in Realms of day."

WILLIAM BLAKE, *Auguries of Innocence*

"*The* electric energy which motivates us is not within our bodies at all. It is a part of the universal supply which flows through us from the Universal Source with an intensity set by our desires and our will."

WALTER RUSSELL

"[W]ithin . . . Self there burns a flame that can never be put out. Beyond the setting sun, beyond the setting moon and stars, the universal Self alone is light. Whether I am weak or strong, do right or wrong; or wander aimlessly along the path, there burns forever that inextinguishable, radiant and universal light within."

WESLEY LA VIOLETTE, *The Creative Light*

"Time and space are but physiological colors which the eye makes, but the soul is light; where it is, is day . . ."

RALPH WALDO EMERSON, *Essays*

"The Lord fashioned man from the earth,
 to consign him back to it.

* * *

He put his own light in their hearts
 to show them the magnificence of his works.

* * *

He set knowledge before them,
 he endowed them with the law of life."

ECCLESIASTICUS 17:1-11

"All that came to be had life in him
and that life was the light of men,
a light that shines in the dark,
a light that darkness could not overpower."

JOHN 1:4-5

"[*W*]ithin you there is an inner seed of radiance waiting to grow."
                                        CHOQUET

"*F*or thou wilt light my candle: the Lord my God will enlighten my darkness."
                                        PSALMS 18:28

"*T*he light of God in the heart of man is the source of his freedom, 'and the spirit of man is the candle of the Lord'."

> GERALD A. KENNEDY, *Who Speaks for God? (quoting Proverbs 20:27)*

"[*T*]he mission of human beings: to give birth to light. This light is not from somewhere else -- from some beneficent being -- but is inherent in oneself, in what I am. 'I am, therefore I think. I am, therefore I create. I am, therefore the world is charged and enlivened by my presence.' This is the potential. This is the invitation."

> MICHAEL EXETER, *Living at the Heart of Creation: Practical Wisdom for Extraordinary Times*

"*W*e are composed of incipient radiance."

> GEORGE GREENSTEIN, *The Symbiotic Universe*

"Grace strikes us when we are in great pain and restlessness. . . . It strikes us when our disgust for our own being, our weakness, our hostility, and our lack of direction and composure have become intolerable to us. It strikes us when, year after year, the longed-for perfection of life does not appear, when the old compulsions reign with us as they have for decades. . . . Sometimes at that moment a wave of light breaks into our darkness, and it is as though a voice were saying 'you are accepted.'"

PAUL TILLICH, The Shaking
of the Foundations

"There is a light seed grain inside.
You fill it with yourself, or it dies."

Jalal-ud-Din RUMI

"The Light is only waiting to be perceived."

KATHERINE TINGLEY, Theosophy:
The Path of the Mystic

"People are like stained-glass windows. They sparkle and shine when the sun is out, but when the darkness sets in, their true beauty is revealed only if there is a light from within."

ELISABETH KUBLER-ROSS

"The soul is light, the mind is light, and the body is light -- light of different grades; it is this relation which connects man with the plants and stars."

HAZRAT INAYAT KHAN

"God puts into creatures, along with a kind of 'sheen,' a reflection of God's own luminous 'ray' which is the fountain of all light."

SAINT   THOMAS   AQUINAS,
Commentary on Dionysius

"There is a light within a man of light and it lights the whole world. If he does not shine, he is in darkness."

THE GOSPEL OF THOMAS 24

"[T]here is some subtle light in the eye of the inspired one . . . which tells you that you are in the presence of one who has bridged the gap which separates the mundane world from the world of spirit."

WALTER RUSSELL

"[T]he Inner Light, the true seed, is no foreign substance added to an undivine human life . . ."

RUFUS JONES

"Everything in temporal nature is descended out of that which is eternal, and stands as a palpable visible outbirth of it, . . . In Eternal Nature, or the Kingdom of Heaven, materiality stands in life and light; it is the light's glorious Body, or that garment wherewith light is clothed, . . ."

WILLIAM LAW, "*An Appeal to All Who Doubt*"

"[T]he manifestation of the Eternal Light is renewed without interruption in the hiddenness of the spirit."

RUYSBROECK,   "*De Ornatu Spiritalium Nuptiarum*"

"There is one light which we perceive through the eye, another by which the eye itself is enabled to perceive; this light by which [outer things] become manifest is certainly within the soul."

ST. AUGUSTINE

"On the death of any living creature the spirit returns to the spiritual world, the body to the bodily world. In this however only the bodies are subject to change. The spiritual world is one single spirit who stands like unto a light behind the bodily world and who, when any single creature comes into being, shines through it as through a window. According to the kind and size of the window less or more light enters the world. The light itself however remains unchanged."

AZIZ NASAFI

"You are the Guardians of God's light. . . ."

Jalal-ud-Din RUMI, *Diwan-i Shams-i Tabriz*

"The light that shines above the heavens and above this world, the light that shines in the highest world, beyond which there are no others, that is the light that shines in the hearts of men."

CHANDOGYA UPANISHAD

C. SPARK OF LIFE

"Man is a stream whose source is hidden. Always our being is descending into us from we know not whence. . . . I am constrained every moment to acknowledge a higher origin for events than the will I call mine.

As with events, so it is with thoughts. When I watch that flowing river, which, out of regions I see not, pours for a season its streams into me, I see that I am . . . not a cause, but a surprised spectator of this ethereal water. . . .

[T]he only profit of that which must be, is that great nature in which we rest, as the earth lies in the soft arms of the atmosphere; that Unity, that Over-Soul, within which every man's particular being is contained and made one with all other; that common heart, of which all sincere conversation is the worship, to which all right action is submission; that overpowering reality which confutes our tricks and talents, and constrains every one to pass for what he is, and to speak from his character and not from his tongue; and which evermore tends to pass into our thought and hand, and become wisdom, and virtue, and power, and beauty."

RALPH WALDO EMERSON, *Essays*

"In many only the spark remains, for the Great Rays are obscured. Yet God has kept the spark alive so that the Rays can never be completely forgotten. If you but see the little spark you will learn of the greater light, for the Rays are there unseen. Perceiving the spark will heal, but knowing the light will create. . . . [T]he spark is . . . as pure as the great light, because it is the remaining call of creation. Put all your faith in it, and God Himself will answer you."

A COURSE IN MIRACLES

"The truth of what we call our knowing is but light and dark. Men are always dying and waking. The rhythm between we call life. . . ."

THE EGYPTIAN BOOK OF THE DEAD

"Our secret creative will divines its counterpart in others, experiencing its own universality, and this intuition builds a road towards knowledge of the power which is itself a spark within us."

DAG HAMMARSKJOLD, *Markings*

"Just to be is a blessing; just to live is holy."

ABRAHAM JOSHUA HESCHEL

"There is no other proof that the sun is shining except this, that we see and feel it. There is no foreign evidence that love is of supreme worth -- nothing except the heart's own testimony. There is no other proof that there is beauty in the world than this, that we perceive it and that our hearts beat with joy at it."

RUFUS JONES

"The fire which serves as pyre for the Phoenix, and cradle where he resumes a new life . . . draws its origins from the highest mountain on earth. . . . This fire is the source of all light which illumines this vast universe: it imparts heat and life to all beings . . ., a Flame that is never consumed."

MICHAEL MAIER

"The One is the Flame of Life.
The Many are the Sparks in the Flame.
The Flame once lighted kindles everything within its sphere.
The Fire is in everything and everywhere. . . ."

SECRET   DOCTRINE   OF   THE ROSICRUCIANS

D. *T*HE WAY

"*H*e who sees the Infinite in all things sees God."

WILLIAM BLAKE, *There is no Natural Religion*

"*I* can only wish that you trustingly and patiently allow that grand solitude to work in you. . . . It will act as an anonymous influence, akin to how ancestral blood constantly moves and merges with our own and links with that of the individual, never to be unlinked."

RAINER MARIA RILKE, *Letters To A Young Poet*

"*I*nspiration comes only to those who seek it with humility toward their own achievements and reverence toward the achievements of God. With love of your work, love of life and reverence for the universal force which gives you unlimited power for the asking, you may sit on the top of the world if you desire to sit there. Flashes of inspiration come only to those who plug in to the universe and become harmonious with its rhythms by communion with it. Inspiration and intuition is the language of Light through which men of God 'intercommunicate.' The universe does not bestow favors upon the few whom it seeks out as its interpreters. It is just the reverse. The universe gives to those who ask without favor."

WALTER RUSSELL

"*R*eunion is reidentification with the Source We Are."

P.M.H. ATWATER, *Future Memory*

"You are what you love."
ST. AUGUSTINE

"Turn your face to the sun and the shadows fall behind you."
MAORI PROVERB

"The winds of grace blow all the time.
All we need to do is set our sails."
RAMAKRISHNA

"Genuine meditation is an act of opening ourselves to . . . Light; it is the art of invoking inspiration at will, by putting ourselves into a state of intuitive receptiveness, in which the gates of the past and the present are open to the mind's eye. . . ."
LAMA ANAGARIKA GOVINDA, "The Problem of Past and Future," Nature, Man, and Society: Main Currents in Modern Thought

"... [To complete ourselves, we must pass into a greater than ourselves."
PIERRE TEILHARD de CHARDIN

"I would advise every searching human being to place his search and to search his place within four general frameworks:

the total universe
total time
the total Earth
the total human family."
ROBERT MULLER, A Planet of Hope

"*D*o not allow yourself to be misled by the surfaces of things. In the great depths all becomes law."

RAINER MARIA RILKE, *Letters To A Young Poet*

"*The* essential thing is to work in a state of mind that approaches prayer."
HENRI MATISSE

"*It* is not we who seek the Way, but the Way which seeks us. That is why you are faithful to it, even while you stand waiting, so long as you are prepared, and act the moment you are confronted by its demands."

DAG HAMMARSKJOLD, *Markings*

"*W*hen we open our eyes, we see beyond ourselves. When we open our ears, we listen beyond ourselves. When we surrender to this attraction, we grow in self-awareness."
SENECA ELDERS

"*The* goal of the hero trip down to the jewel point is to find those levels in the psyche that open, open, open, and finally open to the mystery of your Self being Buddha consciousness or the Christ. That's the journey."
JOSEPH CAMPBELL

"*B*y spiritual force a man can change clay or stone into gold."
NAGARJUNA

"[*B*]eauty is not a need but an ecstasy.

It is not a mouth thirsting nor an empty hand stretched forth,

But rather a heart enflamed and a soul enchanted."

KAHLIL GIBRAN, *The Prophet*

"[*H*]e who has a pact with aloneness can . . . prepare the way for all . . . that in the future may well be possible for many, and can build with hands less apt to err. . . . [E]mbrace your solitude and love it. Endure the pain it causes, and try to sing out with it. For those near to you are distant, you say. That shows it is beginning to dawn around you; there is an expanse opening about you. . . . [W]hen your nearness becomes distant, then you have already expanded far: to being among the stars. Your horizon has widened greatly. Rejoice in your growth."

RAINER MARIA RILKE, *Letters To*
A Young Poet

"*The* truth is born out of the Spring of Light, falsehood from the well of darkness. The dominion of all the children of truth is in the hands of the Angels of Light so that they walk in the ways of Light. The spirits of truth and falsehood struggle within the heart of man, behaving with wisdom and folly. And according as a man inherits truth so will he avoid darkness."

THE DEAD SEA SCROLLS, "*The*
Manual of Discipline"

"*The* path to the source of your and the world's being is not without. You have to go within yourself."

SWAMI RAMDAS

"Constantly remind yourself, 'I am a member of the whole body of conscious things.' If you think of yourself as a mere 'part,' then love for mankind will not well up in your heart; you will look for some reward in every act of kindness and miss the boon which the act itself is offering. Then all your work will be seen as a mere duty and not as the very porthole connecting you with the Universe itself."

MARCUS AURELIUS, *Meditations*

"A new way must be found and it must be a way that overcomes evil with good, that conquers darkness with light, that defeats error with truth and that achieves its gains and advances by the mighty co-operative power of love."

RUFUS JONES, "*An Interpretation of Quakerism*"

"I am a Lamp to thee who beholdest Me,
I am a Mirror to thee who perceivest Me,
I am a Door to thee, who knockest at Me,
I am a Way to thee a wayfarer."

ACTS OF JOHN *(Apocrypha)*

"When we transcend ourselves and become in our ascent towards God so simple that the bare supreme Love can lay hold of us, then we cease, and we and all our selfhood die in God. And in this death we become the hidden children of God, and find a new life within us."

RUYSBROECK, "*De Calculo*"

"From the East House of Light
May wisdom dawn in us
So we may see all things in clarity

From the North House of Night
May wisdom ripen in us
So we may know all from within

From the West House of Transformation
May wisdom be transformed into right action
So we may do what must be done

From the South House of the Eternal Sun
May the right action reap the harvest
So we may enjoy the fruits of planetary being

From Above House of Heaven
Where star people and ancestors gather
May their blessings come to us now

From Below House of Earth
May the heartbeat of her crystal core
Bless us with harmonies to end all war

From the Center Galactic Source
Which is everywhere at once
May everything be known as the light of mutual love

OH YUM HUNAB K'U
EVAM MAY E MA HO!"

JOSE ARGUELLES, *Surfers of the Zuvuya*

"On neither pain nor joy is liberation found.
In neither dark nor light will the spiritual sun appear.
The pairs of opposites distract the eyes of men.
Only the single eye directs the steps
Of the initiate upon the way."

ALICE A. BAILEY *Discipleship in the New Age*

"[T]he Transcendent Life for which we crave is revealed, and our living within it, not on some remote and arid plane of being, in the cunning explanations of philosophy; but in the normal acts of our diurnal experience, suddenly made significant for us. Not in the backwaters of existence, not amongst subtle arguments and occult doctrines, but in all those places where the direct and simple life of earth goes on. It is found in the soul of man so long as that soul is alive and growing: it is not found in any sterile place."

EVELYN UNDERHILL, *Mysticism*

The Grace Prayer

For Thee I Thirst.
Into Thy hands I commit my Spirit
(my soul, my body, my life, this problem, all unforgiven states).

Thy Will is my will.
Thy Will be done through me!
Heal me at depth.

Reveal that which needs to be revealed.
Heal that which needs to be healed,
so I can gorify You, God, and live in the fullness of grace.
It is finished.

DIADRA PRICE

E. TRUTH AND WISDOM

"Eternity is in love with the productions of time.
The busy bee has no time for sorrow.
The hours of folly are measur'd by the clock, but of wisdom: no clock can measure."

WILLIAM BLAKE, *The Marriage of Heaven and Hell*

"*We* know the truth, not only by reason but also by the heart."
BLAISE PASCAL

"*Truth* is within ourselves;
it takes no rise from outward things,
whate'er you may believe.
There is an inmost centre in us all,
Where truth abides in fullness."
ROBERT BROWNING, *Paracelsus*

"*Behold*, Thou dost desire truth in the innermost being,
And in the hidden part Thou wilt make me know wisdom."
PSALM 51:6

"*One* has to realize the truth within oneself."
SUTRALAMKARA

"[*The*] man who lives by the truth comes out into the light. . ."
JOHN 3:21

"*Truth* is as impossible to be soiled by any outward touch as the sunbeam."
JOHN MILTON

"Education is, or should be, a continuing process from birth to death concerned not so much with the acquisition of knowledge as with the expansion of consciousness. Knowledge of itself is a dead end, unless it is brought into functioning relationship with environment, social responsibilities, historical trends, human and world conditions and, above all, with the evolution of consciousness which brings the infinite vastness of an unknown universe within the range of the finite human mind.

... [E]ducation is a continuous process of learning how to reconcile the human and the divine elements in the constitution of man, creating right relationship between God and man, spirit and matter, the whole and the part."

ALICE A. BAILEY, *Education in The New Age*

"All energy or nerve-force within the human system is illuminated by knowledge, and so becomes the lamp to light us on the Way."

WESLEY LA VIOLETTE, *The Creative Light*

"Cultivate The Way yourself; and your virtue will be
    genuine;
Cultivate it in your home; and its virtue will overflow;
Cultivate it in your village; and your village will prosper;
Cultivate it in your country; and your nation will flourish;
Cultivate it in the whole world; and virtue will be
    universal."

GERAINT AP IORWERTH (*Order of Sancta Sophia*), "*Honouring the Divine Wisdom: Challenging Humanity to Follow The Way*"

"*He* who knoweth the truth knoweth that Light: and who knoweth it, knoweth eternity. Love knoweth it."

ST. AUGUSTINE, *Confessions*

"[*W*]ith their thoughts guided by holy wisdom do the Sons of Men build a bridge of light . . . to reach God."

THE ESSENE GOSPEL OF PEACE

XI.

𝒩EW GENESIS

"𝓜ay the kind divine providence help us start a new history and prepare the advent of a new age, a new world, a new philosophy and new human relationships, as we approach the bimillennium.

Let us all coalesce with all our strength, mind, heart and soul around a New Genesis, a true global, God-abiding political, moral and spiritual renaissance to make this planet at long last what it was always meant to be: the Planet of God."

ROBERT MULLER, *New Genesis:*
Shaping a Global Spirituality

A. GOLDEN RACE

"*N*ow the last stage is coming. . . .
A new line is sent down to us from the skies
For whom they will beat their swords into ploughshares,
For whom the golden race will rise, the whole world new."

VIRGIL, *Fourth Eclogue*

"*T*o those who . . . . find that inner joyousness which comes from that miracle of discovery of the Self which is within every man, comes something also which is greater than success. To them comes the Life Triumphant. . . .

[T]he Life Triumphant . . . transcends all material success. The Life Triumphant is that which places what a man gives to the world in creative expression far ahead of that which he takes from it of the creations of others.

[I]t should be every man's greatest ambition to be that kind of man. With that desire in the heart of every man there could be no greeds or selfish unbalance, nor could there be exploitation of other men, or hatreds, or wars or fear of wars.

The impregnation of that desire . . . will be the makings of a new race of men which will mark the next stage of . . . [the] journey from the jungle of . . . beginnings to a full awareness of the Light of God which awaits all mankind on the mountain top of its journey's end."

WALTER RUSSELL, *The Man Who Tapped the Secrets of the Universe*

". . . [*A*] new race is in the act of being born from us, and in the near future it will occupy and possess the earth."

RICHARD   BUCKE,   *Cosmic Consciousness*

"*A*ll will grow great and proper again:
the seas be wrinkled and the land be plain,
the trees gigantic and the walls be low;
and in the valleys, strong and multiform,
a race of herdsmen and of farmers grow.

No churches to encircle God as though
he were a fugitive, and then bewail him
as if he were a captured wounded creature, --
all houses will prove friendly, there will be
a sense of boundless sacrifice prevailing
in dealings between men, in you, in me.

No waiting the beyond, no peering toward it,
but longing to degrade not even death;
we shall learn earthliness, and serve its ends,
to feel its hands about us like a friend's."

RAINER MARIA RILKE, *The Book of Hours*

"[T]he story of man's spirit ends in a garden: in a place of birth and fruitfulness, of beautiful and natural things. . . . It ends with the coming forth of divine humanity, never again to leave us: living in us, and with us, a pilgrim, a worker, a guest at our table, a sharer at all hazards in life. The mystics witness to this story: waking very early they have run on before us, urged by the greatness of their love. We, incapable as yet of this sublime encounter, looking into their magic mirror, listening to their stammered tidings, may see far off the consummation of the race."

EVELYN UNDERHILL, *Mysticism*

B. NEW AGE

"The Germ within the Cosmic Egg takes unto itself Form. The Flame is re-kindled. . . . The World Soul is born, and awakens into manifestation. The first rays of the new Cosmic Day break over the horizon."

SECRET DOCTRINE OF THE ROSICRUCIANS

"Send victory like dew, you heavens,
and let the clouds rain it down.
Let the earth open
for salvation to spring up,
Let deliverance, too, bud forth
which I, Yahweh, shall create."

ISAIAH 45:8

"[T]he new rising sociocultural order promises to shelter a spontaneous unification of religion, philosophy, science, ethics and the fine arts into one integrated system of values based on truth, goodness and beauty. . . . [T]his unification means the beginning of a new organic era in the history of mankind."

PITIRIM A. SOROKIN, "*Three Basic Trends of Our Times,*" *Nature, Man, and Society: Main Currents in Modern Thought*

"As people were mistaken so long about the movement of the sun, so it is that people are yet mistaken about the movement of what is to come. The future stands firm and still . . . but we are moving in infinite space."

RAINER MARIA RILKE, *Letters To A Young Poet*

"When peaceful silence lay over all,
and night had run the half of her swift course,
down from the heavens, from the royal throne, leapt your
  all-powerful Word;
into the heart of a doomed land the stern warrior leapt."

BOOK OF WISDOM 18:14-15

"Apocalypse does not point to a fiery Armageddon, but to our ignorance and complacency coming to an end."

JOSEPH CAMPBELL

"*A*rise, shine out, for your light has come,
the glory of Yahweh is rising on you,
though night still covers the earth
and darkness the peoples."

ISAIAH 60:1-2

"*R*emember that you are at an exceptional hour in a unique epoch, that you have this great happiness, the invaluable privilege of being present at the birth of a new world."

THE MOTHER, *The Mind of the Cells*

"*B*eautiful woman, blessed be you and your wondrous child and that which you bring forth upon this planet for all who bring forth from their wombs this time forward bring masters. They are Gods that will herald in the new age, for they are the livers of the New Age, they are advance entities of higher cause. And that which you carry in your beloved womb, Entity, be not a primitive; it be a wondrous master already understood. All like you will bring forth great fruit that will bring forth an age called the 'Age of Spirit, Age of Light,' on this planet."

RAMTHA, *Ramtha: An Introduction*

"*T*he emergence of the future fifth world has begun. You can read this in the earth itself. Plant-forms from previous worlds have begun to spring up as seeds. . . . The same kinds of seeds are being planted in the sky as stars. The same kinds of seeds are being planted in our hearts. All these are the same, depending on how you look at them. This is what makes the emergence to the next, fifth world."

HOPI INDIAN PROPHECY

"[M]an . . . must perceive his right, miraculous place in the splendor of God's creation. We must manage our globe so as to permit the endless stream of humans admitted to the miracle of life to fulfill their lives physically, mentally, morally and spiritually as has never been possible before in our entire evolution. Global education must prepare our children for the coming of an interdependent, safe, prosperous, friendly, loving, happy planetary age as has been heralded by all great prophets. The real, the great period of human fulfillment on planet Earth is only now about to begin."

ROBERT MULLER, *New Genesis:*
Shaping a Global Spirituality

"Your sun will set no more
nor your moon wane,
but Yahweh will be your everlasting light
and your days of mourning will be ended."
ISAIAH 60:20

"Your old men shall dream dreams, your young men shall see visions."
JOEL 2:28

"The slow evolution of mother-love -- and, trailing behind it, father-love -- runs like a shining thread through the whole process. The coming of persons within the World-Process -- persons of the spirit-type who live for ideal ends and who love for love's sake -- seems to indicate that something in and behind the World-Process has <u>backed</u> the arrival of this sublime reality."

RUFUS JONES, *Spirit in Man*

"There are now no more horizons. And with the dissolution of horizons we have experienced and are experiencing collisions, terrific collisions, not only of peoples but also of their mythologies. It is as when dividing panels are withdrawn from between chambers of very hot and very cold airs: there is a rush of these forces together . . . That is just what we are experiencing; and we are riding it: riding it to a new age, a new birth, a totally new condition of mankind -- to which no one anywhere alive today can say that he has the key, the answer, the prophecy, to its dawn. Nor is there anyone to condemn here. . . . What is occurring is completely natural, as are its pains, confusions, and mistakes."

JOSEPH CAMPBELL, *Myths to Live By*

"The New Creation is our present ordinary world, but as experienced in depth, illumined by the divine Light."

R. MELVIN KEISER, "*Inward Light and The New Creation*"

"The call from the Cosmic Heart is vibrating throughout the Earth, the New Age is here, and the Spiritual vibrations are refreshing the earth and all living things."

ELIZABETH DELVINE KING, *The Higher Metaphysics*

C. *R*EBIRTH AND REAWAKENING

"*I* think it not improbable that man, like the grub that prepares a chamber for the winged thing it never has seen but is to be -- that man may have cosmic destinies that he does not understand. And so beyond the vision of battling races and an impoverished earth, I catch a dreaming glimpse of peace."

> OLIVER WENDELL HOLMES,
> *Speech at Harvard Law*
> *School Association of New*
> *York (February 15, 1913)*

"*F*rom the beginning till now the entire creation, as we know, has been groaning in one great act of giving birth; and not only creation but all of us who possess the first-fruits of the Spirit. . . ."

> ROMANS 8:22-24

"*A*ll this world is heavy with the promise of greater things, and the day will come, one day in the unending succession of days, when beings who are now latent in our loins shall stand upon this earth as one stands upon a footstool and shall touch the stars."

> H. G. WELLS, *The Open*
> *Conspiracy: Blueprints for a*
> *World Revolution*

"The journey into self circles downward and inward until we realize we are trapped within an illusion that has been woven around us since birth -- the illusion that we are separate selves. The truth is that we are single selves who exist only within a community of interdependent beings. There is no I without a thou. As we become aware of how isolated we have been we begin to feel our loneliness for the first time and are filled with a longing for reunion. The prodigal son awakes alone in a strange land and begins to dream of going home."

SAM KEEN, *Fire in the Belly: On Being a Man*

"Humanity is the vehicle through which the earth is becoming conscious of itself. In our awakening, the earth awakens as well."

DUANE ELGIN, "*Awakening Earth*"

"Just as in night-dreams the first symptom of waking is to suspect that one is dreaming, the first symptom of waking from the waking state -- the second awakening of religion -- is the suspicion that our present waking state is dreaming likewise. To be aware that we are only partially awake is the first condition of the coming and making ourselves more fully awake."

A. R. ORAGE

"Lo, I tell you a mystery. We shall not all sleep, but we shall all be changed, in a moment, in a twinkling of an eye, at the last trumpet."

1 COR. 15:51

"Root and branch shall change places and the newness of the thing shall pass as a miracle."

MERLIN THE WIZARD, "*Book of Prophecies*," *Verse 88*

"'Tis Time
New hopes should animate the world, new light
Should dawn from new revealings to a race
Weighed Down so long, forgotten so long."

ROBERT   BROWNING,
Paracelsus

"The idea of generation, birth and subsequent manifestation runs like a guiding thread through all esoteric thought. The ancient teachers of the race . . . employed the symbolism of natural process in order to illustrate and make clear the needed instruction, and lay that spiritual foundation of truth which will in the coming age lead the race into new ways and a new manner of thought. . .   There is the process of birth into the darkness of physical incarnation which -- in its turn -- is the foreordained preparatory process which leads to birth into light, carried forward in the light and producing the externalisation of the body of light.   This continuing process (for in all ages this birth into light has been going forward) will produce that future world of light which it is the purpose of the natural process of evolution to reveal.   This is the 'second birth' spoken of in the New Testament, in which a man is 'born again' into the world of light and love."

ALICE A. BAILEY, *Education*
in The New Age

"*A* new world is born. It is not the old world that is changing. It is a new world which is born. And we are right in the middle of the transition period, when the two overlap, when the old is still all-powerful and entirely controlling the ordinary consciousness. But the new slips in, still very modest and unnoticed -- so unnoticed that externally it disturbs hardly anything . . . For the moment, it is even absolutely imperceptible in the consciousness of most people. But it is working, it is growing."

THE MOTHER, *The Mind of the Cells*

"*The* Light convinces us to open to this whole world. To respond to the Light is to come into unity not only with God but with the world. But this is not the world at the surface; the New Creation is the world in its depths. Beneath our surface life the world exists in our depths as originally created. . . . Light opens us to our depths and there we are brought into touch with the original matrix of our being."

R. MELVIN KEISER, "*Inward Light and The New Creation*"

"*They* will manage to cross the ocean of becoming."

THE MAITREYAVYAKARANA

"[*E*]ach age is a dream that is dying,
Or one that is coming to birth."

ARTHUR WILLIAM EDGAR O'SHAUGHNESSY, "*Ode*"

"*We* are reclaiming our Divine Birthright and Heritage, remembering that we are Angels incarnate, vast starry beings of Light who are no longer limited to and bound by the illusions of time, space and matter."

SOLARA, *11:11: Inside the Doorway*

"At this time of . . . darkness one has to, in the theological sense, remember the light; to remember it as the awe, the wonder, the gratitude, and the joy that surround us and that give us energy."

MATTHEW FOX

"The universe is reinvented in every second."

Jalal-ud-Din RUMI

"What if you slept, and what if in your sleep you dreamed, and what if in your dream you went to heaven and there plucked a strange and beautiful flower, and what if when you awoke you had the flower in your hand?

Ah, what then?"

SAMUEL TAYLOR COLERIDGE

"We do not 'arrive,' we process.
We do not 'learn,' we remember.
We do not 'become,' we are.

P.M.H. ATWATER, *Future Memory*

D. Homeward Bound

"Our own personal myths are internalized and renewed if we are in touch with our source in nature, for nature is the point of contact between the finite and the infinite. Life is radically more than the experiences of a lifetime, it is an invitation to a journey back to our origin in God, and our own personal memories form the unique stuff of that quest."

MEINRAD CRAIGHEAD

"Evolution strives toward higher and higher levels of consciousness, while the contractions of involution condemn it to insentient equilibrium -- a kind of unconscious entropy. The Hindu sages inform us that existence is all 'Leela' -- or God's infinite play. The essence of this divine comedy lies in self-forgetting. By becoming a separate wave, God is playing hide-and-seek with himself. The play revolves around the exquisite piquancy of the 'remembrance' -- that moment when God comes rushing around the corner and catches sight of Itself in the mirror. The final aim of evolution is for existence to re-awaken as Primal Consciousness, having tasted the novelty of creation, the restrictions and the sufferings from the contraction and the ultimate beauty of that image in the mirror. Evolution is simply the way back home."

YATRI, *Unknown Man: The Mysterious Birth of a New Species*

"*Through* many dangers, toils and snares
We have already come.
'Twas grace that brought us safe thus far
And grace will lead us home."

JOHN NEWTON, "*Amazing Grace*"

"*If* God is God, which means in other words, Spirit, Life of our lives, Love at the heart of things, the over-arching, under-girding Source of all that is eternally Real and True and Beautiful and Good, then we already have a two-storied universe with a Home in it for all we love and a Garden in it greater than Eden, where transplanted human worth will bloom to profit otherwhere. This faith . . . may 'call home our hearts to quietness'."

RUFUS   JONES,   "*The Radiant Life*"

"*We* are the joint will of the Sonship, whose wholeness is for all. We begin the journey back by setting out together, and gather in our brothers as we continue together."

A COURSE IN MIRACLES

"*In* this Age of Aquarius we are all on a journey towards expanded awareness. We are all on this path whether our conscious mind agrees or not. Slowly, but surely, the clouds of illusion become thinner and less imposing. For at the end of our journey, at last there is only the true basic reality: 'light'."

RABBI PHILIP S. BERG, *Miracles, Mysteries & Prayer*

"There is a nascent, latent sense in each of us that silently, yet ever surely and inevitably, tells us that earth is not our home eternally. This inner knowing is the evidence of things not seen, of a dwelling not made with hands but always existent at the level of the individual awareness or consciousness. Eventually the noise and confusion that all of Time makes while we are passing by must yield its place to an eternal silence we shall hear when we listen to the voice of God. That hour can be now."

WESLEY LA VIOLETTE, *The Creative Light*

"The New Creation is neither a past act, the beginnings of the world, nor a future event, the heavenly world at the end of time. It is the present context of our being. As such it is in fact one with the primordial and eschatological creation, but the stress falls on divine and human presence in the present."

R. MELVIN KEISER, *"Inward Light and The New Creation"*

"Unfold your wings of light, and in the eye of your thought, soar with the stars into the farthest reaches of heaven where untold suns blaze with light. And you shall be one with it, and the power of the Holy Light Stream will fill your whole body."

THE ESSENE GOSPEL OF PEACE

XII.

QUEST RENEWED

"*We* have it in our power to begin the world again."

THOMAS PAINE, *Common Sense*

A. PASSING THE TORCH

> "The transformation of the world is in our hands."
> DADI JANKI

"We can change ourselves. We can change our communities. We have incredible spirit. We can brave life's pains and enjoy the triumphs. Generation after generation of human beings have walked this earth. They have known hunger, fear, ignorance and pestilence, war and rape. But they endured. You and I are here, thanks to them. They bequeathed to us the will to go forward. Whatever dragons we face, we can slay. Our dead mothers and fathers believed we would go forward. They did what they did with little hope of immediate reward but with the hope that life would be better for their children and their children's children. We are those children's children. We cannot fail."

RITA MAE BROWN, *The Courage of Conviction*

"Don't let the light go out
It's lasted for so many years
Don't let the light go out
Let it shine through our love and tears."

PETER YARROW, "*Light One Candle*"

B. NEW GENERATION

"We are members of a world team. We are partners in a grand adventure. We are offered the most challenging opportunity of all history: the chance to help create a new society in which men and women the world around can live and grow invigorated by independence and freedom."

WENDELL WILLKIE, *One World*

"In our time the journey begins when men and women hear and respond to a common vocation to come together to create a new kind of social order that is not based on enmity and the hope of conquest."

SAM KEEN, *Fire in the Belly: On Being a Man*

"Why concern ourselves so much about our beans for seed, and not be concerned at all about a new generation of men?"

HENRY DAVID THOREAU, *Walden*

"When I allow myself to hope that the world will emerge from its present troubles, and that it will someday learn to give the direction of its affairs, not to cruel mountebanks, but to men possessed of wisdom and courage, I see before me a shining vision: a world where none are hungry, where few are ill, where work is pleasant and not excessive, where kindly feeling is common, and where minds released from fear create delight for eye and ear and heart. Do not say this is impossible. It is not impossible . . . [I]t could be done . . . if men would bend their minds to the achievement of the kind of happiness that should be distinctive of man. . . . True happiness for human beings is possible only to those who develop their godlike potentialities to the utmost. For such men, in the world of the present day, happiness must be mixed with much pain, since they cannot escape sympathetic suffering in the spectacle of the sufferings of others. But in a society where this source of pain no longer existed, there could be human happiness more complete, more infused with imagination and knowledge and sympathy, than anything that is possible to those condemned to live in our present gloomy epoch.

* * *

Man . . . is . . . the child of the starry heaven. Man, though his body is insignificant and powerless in comparison with the great bodies of the astronomer's world, is yet able to mirror that world, is able to travel in imagination and scientific knowledge through enormous abysses of space and time. . . [I]f he continues on his present course, what he will know a thousand years from now will be . . . beyond what we can imagine. But it is not only, or even principally, in knowledge that man at his best deserves admiration. Men have created beauty; they have had strange visions that seem like the first glimpse of the land of wonder, they have been capable of love, of sympathy for the whole human race, of vast hopes for mankind as a whole. These achievements, it is true have been those of exceptional men, and have very frequently met with hostility from the herd. But there is no reason why, in the ages to come, the sort of man who is now exceptional should not become usual. . . ."

BERTRAND RUSSELL, *Human Society in Epochs and Politics*

"Those who really desire to understand, who are looking to find that which is eternal, without a beginning and without an end, will walk together with greater intensity, and they will be a danger to everything that is inessential, to unrealities, to shadows."

J. K. KRISHNAMURTI

C. REVOLUTION OF SPIRIT

"It is not seeing with the eye but seeing with the mind that gives us a basis for belief, and in this way science and religion are one. We are now entering an age when we will hold the power of life in our hands, and if it is to be used properly it must be in a world dominated by love. What we must have in the world today is a chain reaction of the human spirit. If we can feel this vision and if we can act on it, if we can transmit this vision to others and persuade everyone that living in terms of the spirit is the only answer, then we can change the face of the world."

DONALD HATCH ANDREWS

"At our stage of evolution, there will be growing numbers of enlightened, universal beings. Some day peaceful, serene saints will be the majority of this Earth's inhabitants."

ROBERT MULLER, *A Planet of Hope*

"All bonafide revolutions are of necessity revolutions of the spirit."

SONIA JOHNSON, *Going Out of Our Minds*

"A man must go on a quest
to discover the sacred fire
in the sanctuary of his own belly
to ignite the flame in his heart
to fuel the blaze in the hearth
to rekindle his ardor for the earth."

SAM KEEN, *Fire in the Belly: On Being a Man*

"[We need] a deep mystical awakening the likes of which the planet has never witnessed before -- a mystical awakening that is truly planetary, that draws out the wisdom and the mystic, the player and the justice maker from the wisdom traditions of all religions and cultures. Such a mystical awakening would surely birth that 'peace on earth' for which creation longs -- the promise given two thousand years ago in Bethlehem. Peace on earth cannot happen without peace with the earth and peace among all earth creatures."

MATTHEW FOX, *The Coming of the Cosmic Christ*

"The only way out is a spiritual, intellectual, and emotional revolution in which, finally, we learn to experience, first-hand, the interlooping connections between person and person, organism and environment, action and consequence."

GREGORY BATESON

"[W]e shall never have a 'new world' here until we wake up and want it and are ready to pay the high price which it will cost. . . . It will come only as we make experiments with another way of living. The process of advance begins with a vision of advance. The little heroic band . . . must make the stand, fling out their banner and dare the venture. It means . . . the practice of a new spirit rather than the abstract formulation of a new theory of society. It means the brave adoption of a new way of living. It involves greater simplicity of life, more sacrifices, more love and sympathy, less selfishness and rivalry. . . . [T]o build the better world . . . to rebuild the house while we are still living in it, . . . [requires] sensitive hearts, awakened minds and brave spirits to dare the forward step when they see it."

RUFUS JONES, *The Faith and Practice of the Quakers*

D. NEW ORDER OF THE AGES

"The illuminator of our hearts
is coming
the lamp of Light
brightening even those in darkness."

"*The Illuminator of our Hearts*"
(Manichean Poem)

"There is a stage in [the] upward climb of our strange Jacob's ladder of spirit when we can see and can enjoy realities which to a certain degree are spiritual in their own sovereign right. I mean of course the intrinsic values of Beauty, Truth, Goodness, and Love, . . . A mind which can see and appreciate those realities has already transcended the realm of time and space and matter and <u>sensa</u> and the biological order, and belongs already to an intrinsic, that is, an eternal, order. These ideal values are the unmoved movers which shape our destiny; and in the realm of the spirit they are eternal, i.e., they are time-transcending realities."

RUFUS JONES, *Spirit in Man*

"When Earth's last picture is painted,
And the tubes are all twisted and dried,
The oldest of colors have faded
And the youngest of critics have died,
We shall rest
And well shall we need to
Lie down for an eon or two
'Til the master of all good workmen
Shall put us to work anew.

Then only the master shall praise us,
And only the master shall blame,
No one will work for money,
And no one will work for fame.
But all for the love of the working
And each in his separate star
Shall draw the thing as he sees it
For the God of things as they are."

RUDYARD KIPLING, "*L'Envois*"

"*We* must recognize that the season has turned. . . . We can read in . . . signs the beginning of a new order, as we might read in the first crocus the coming of spring. Something in the world has changed profoundly -- a shift is underway as fundamental as the movement from winter to spring.

The possibility of building a society that works -- . . . is real, and not in some distant, imaginary land, but here, on this earth, beneath these feet. Built with these hands."

MARJORIE KELLY, "*The Million Hands of God*"

"*As* our religions embrace feminine values, we will honor the earth, harmonizing with nature rather than seeking to conquer it. We will live with a sense of completion, acceptance, and forgiveness rather than with a competitiveness that divides nations. With this sensibility, we will give birth to a planetary civilization based on cooperation and goodwill."

JUNE SINGER

"*Everywhere* on Earth, at this moment, in the new spiritual atmosphere created by the idea of evolution, there float, in a state of extreme mutual sensitivity, love of God and faith in a new world: the two essential components of the ultra human. These two components are everywhere in the air . . . sooner or later there will be a chain reaction."

PIERRE TIELHARD de CHARDIN, *The Phenomenon of Man*

"These are the promised days when 'old things will pass away and all things become new.' These are the times when things which have been hidden for thousands of years will be revealed through science, general knowledge and spiritual apprehension. For thousands of years, millions of the devout have prayed and believed that this time eventually would come."

WESLEY LA VIOLETTE, *The Creative Light*

"There is now no choice before us: either we must succeed in providing a rational co-ordination of impulses and thoughts, or for centuries civilization will sink into a mere welter of minor excitements. We must produce a great age, or see the collapse of the upward striving of our race."

A. N. WHITEHEAD, *Preface to Business Adrift*

"[T]here is a new world to be won -- a world of peace and goodwill, a world of hope and abundance."

JOHN F. KENNEDY, *Televised Press Conference (July 4, 1960)*

"[T]he new and higher life entail a spirit and . . . a way of life that practices love and forbearance. It seeks to give rather than to get. It conquers by grace and gentleness. It prefers to suffer injustice than in the slightest degree to do it. It wins and triumphs by sacrifice and self-giving. It spreads abroad an atmosphere of trust and confidence and proposes to prepare the way for a new world by creation of a new spirit -- . . . 'a covenant of peace'."

RUFUS JONES, *The Faith and Practice of the Quakers*

"**D**espite all the efforts of tyranny, despite the violence and trickery of the priesthood, despite the vigilant efforts of all the enemies of mankind, the human race will attain enlightenment; nations will know their true interest; a multitude of rays, assembled, will form one day a boundless mass of light that will warm all hearts, that will illuminate all minds."

HOLBACH, *Essai sur les prejuges*

E. CALL TO ACTION

"**W**ith a good conscience our only sure reward, and with history the final judge of our deeds, let us go forth to lead the land we love, asking His blessing and His help, but knowing that here on earth God's work must truly be our own."

JOHN F. KENNEDY, *Inaugural Address (January 20, 1961)*

"**D**estiny is not a matter of chance; it is a matter of choice. It is not a thing to be waited for; it is a thing to be achieved."

WILLIAM JENNINGS BRYAN

". . . **I** strive to discover how to signal my companions . . . to say in time a simple word, a password, like conspirators: Let us unite, let us hold each other tightly, let us merge our hearts, let us create for Earth a brain and a heart, let us give a human meaning to the superhuman struggle."

NIKOS KAZANTZAKIS

"Nature all around us is so beautiful. It is real magic. But what is behind it is probably even more beautiful. It is the transcendent beauty and meaning which we must seek at this stage of our evolution. And for that purpose we must settle our earthly problems and differences as quickly as possible. We are losing much precious time."

ROBERT MULLER, *A Planet of Hope*

"Come, my friends,
Tis not too late to seek a newer world . . .
for my purpose
holds to sail beyond the sunset, and the baths
Of all the western stars, until I die."

ALFRED, LORD TENNYSON

"The ancients knew that you could entrance the gods. You could entrance the energies wherever they are. You can heighten the frequencies to come toward you, or you can draw them in. But you have to start by being entrancing.

You have to enchant. You have to call. You have to sing it. You have to dance it. You have to know that the human heart can go to the lengths of God."

JEAN HOUSTON, "*The Promise of The New Millennium*"

"This may well be mankind's last chance to choose between chaos and community."

MARTIN LUTHER KING, JR.

"If each of us can believe that he is working so that the Universe may be raised, in him and through him, to a higher level, then a new spring of energy will well forth in the heart of Earth's workers. The whole organism, overcoming a momentary hesitation, will draw its breath and press on with strength renewed."

PIERRE TEILHARD de CHARDIN,
The Future of Man

"Yet there are those who wonder. There are those who have gentle stirrings. And there are those who have stepped upon the beautiful threshold of awareness -- all on the verge of perceiving that which is there to see. To these ones, I say, open your exquisite senses. Look with fine clarity into that which is beyond and beneath, within and without. In these coming critical times, listen to and heed the directives of your spirits that retain the high wisdom you are just now perceiving."

MARY SUMMER RAIN, *Phoenix Rising*

"We live in an epic age. We play in by far the greatest drama the human race has ever staged; and we determine whether the outcome is tragedy."

SUMNER H. SLICHTER, "*The Word of Tomorrow*"

"If you want great wealth,
 and that which lasts forever,
Wake up!
If you want to shine
 with the love of the Beloved,
Wake up!
You've slept a hundred nights,
 And what has it brought you?
For your Self, for your God,
Wake up! Wake up!
Sleep no more."

Jalal-ud-Din   RUMI,   *Diwan-i Shams-i Tabriz*

"It is the future which draws, not the past which pushes."

SRI AUROBINDO GHOSE

"The forces of light and darkness, ignorance and intelligence, were never more arrayed against each other than during this century. But that darkness, that light, is in the consciousness and life of each individual who must now decide upon which path he wishes to walk. Ultimately there is only one path, and we make our decision as to when we shall begin to walk upon the path of light."

WESLEY LA VIOLETTE, *The Creative Light*

"[O]f those to whom much is given, much is required. And when at some future date the high court of history sits in judgment on each of us, recording whether in our brief span of service we fulfilled our responsibilities . . . our success . . . will be measured by the answers to four questions:

First, were we truly men of courage . . .
Second, were we truly men of judgment . . .
Third, were we truly men of integrity . . .
Finally, were we truly men of dedication . . . ?"

> JOHN F. KENNEDY, *Address to*
> *Massachusetts State Legislature*
> *(January 1961)*

"Leave your country behind, leave your people behind, and go to the land I will guide you to."

> GENESIS 12:1

". . . [T]he free association of men and women of like spirit . . . not a handful but a thousand heroes, ten thousand heroes . . . will create a future image of what humankind can be."

> JOSEPH CAMPBELL

"Man has been able to extend the power of his hands with incredible machines, of his eyes with telescopes and microscopes, of his ears with telephones, radio and sonars, of his brain with computers and automation. He must now also extend his heart, his sentiments, his love and his soul to the entire human family, to the planet, to the stars, to the universe, to eternity and to God."

> ROBERT MULLER, *New Genesis:*
> *Shaping a Global Spirituality*

"*We* can if we will, set our sails to the divine breezes and move away from the shallow waters . . ."

RUFUS   JONES,   "*Original Quakerism, A Movement not a Sect*"

"*The* longest journey is the journey inwards of him who has chosen his destiny -- who has started upon his quest for the source of his being."
DAG HAMMARSKJOLD

"*The* mystics . . . are our guarantee of the end towards which the Immanent Love, the hidden steersman which dwells in our midst, is moving: our 'lovely forerunners' on the path towards the Real. . . . We, longing for some assurance, and seeing their radiant faces, urge them to pass on their revelation if they can. It is the old demand of the dim-sighted and incredulous: --

'Dic nobis Maria
Quid vidisti in via?'

But they cannot say: can only report fragments of the symbolic vision:

-- 'Angelicos testes, sudarium, et vestes' --

not the inner content, the final divine certainty. We must ourselves follow in their footsteps if we would have that."
EVELYN UNDERHILL, *Mysticism*

"[*T*]he time is now. The Call to Awaken has already resounded across the Celestial Vastness calling us to remember and ultimately, to embody, that which we truly are in our full magnificence and empowerment."
SOLARA, *11:11: Inside the Doorway*

"Confronted by the dangers with which the advances of science can, if employed for evil, face him, man has need of a 'supplement of soul' and he must force himself to acquire it promptly before it is too late. It is the duty of those who have the mission of being the spiritual or intellectual guides of humanity to labour to awaken in it this supplement of the soul."

KEN WILBER, *Quantum Questions: Mystical Writings of the World's Great Physicists*

"Spiritual maturing in the New Creation is learning a new language, a new form of life. It is learning to be at home in the silence of being and to speak its language of Light -- of the depth and the love and the fullness of being in the world."

R. MELVIN KEISER, *"Inward Light and The New Creation"*

"It is an extreme time and it requires extreme lives, and extreme love."

ANDREW HARVEY, *The Way of Passion, a Celebration of Rumi*

F. LET US BEGIN

"The glory that can be seen faintly shining in humanity, and the dim light which flickers within the human form, must give place to the radiance which is the glory of the developed son [and daughter] of God. Only a little effort is needed, and the demonstration of a steady staying power . . . to evidence the radiant light, and to establish upon the earth a great station of light which will illumine the whole of human thought. Always there have been isolated light bearers, down the ages. Now the group light bearer will shortly be seen. Then shall we see the rest of the human family . . . having their progress facilitated towards the path. . . . The work will still be slow, and much yet remains to be done; but if all the aspirants of the world and all the disciples at work in the world today will submerge their personal interests in the task immediately ahead, we shall have . . . the opening of a great station of light on earth, . . . a power house which will greatly hasten the evolution and elevation and humanity, and the unfoldment of the human consciousness."

ALICE A BAILEY, *Esoteric Psychology*
I: A Treatise on the Seven Rays

"[I]f we wait for the moment when everything, absolutely everything is ready, we shall never begin."

IVAN TURGENEV

"All this will not be finished in the first hundred days. Nor will it be finished in the first thousand days, nor in the life of this administration, nor even perhaps in our lifetime on this planet. But let us begin."

JOHN F. KENNEDY, *Inaugural*
Address (January 20, 1961)

"Join me in a vision of a world in which the Good Life is expressed as it was intended from the beginning. I see a world in which there is no dichotomy between what is idealized and what is condoned, where the will of men and the Will of God are One Will. In this new, bright world, nature is honored and revealed as a loving friend, and not a threat. Here, there is nothing to conquer, for all forces are realized to be Holy, harmoniously working for mutual good. The foot that was turned astray is once again set firmly on the path of wholeness, and all who walk this path shine with the Love that the world has ignored, but could never be forgotten."

ALAN COHEN, *The Dragon Doesn't Live Here Anymore*

"If I am not for myself, who will be for me? If I am only for myself, what good am I? If not now, when?"

Ethics of the Fathers

"There is no greater power than that of an idea whose time has come."
VICTOR HUGO

"We must no longer wait for tomorrow; it has to be invented."
GASTON BERGER

"There are only two mistakes one can make along the road to truth:

1. Not going all the way.
2. Not starting."

GUATAMA SIDDHARTHA (THE BUDDHA)

"*W*hatever you can do or dream you can, Begin it. Boldness has genius, power and magic in it. BEGIN IT NOW."

JOHANN   WOLFGANG   VON
GOETHE, *A Tragedy*

"*W*ithout an organizing center, postmodern man is lost, wandering in a wilderness of confusing plurality. But, paradoxically, being bereft of set moral landmarks, he is in a unique position to undertake a new journey."

SAM KEEN, *Fire in the Belly: On Being a Man*

"*B*egin difficult things
   while they are easy,
Do great things
   when they are small.
The difficult things of the world
   must once have been easy;
The great things
   must once have been small . . .
A thousand mile journey
   begins with one step."

LAO TZU

"*T*he present . . . [is] the only time. Here in the present is the world set free."

A COURSE IN MIRACLES

"*W*e cannot wait for the world to turn, for times to change that we might change with them, for the revolution to come and carry us around in its new course. We ourselves are the future. We are the revolution."

BEATRICE BRUTEAU

"The sun will rise or set on humanity by what we do or fail to do this decade. Now is the moment for an unprecedented movement to bring this extraordinary message and understanding to every person on earth."
RENNIE DAVIS

"The time is always right to do what is right."
MARTIN LUTHER KING, JR.

"[To the same degree that we as individuals begin to explore life, to that degree shall . . . deep things surface for each of us in great intimacy. The responsibility that the difficult work of love demands of our evolvement overwhelms us; it is larger than life. . . . If we persevere after all, and take this love upon us, accepting it as a burden and a time of training, instead of losing ourselves to the frivolous and careless game behind which people have hidden themselves, not willing to face the most serious question of their being -- then perhaps shall a small bit of progress be perceptible as well as some relief for those to come after us. That would be a great deal."
RAINER MARIA RILKE, *Letters To A Young Poet*

"At the day of judgment, we shall not be asked what we have read but what we have done."
THOMAS A. KEMPIS

"All mankind waits upon our decision. A whole world looks to see what we will do. We cannot fail their trust. We cannot fail to try."
JOHN F. KENNEDY, *Acceptance Speech at Democratic National Convention (July 14, 1960)*

"[I]t falls to men and women today to begin a journey. As it was at the beginning of every pivotal era in human history, so it is in ours -- only the starting point of the journey is known, and not its conclusion."

SAM KEEN, *Fire in the Belly: On Being a Man*

"I heard, or seemed to hear, the chiding sea say, 'Pilgrim, why so slow and late to come?'"

RALPH WALDO EMERSON

"The sum of all our days is just our beginnings."

LEWIS   MUMFORD,   *The Transformations of Man*

XIII.

COMMON PRAYER

"Arise, O Children of the Earth; be strong.

The Light is breaking on the hills.

Stand up, be unafraid, ... and see yourselves as Light --

Children of Divinity."

WESLEY LA VIOLETTE,
Wings Unfolding

THE GREAT INVOCATION

"From the point of Light within the Mind of God
Let light stream forth into the minds of men.
Let Light descend on Earth.

From the point of Love within the Heart of God
Let love stream forth into the hearts of men.
May Christ return to Earth.

From the centre where the Will of God is known
Let purpose guide the little wills of men --
The purpose which the Masters know and serve.

From the centre which we call the race of men
Let the Plan of Love and Light work out.
And may it seal the door where evil dwells.

Let Light and Love and Power restore the Plan on Earth."

AUTHOR UNKNOWN

"As the blessing of your presence encircles the earth,
   may it awaken in all people
   a great desire to serve one another
   in humble and loving ways.
May it call proud hearts to gentleness
   and awaken the child in those
   who seek to hold power over others.

Inflame those hearts that have grown cold;
   reawaken within the weary of soul
   your spirits of youthfulness and joy.
Stir up your breath of freshness and enthusiasm
   that slumbers in tired hearts."

EDWARD HAYS, *Prayers for a Planetary Pilgrim*

"[H]is peace descended upon them; and in their heart the angel of love, in their head the wisdom of law, and in their hands the power of rebirth, they went forth among the Sons of Men, to bring the light of peace. . . . And they parted, wishing, one to another:
'PEACE BE WITH YOU'."
THE ESSENE GOSPEL OF PEACE

"Oh, let not the flame die out! Cherished age after age in its dark caverns, in its holy temples cherished. Fed by pure ministers of love -- let not the flame die out."

EDWARD CARPENTER

$\mathcal{A}$PPENDICES

$\mathscr{S}$ELECTED[1] WISDOM SOURCES

$\mathscr{I}$NDIVIDUALS

ABU SAID IBN ABI'L-KHAYR (A.D. 967-1049) Persian Sufi Master, mystic, poet.

ADAMS, JOHN (1735-1826) 2d President of the United States.

ADLER, ALFRED (1870-1937) Austrian psychiatrist, associate of Sigmund Freud.

AHMAD, AIJAZ Ghalib scholar, translator, author.

AMIEL, HENRI FREDERIC (1821-81) Swiss poet, philosopher.

ANDERSON, CAROLYN Director and Co-Founder of Global Family, author.

ANDREWS, DONALD HATCH Professor of chemistry, Johns Hopkins University, author.

APOLLONIUS OF TYANA (A.D. 1st century) Greek Neopythagorean philosopher.

APPOLLINAIRE, GUILLAUME (1880-1918) French surrealist poet, critic.

AQUINAS, SAINT THOMAS (1226-74) Italian scholastic, Dominican theologist, canonized 1323.

ARGUELLES, JOSE (b. 1939) Artist, Mayan historian, mystic, author.

ARISTOTLE (384-322 B.C.) Greek philosopher.

Failure to cite any source is not intended in any way as reflective on the value of or appreciation for the source's contribution.

ARJUNA (5th century B.C.) Indian philosopher.

ASRANI, U. A. Indian mystic, physicist, author.

ATTAR, FAVID-UD-DIN (1140-1234) Persian mystic poet, Sufi biogrophie.

ATWATER, P.M.H. Author, multiple near death experiences.

AUGUSTINE, SAINT (A.D. 354-430) Bishop of Hippo, philosopher, theologian. Also known as Aurelius Augustinus.

BABAJI (A.D. 8th century) Deathless Himalayan saint, guru of Lahiri Mahasaya.

BACH, RICHARD American spiritual writer.

BAHA' U' LLAH OF PERSIA (1817-92) Persian religious leader, founder of Baha'i.

BAILEY, ALICE (1880-1949) English-born occultist, New Age prophet, mystic.

BALDWIN, JAMES (1924-87) American author.

BANYACYA, THOMAS Hopi tribal leader, interpreter of Hopi prophecies.

BATESON, GREGORY (1904-80) Psychiatrist, consciousness researcher, author.

BAYAZID AL-BISTAMI (d. A.D. 875) Persian Sufi authority, founder of Ecstatic School of Sufism.

BEECHER, HENRY WARD (1813-87) American preacher, theologian.

BENEDICT, SAINT (A.D. 480-543) Italian monk, founder of Benedictine Order.

BENTHAM, JEREMY (1748-1832) English jurist, philosopher.

BENTON-BANAIE, EDDIE Ojibway Indian.

BERDYAEV, NIKOLAI (1874-1948) Russian theologian, mystic, philosopher.

BERG, RABBI PHILIP S. Ordained Orthodox Rabbi, lecturer and author on mystical Kabbalah.

BERGSON, HENRI LOUIS (1859-1941) French philosopher, Nobel Prize winner.

BERNARD OF CLAIRVAUX, SAINT (1090-1153) French Doctor of the Church, founder of Cistercian monastery, mystic, abbot. Also known as "Thaumaturgus of the West."

BERNARD, de CHARTRES (d. 1130) French Platonist, scholastic philosopher, writer.

BERRY, THOMAS (b. 1914) Catholic ego-theologian, cultural historian

BERRY, WENDELL (b. 1934) Poet, novelist, farmer, essayist.

BESANT, ANNIE (1847-1933) English-born theosophist and social reformer.

BESTON, HENRY (1888-1968) American writer and naturalist.

BHAGAT, SHANTILAL P. Ordained minister in Church of the Brethren, ego-justice advocate, speaker, agronomist, prophetic author.

BLACK ELK (1863-1950) Priest, holy man of Oglala Sioux.

BLACKSTONE, WILLIAM (1723-80) English jurist, writer.

BLAKE, WILLIAM (1757-1827) English poet, painter, visionary, prophet.

BLAVATSKY, HELENA PETROVNA (1836-91) Russian-born co-founder of Theosophical Society, mystic, spiritualist.

BLY, ROBERT (b. 1926) American poet.

BOEHME, JAKOB (1575-1624) German mystic.

BOHM, DAVID (1918-1992) Theoretical physicist, scholar, author.

BONAPARTE, NAPOLEON (1769-1821) French General and Emperor.

BONHOEFFER, DIETRICH (1906-45) German Lutheran clergyman, theologian.

BOODIN, JOHN ELOF American environmentalist, author, deep ecologist.

BORGESE, G. A. (1882-1952) Italian-American novelist, scholar, critic.

BRADEN, GREGG Speaker, engineer, author, and guide to sacred sites.

BRANDEIS, LOUIS D. (1856-1941) Associate Justice of the United States Supreme Court, legal scholar.

BRIDGMAN, PERCY W. (1882-1961) American physician, Nobel prize winner.

BROWN, LESTER R. American author, lecturer, environmentalist, founder of Worldwatch Institute.

BROWN, RITA MAE (b. 1944) American author, human rights activist.

BROWNE, SIR THOMAS (1605-82) English physician, scholar, author.

BROWNING, ROBERT (1812-89) English poet.

BRUNTON, PAUL (1898-1981) Author of thirteen books on spirituality, Eastern religion and mysticism, as well as comprehensive survey on the art of meditation.

BRYAN, WILLIAM JENNINGS (1860-1925) American political leader.

BUBER, MARTIN (1878-1965) Jewish philosopher, theologian, scholar.

BUCK, PEARL S. (1892-1973) American novelist, Nobel Prize winner.

BUCKE, RICHARD (1837-1902) Author, cosmologist, Canadian physician.

BUDDHA (see Sidharta, Gautama)

BUNCHE, RALPH J. (1904-71) American diplomat, United Nations representative, Nobel Peace Prize winner.

BURKE, EDMUND (1729-97) Irish statesman, orator, writer.

CADDY, EILEEN (b. 1908) Co-founder of Findhorn Foundation.

CAMPBELL, JOSEPH (1904-87) Mythologist, speaker, writer.

CAMUS, ALBERT (1913-60) French thinker, novelist, Nobel Prize winner.

CAPRA, FRITJOF (b. 1939) Austrian-born physicist, founder of Elmwood Institute (ecological think tank), author.

CARLYLE, THOMAS (1795-1881) Scottish essayist, historian.

CARPENTER, EDWARD (1844-1929) English poet, essayist, socialist, mystic.

CARREL, DR. ALEXIS (1873-1944) French surgeon, biologist, Nobel Prize winner.

CARSON, RACHEL (1907-64) American marine biologist, ecological activist.

CASALS, PABLO (1876-1973) Spanish conductor, composer, author.

CASTANEDA, CARLOS (b. 1934) Anthropologist, apprentice sorcerer, writer.

CAUSSADE, JOHN PIERRE de (1675-1751) French priest, mystic.

CHANNING, WILLIAM ELLERY (1780-1842) American Unitarian clergyman, writer.

CHAPLIN, RALPH (1887-1961) American writer, labor movement leader.

CHARON, JEAN E. Physicist, author, professor.

CHESTERTON, G. K. (1874-1936) English essayist, critic, novelist.

CHIEF JOSEPH (1840-1904) Indian leader of 1,000 mile march. Also known as Nez Perce.

CHOPRA, DEEPAK Indian-born holistic medical doctor, author.

CHUANG, TZU (369-286 B.C.) Chinese thinker, writer, follower of Lao Tzu.

CHURCHILL, WINSTON (1874-1965) English statesman, writer.

CLARKE, ARTHUR C. (b. 1917) English science fiction writer.

CLEMENCEAU, GEORGES (1841-1929) French Premier.

CLEMENT OF ALEXANDRIA, SAINT (A.D. 150-215) Greek Christian theologian.

COHEN, ALAN New Age spiritual writer, author, speaker.

COHEN, LEONARD American composer, song writer, folk singer.

COLERIDGE, SAMUAL TAYLOR (1772-1834) English poet, philosopher and critic.

COMMONER, BARRY (b. 1917) Urban ecologist, environmental activist.

CONFUCIUS (551-478 B.C.) Chinese philosopher, teacher, founder of Confucianism. Also known as Kung Fu-Tze.

COOMERASWAMY, ANANDA K. (1877-1947) Art historian, Indian doctrine scholar, author.

COUSINS, NORMAN (1915-90) American editor, writer.

COUSTEAU, JACQUES (1910-97) French author, writer.

CRAIGHEAD, MEINRED Artist, teacher, former Catholic nun, poet, mystic.

CURIE, MARIE (1867-1934) Polish-French physicist, first female Nobel Prize winner, discoverer of radium, charted radioactivity.

DALAI LAMA [14th] (b. 1935) Tibetan religious and political leader in exile since 1959, Nobel Prize winner. Also known as Tensin Tsering and Tenzin Gyatso.

DANTE, ALIGHIERI (1265-1321) Italian poet, author, mystic.

DARION, JOE (b. 1917) Music lyric composer.

DASS, BABA HARI Indian yogi, founder of Hanuman Fellowship.

DAY, CLARENCE SHEPARD, JR. (1874-1935) American essayist, humorist.

DAVIS, RENNIE (b. 1941) Peace activist, Divine Light Mission organizer, coordinator for the U.S. anti-war movement coalition The National Mobilization.

DENVER, JOHN (b. 1943) American songwriter, singer, environmental and peace activist.

DEVALL, BILL Environmentalist, author, deep ecologist.

DEVOE, ALAN (1909-55) American naturalist, author.

DEWEY, JOHN (1859-1952) American philosopher, educator, psychologist.

DICKENS, CHARLES (1812-70) English novelist.

DICKINSON, EMILY (1830-86) American poet.

DILLARD, ANNIE (b. 1945) Writer, teacher, professor, winner of Pulitzer Prize for nonfiction.

DIMNET, ERNEST (1866-1954) French literary critic, essayist, biographer.

DIONYSIUS THE AREOPAGITE (A.D. 1st century) Athenian scholar, Neoplatonist philosopher.

DIOUM, BABA Seneca Indian.

DISRAELI, BENJAMIN (1804-81) British Prime Minister.

DONNE, JOHN (1573-1631) English poet, clergyman.

DOSTOYEVSKI, FYODOR (1821-81) Russian novelist, mystic.

DOUGLAS, FREDRICK (1817-95) American abolitionist.

DRUMMOND, HENRY (1854-1907) Canadian poet.

DYLAN, BOB (b. 1941) American folk-rock singer, songwriter, human rights
and peace activist.

DUMAS, ALEXANDRE (1802-70) French author, dramatist.

EASTMAN, CHARLES ALEXANDER (1858-1939) Santee Sioux Indian,
author, physician.

EASWARAN, EKNATH Lecturer, writer, English professor, founder of Blue
Mountain Center of Meditation in Berkeley, California.

ECKHART, MEISTER (1260-1328) German mystic, Dominican Order
scholar, priest, writer. Also known as Johannes Eckehart.

EDDINGTON, SIR ARTHUR STANLEY (1882-1944) English astronomer,
physicist, writer.

EDDY, MARY BAKER (1821-1910) Founded Church of Christ Scientist,
spiritual author.

EHRMANN, MAX (1872-1945) Poet.

EINSTEIN, ALBERT (1879-1955) American physicist, Nobel Prize winner,
peace advocate.

ELGIN, DUANE Author, Director of Choosing Our Future, former SRI
Senior Researcher on alternative futures.

ELIOT, T. S. (1888-1965) British poet, critic, Nobel Peace Prize winner.

ELLIS, HAVELOCK (1859-1939) English psychologist, author.

EMMANUEL Spiritual entity channeled by Pat Rodegast.

EMERSON, RALPH WALDO (1803-82) transcendentalist, essayist, poet, mystic.

ERASMUS, DESIDERIUS (1466-1536) Dutch humanist, theologian.

ERIGENA, JOHANNE SCOTUS (810-877) Irish philosopher, theologian. Name also spelled Eriugena.

EURIPIDES (485-406 B.C.) Greek dramatist.

EXETER, MICHAEL Eighth Marquess of Exeter, Executive Director of International Emissary Network.

FABRE D'OLIVET, ANTOINE Pythagorean scholar, author.

FABRE, JEAN HENRI (1823-1915) French entomologist, writer.

FAULKNER, WILLIAM (1897-1962) American novelist, Nobel Prize winner.

FERGUSON, MARILYN (b. 1938) Brain mind researcher, transformational writer.

FOSDICK, HARRY EMERSON (1878-1969) American preacher, author.

FOX, EMMET (1886-1951) Spiritualist, author.

FOX, GEORGE (1624-91) English religious leader, founder of Society of Friends or Quakers, mystic, originator of doctrine of Inner Light.

FOX, MATTHEW Dominican priest, writer on "creation spirituality," speaker, church reform advocate, educator.

FRANCIS OF ASSISI, SAINT (1182-1226) Italian friar, founder of Franciscan Order.

FRANKLIN, BENJAMIN (1706-90) American statesman, inventor.

FRANKL, VIKTOR (b. 1905) German-born analyst.

FREIRE, PAULO Brazilian educator, author.

FROMM, ERICH (1900-80) American psychoanalyst, social philosopher, author.

FROST, ROBERT (1874-1963) American poet.

FULLER, R. BUCKMINSTER (1895-1983) Ecologist, engineer, designer, architect, futurist.

GALSWORTHY, JOHN (1867-1933) English novelist, dramatist, Nobel Prize winner.

GANDHI, MOHANDAS K. (1869-1948) Hindu religious leader, social reformer, lawyer, mystic, nonviolence advocate.

GARRISON, LLOYD (1805-79) American abolitionist, editor.

GARY, ROMAIN (1914-80) Russian-born French novelist.

GAWAIN, SHAKTI (b. 1947) Spiritual author, teacher.

GEBER (A.D. 721-776) Arab scholar, alchemist, mystic. Also known as Jabir ibn Hayyan.

GEORGE, HENRY (1839-1897) American economist.

GHALIB (1797-1869) Indian Sufi mystic, poet.

GHAZZALI, ABU HAMID MUHAMMAD IBN MUHAMMED AL-TUSI AL (1058-1111) Arab Sufi, theologian, jurist, mystic, philosopher. Name also spelled Ghazali.

GHOSE, SRI AUROBINDO (1872-1950) Indian scholar, mystic, spiritual leader, poet.

GIBRAN, KHALIL (1883-1931) Lebanese poet, mystic, dramatist, artist. Also known as Jubran Khalil Jubran.

GIDE, ANDRE (1869-1951) French writer, Nobel Prize winner.

GOETHE, JOHANN WOLFGANG VON (1749-1832) German poet, dramatist, naturalist.

GOLDMAN, EMMA (1869-1940) American anarchist leader.

GOODMAN, PAUL (1911-72) Anarchist, educator.

GOULD, STEPHEN JAY (b. 1941) American palentologist, science popularizer.

GORBACHEV, MIKHAIL (b. 1931) Former President of Soviet Union, Nobel Peace Prize winner.

GOVINDA, LAMA (b. 1898) Anagarika Brahmacari teacher of Arya Maitreya Mandala.

GRANT, ULYSSES SIMPSON (1822-85) American Civil War Union general, 18th President of the United States.

GREENSTEIN, GEORGE Professor of Astronomy at Amherst College, theoretical astrophysicist, author.

GREGORIOS, PAULOS MAR Syrian orthodox metropolitan of New Delhi, India, President of World Council of Churches for Asia, theologian, author.

GREGORY, DICK (b. 1932) Comedian, civil rights and peace activist, speaker, writer.

GRIFFIN, SUSAN Naturalist, philosopher, feminist critic.

GROF, CHRISTINA and STANISLAV Psychologists, consciousness researchers, authors.

GUMBS, HARRIETT STARLEAF Shinnecock Indian elder, tribal spokesman, historian, teacher.

GUTIERREZ, GUSTAVO (1859-95) Mexican poet.

HAMMARSKJOLD, DAG (1905-61) Swedish statesman, Secretary General of United Nations, Nobel Peace Prize winner.

HAND, LEARNED (1872-1961) American jurist.

HANH, THICH NHAT (b. 1926) Vietnamese Zen master, poet, peace activist.

HARMAN, WILLIS Ph.D. (1918-97) Futurist, scientist, President of Institute of Noetic Sciences, Founding Trustee of World Business Academy, Emeritus Professor of Engineering-Economic Systems at Stanford University.

HASTIE, WILLIAM HENRY (1904-76) American jurist, first black Judge of U.S. Circuit Court of Appeals.

HAVAL, VACLAV (b. 1936) Czech dramatist, activist for democracy, former President of Czechoslovakia.

HAYAKAWA, S. I. (1906-92) American semanticist, educator, politician.

HAYWARD, JEREMY Ph.D. Nuclear physicist, molecular biologist, lecturer on Buddhism, author.

HEIDEGGAR, MARTIN (1889-1976) German philosopher.

HENRY, PATRICK (1736-99) American patriot, orator.

HENSON, MATTHEW A. (1832-1902) English journalist, novelist.

HERACLITUS OF EPHESUS (540-470 B.C.) Greek philosopher, sage.

HESCHEL, ABRAHAM JOSHUA (1907-72) Polish-born mystic rabbi.

HESSE, HERMANN (1877-1962) German writer, Nobel Prize winner.

HILDEGARDE OF BINGEN (1098-1179) German contemplative, doctor, pharmacist, poet, mystic, playwright.

HOLBACH, PAUL HENRY THIRY D' (1723-89) German-born philosopher, skeptic, French baron.

HOLMES, OLIVER WENDELL (1809-94) American author, physician, professor at Harvard Medical School, writer.

HOLMES, OLIVER WENDELL (1841-1935) Associate Justice of the United States Supreme Court, legal scholar.

HOMER (7th century B.C.) Greek epic poet, reputed author of Iliad and Odyssey.

HOUSTON, JEAN Writer, Director of Foundation for Mind Research, transpersonal psychologist.

HUBBARD, BARBARA MARX (b. 1930) New Age author, speaker, teacher, visionary, political scientist, President of Foundation for Co-Creation.

HUGHES, LANGSTON (1902-67) American novelist, poet.

HUGO, VICTOR (1802-85) French poet, dramatist, novelist.

HUGH OF ST. VICTOR (1100-41) German philosopher, theologian.

HUMPHREY, HUBERT H. (1911-78) Vice President of United States, civil rights supporter.

HUXLEY, ALDOUS (1894-1963) English novelist, essayist.

HUXLEY, THOMAS HENRY (1825-95) English biologist, writer.

IBN ARABI (1165-1240) Sufi metaphysic, sage, writer, Muslim exponent of metaphysical doctrine.

INGERSOLL, ROBERT G. (1833-99) American lawyer, political leader, orator.

IRENAEUS, AGNOSTUS (A.D. 17th century) German Rosicrucian.

IRENEUS, SAINT (A.D. 130-202) Bishop of Lyons, theologian.

IYER, RAGHAVAN Gandhi scholar, author.

JACKSON, ANDREW (1767-1845) 7th President of the United States.

JACKSON, HOLBROOK (1874-1948) English literary scholar, editor, author.

JAMES, HENRY (1811-82) American philosopher.

JAMES, WILLIAM (1842-1910) Psychologist, philosopher.

JAMI, NURAD-DIN ABD UR-RAHMAN IBN AHMAD (1414-92) Famous Persian Sufi poet.

JANKI, DADI (b. 1918) Indian social reformer, educator.

JEAN, SIR JAMES (1877-1946) Mathematician, physicist, astronomer, author.

JEFFERSON, THOMAS (1743-1826) 3d President of the United States, inventor, architect.

JESUS OF NAZARETH (4 B.C. - A.D. 30 ?) Judean Jewish prophet, healer, martyr. Also known as Jesus Christ.

JOHN, SAINT (A.D. 1st-2d century) Son of Zebedee, brother of James, mystical gnostic Christian gospelist, disciple of Jesus of Nazareth. Also known as St. John the Evangelist, St. John the Divine, the Beloved Disciple.

JONES, RUFUS M. (1863-1948) American Quaker, teacher, author, humanitarian, mystic.

JOYCE, JAMES (1882-1941) Irish writer.

JULIAN OF NORWICH (1343-1413) Lady Julian, anchoress at Norwich, mystic.

JUNG, C. G. (1875-1961) Swiss psychiatrist, scholar, author.

KABIR, HUMAYUN (1440-1518) Spiritual leader, Indian mystic poet of Benares, philosopher, teacher of Nanak.

KAHN, HAZRAT INAYAT (1882-1927) Founder of Sufi Order.

KANT, IMMANUEL (1724-1804) Prussian philosopher.

KAZANTZAKIS, NIKOS (1883-1957) Poet, novelist.

KEATS, JOHN (1795-1821) English poet.

KEEN, SAM Storyteller, author, speaker.

KELLER, HELEN (1880-1968) American lecturer, author.

KEMPIS, THOMAS A. (1379-1471) German ecclesiastic, author. Also known as Thomas Hamerken Von Kempen.

KENNEDY, JOHN F. (1917-63) 35th President of the United States.

KENNEDY, ROBERT F. (1925-68) American political leader, younger brother of John F. Kennedy.

KIERKEGAARD, SOREN (1815-55) Danish philosopher.

KING, MARTIN LUTHER (1919-68) American Baptist minister, civil rights leader, Nobel Peace Prize winner.

KIPLING, RUDYARD (1865-1936) English author, Nobel Prize winner.

KRISHNAMURTI, J. K. (1895-1986) Indian-born theosophist, mystic, spiritualist.

KRUTCH, JOSEPH WOOD (1893-1970) American critic, biographer, naturalist, essayist, teacher, nature writer, winner of John Burroughs medal.

KUBLER-ROSS, ELIZABETH Psychiatrist, author and lecturer on after-death consciousness, spiritualist.

LAING, R. D. (1927-89) Scottish psychiatrist.

LAO TZU (6th Cent. B.C.) Founder of Taoism, author of Tao-Te-Ching. Also known as Lao Tse and Lao Tsu.

LASZLO, ERWIN General systems analyst, author.

LA VIOLETTE, WESLEY (1894-1978) American composer, conductor, educator, philosopher, poet and lecturer.

LAW, WILLIAM (1686-1761) English religious writer, mystic.

LAWRENCE, D. H. (1885-1930) English novelist.

LEONARD, GEORGE (b. 1923) Educational reformer.

LEOPOLD, ALDO (1886-1948) American author, father of deep ecology movement, essayist, conservationist, winner of John Burroughs medal.

LEWIS, C. S. (1898-1963) English novelist, essayist.

LILLIENTHAL, DAVID E. (1899-1981) American public administrator.

LINCOLN, ABRAHAM (1809-65) 16th President of the United States, lawyer, civil rights advocate.

LINDBERG, CHARLES (1902-74) American aviator, writer.

LIPPMANN, WALTER (1889-1974) American journalist.

LONGFELLOW, HENRY WADSWORTH (1807-82) Poet, romanticist, translator, professor.

LORDE, AUDRE (1934-92) Black American poet, teacher.

LORENZ, KONRAD Z. (1903-89) Austrian zoologist, ethologist, author, Nobel Prize winner.

LOWELL, JAMES RUSSELL (1819-91) American poet, essayist, diplomat.

LUTHER, MARTIN (1483-1546) German leader of protestant reformation.

LYONS, CHIEF OREN Onandago Indian, Faithkeeper of the Turtle Clan of Onandago Nation, spokesman for Six Nations Iroquis Confederacy.

MA, ANANDAMAYI (1896-1982) Indian mystic, saint known as Beloved Mother.

MACY, JOANNA ROGERS Professor of religion and philosophy, peace and environmental activist, author, eco-philosopher.

MADISON, JAMES (1751-1836) 4th President of the United States.

MAHARSHI, RAMONA (1879-1950) Hindu sage, saint.

MAIMONIDES (Moses ben Maimon)(1135-1204) Jewish philosopher, jurist. Also known as Rambam.

MALCOLM X (1925-65) American civil rights activist, black power advocate, black Muslim leader. Also known as El-Hajj Malik El-Shabazz.

MANDELA, NELSON ROLIHLAHLA (b. 1918) Attorney, State President of South Africa, President of the African National Congress, co-recipient of 1993 Nobel Peace Prize, and long imprisoned for his civil disobedience and political activities against Apartheid.

MANN, HORACE (1796-1859) American education reformer.

MANN, THOMAS (1875-1955) German novelist, Nobel Prize winner.

MARCEL, GABRIEL (1889-1972) French philosopher, dramatist.

MARCUS, AURELIUS ANTONINUS (A.D. 121-180) Stoic philosopher, Emperor of Rome.

MARGENAU, HENRY Physicist, philosopher, author.

MASLOW, ABRAHAM H. (1908-70) Humanist, psychologist.

MASON, GEORGE (1725-92) American revolutionary statesman, author of Virginia Declaration of Rights.

MATISSE, HENRI (1869-1954) French painter, sculptor, lithographer.

MATTHEW, SAINT (A.D. 1st century) Tax collector from Capernaum, gospelist, disciple of Jesus of Nazareth. Also known as Levi.

MAXIMUS (A.D. 508-662) Christian theologian.

MAY, ROLLO (b. 1909) Psychologist.

MAYUR, DR. RASHMI Indian global environmental activist, advisor to United Nations, author, speaker.

MCLUHAN, MARSHALL (1911-80) Canadian philosopher, cultural historian.

MEAD, MARGARET (1901-78) American anthropologist.

MECHTILD OF MAGDEBURG (1212-99) German contemplative, writer, Dominican nun.

MEHER BABA (1894-1969) Indian-born prophet, teacher of Sufi wisdom.

MELVILLE, HERMAN (1819-91) American writer, adventurer.

MENCIUS (372-289 B.C.) Chinese philosopher.

MENNINGER, KARL (1893-1990) American psychiatrist, prison reformist, author.

MERLIN Celtic Romance bard and mystical sage who tutored King Arthur of ancient Britain, likely instigator of Quest for the Holy Grail, author of book of prophecies.

MERTON, THOMAS (1915-68) Zen commentator, Trappist monk.

METZGER, DEENA (b. 1936) Author, spiritualist, poet.

MILAREPA (1052-1135) Tibetan saint, Buddhist sage.

MILL, JOHN STUART (1806-73) English philosopher.

MILLER, HENRY (1891-1980) American novelist.

MILTON, JOHN (1608-74) English poet, essayist.

MITCHELL, EDGAR D. (b. 1930) Astronaut, moonwalker, Founder of Institute of Noetic Sciences.

MONTAIGNE, MICHEL de (1533-92) French essayist.

MOTHER THERESA OF CALCUTTA (b. 1910) Roman Catholic nun and Indian missionary, Nobel Peace Prize winner, Saint of Loreto Order, founder of Missionaries of Charity. Also known as Agnes Gonxha Bojaxhiu.

MUHAMMAD (A.D. 570-632) Arab prophet, founder of Islam. Also known as Muhammad ibn 'Abd Allah ibn 'Abd al-Muttalib.

MUIR, JOHN (1838-1914) Scottish-born American naturalist, writer, founder of Sierra Club.

MUKTANANDA, SWAMI (1908-82) Indian spiritual teacher, guru.

MULLER, ROBERT (b. 1923) Social theorist, educator, global spiritualist, chancellor of University for Peace in Costa Rica, former U. N. Assistant Under Secretary General.

MUMFORD, LEWIS (1895-1990) American author, social scientist.

MURROW, EDWARD R. (1908-65) American newscaster.

MYRDAL, GUNNAR (1898-1987) Swedish economist, sociologist, diplomat, Nobel Prize winner.

NAGARJUNA (A.D. 2d century) Buddhist patriarch, Indian sage, philosopher, author, founder of Mahayana Buddhism. Also known as Nagasena.

NANAK, BABA (1469-1539) Indian teacher, founder of Sikh Dharma. Also known as Guru Nanak.

NASAFI, AZIS IBN MUHAMMUD AL- (A.D. 7th-8th century) Sufi master, disciple of Najm al-Din Kubra.

NERUDA, PABLO (1904-73) Chilean poet, diplomat, Nobel Prize winner.

NEWMAN, JOHN (1801-90) English clergyman, Roman Catholic Cardinal, writer.

NEWTON, JOHN (1725-1807) English clergyman, hymn writer.

NIEBUHR, REINHOLD (1892-1971) American theologian, philosopher.

NIETZSCHE, FRIEDRICH (1844-1900) German philosopher, poet.

NITSCH, TWYLAH Keeper of the Tradition of the Wolf Clan of Seneca Indians, teacher.

NOVALIS (1772-1801) German poet, visionary, aphorist, metallurgist, philosopher.

OKEN, LORENZ (1779-1851) German naturalist, philosopher.

O'LEARY, BRIAN Ph.D., Former astronaut, international speaker, author, co-founder of International Association for a New Science.

O'NEILL, EUGENE (1888-1953) American playwright, Nobel Prize winner.

ORAGE, A. R. (1871-1932) Editor, student of Gurdjieff.

ORTEGA Y GASSET JOSE (1885-1955) Spanish philosopher, statesman.

OSLER, SIR WILLIAM (1849-1919) Canadian physician, medical historian, teacher.

OTTO, RUDOLF (1869-1937) Naturalist, spiritualist.

OUSPENSKY, P. D. (1878-1947) Russian mathematician, philosopher, disciple of Georges Ivanovitch Gurdjieff, proponent of method of learning known as the "Fourth Way."

PAINE, THOMAS (1737-1809) English-born rebel, American patriot, political writer.

PASCAL, BLAISE (1623-62) French philosopher, mathematician.

PASTEUR, LOUIS (1822-95) French chemist, bacteriologist.

PATANJALI (2d century B.C.) Indian scholar, philosopher.

PAUL, SAINT (A.D. 1st century) Tentmaker, converted following mystical vision on road to Damascus, apostle of Jesus of Nazareth, Christian missionary, author of letters and epistles. Also known as Saul of Tarsus.

PENINGTON, ISAAC (1616-79) English Quaker, father-in-law of William Penn.

PERICLES (495-429 B.C.) Athenian statesman.

PERLS, FRITZ (1893-1970) German-born psychiatrist, developer of Gestalt therapy.

PETER, PAUL & MARY (1961-) American folk-rock group of Peter Yarrow, Paul Stookey and Mary Ellen Travers, peace and environmental activists.

PHILO, JUDAEUS (20 B.C. - A.D. 50) Alexandrian Jewish theologian, philosopher.

PLATO (427-347 B.C.) Greek philosopher, reputed member of secret brotherhood -- "Illuminati."

PLOTINUS (A.D. 205-270) Roman philosopher, founder of Neoplatonism.

PLUTARCH (A.D. 46-120) Greek biographer.

POPE, ALEXANDER (1688-1744) English poet, animist philosopher.

PREM, SRI KRISHNA Yoga theosophist, scholar on Kathopanishads, author.

PRICE, DIADRA Co-founder of Wings of Spirit Foundation, author, teacher, Unity minister, spiritual intuitive.

PRICE, JOHN RANDOLPH Spiritual writer, mystic, founder of Quartas Foundation.

PRIESTLY, J. B. (1894-1984) English writer, literary critic.

PRIGOGINE, ILYA (b. 1917) Russian-born chemist, theorizer of self-organizing process of natural world.

PYTHAGORAS (5th century B.C.) Greek philosopher, mathematician, precursor of gnosis, spiritual mystic, reputed member of secret brotherhood -- "Illuminati."

RAIN, MARY SUMMER New Age author, visionary.

RAINE, KATHLEEN (b. 1909) Poet, author.

RAJNEESCH, BHAGWAN SHREE (1931-90) Indian-born teacher of Tantric Sufi heritage.

RAM DASS, BABA (b. 1932) Seeker, teacher, spiritual author, student of guru Maharajji, creator of Hanuman Foundation, co-founder of Seva Foundation. Also known as Dr. Richard Alpert.

RAMAKRISHNA, SRI (1836-86) Hindu religious reformer, mystic.

RAMDAS, SWAMI (1886-1963) Hindu bhakta.

RAMTHA Ancient Lemurian entity channeled by J. Z. Knight.

RANK, OTTO (1884-1939) Austrian psychoanalyst.

RAVINDRA, RAVI Author, philosopher, professor of physics and religion.

RAY, MICHAEL Professor of Creativity and Innovation at Stanford University Graduate School of Business, author, social psychologist.

RICH, ADRIENNE (b. 1929) Teacher, poet.

RICHARD OF SAINT-VICTOR (12th century) Medieval Scot mystic, philosopher, theologian.

RICHARDS, M.C. Author, poet, artisan.

RILKE, RAINER MARIA (1875-1926) German poet, mystic.

ROLLING THUNDER Shoshone Indian spiritual leader, healer, environmental activist, protector of Indian lands, tribal spokesperson, keeper of tribal secrets. Also known as John Pope.

ROOSEVELT, ELEANOR (1884-1926) American diplomat, author, advocate for human rights.

ROOSEVELT, FRANKLIN (1882-1945) 32d President of the United States.

ROSZAK, THEODORE American author on counter culture, sociology, postindustrial society.

ROUSSEAU, JEAN-JACQUES (1712-78) French philosopher, social reformer.

RUMI, JALAL-UD-DIN (1207-73) Mystical sufi poet of Persia.

RUSH, BENJAMIN (1745-1813) American physician, political leader.

RUSKIN, JOHN (1819-1900) English author, art critic, social reformer.

RUSSELL, BERTRAND (1872-1970) English philosopher, mathematician, Nobel Prize winner.

RUSSELL, WALTER (1871-1963) Artist, sculptor, philosopher, metaphysician.

RUYSBROECK, JOHN (1293-1381) Flanders mystic.

SAGAN, CARL (1934-96) American astronomer, scientist, writer.

SALK, JONAS (1914-1995) American bacteriologist.

SALT, HENRY S. English 19th century animal rights author, activist.

SANA'I, HAKIM ABU (1118-52) Sufi author.

SANKARACHARYA, SRI (A.D. 789-821) Hindu Vedantist, philosopher, teacher, metaphysician.

SASS, HERBERT RAVENEL (1884-1958) American nature writer.

SATPREM Scholar, author, philosopher of mind.

SCHELL, JONATHAN (b. 1943) Author, ecologist, peace activist.

SCHRODINGER, ERWIN (1887-1961) Austrian physicist, Nobel Prize winner.

SCHWEICHART, RUSTY American Apollo 9 astronaut.

SCHWEITZER, ALBERT (1875-1965) Writer, missionary, doctor, Nobel Peace Prize winner.

SCOTT, HAZEL (b. 1920) Black American pianist, entertainer.

SEATTLE, CHIEF (1790-1866) Suquamish Indian leader, scholar, speaker. Also known as Chief Sealth.

SEED, JOHN Hungarian-born deep ecologist.

SENECA, LUCIUS ANNAEUS (4 B.C. - A.D. 65) Roman statesman, stoic philosopher.

SESSIONS, GEORGE (b. 1938) Philosopher, deep ecologist.

SHABISTARI (1250-1320) Persian Sufi poet.

SHAKESPEARE, WILLIAM (1564-1616) English poet, dramatist.

SHANKARA (A.D. 686-718) Indian yogi, philosopher, founder of Advaita Vedanta.

SHAW, GEORGE BERNARD (1856-1950) Irish writer, Nobel Prize winner.

SHELLEY, P. B. (1792-1822) English poet.

SHENANDOAH, CHIEF LEON Keeper of the Central Fire, Speaker of House of Grand Council of Six Nations Iroquois Confederacy, activist for peace, consultant to the United Nations.

SIDDHARTHA, GUATAMA (566-480 B.C.) Indian religious leader, founder of Buddhism. Also known as the "Buddha."

SIEGEL, BERNIE (b. 1932) Surgeon, pediatrician, holistic healer.

SILESIUS, ANGELUS (1624-77) German theosophist. Also known as Johannes Schoffler.

SIVANANDA, SWAMI (1887-1963) Hindu exponent of Japa.

SKORPEN, ERLING American professor of philosophy.

SKUTCH, ALEXANDER FRANK (b. 1904) American naturalist, oronothologist, winner of John Burroughs medal.

SMITH, HUSTON American professor of religion and philosophy.

SNYDER, GARY (b. 1930) Pulitzer Prize winner, poet, author, Buddhist wanderer.

SOLARA New Age visionary, spiritualist.

SOROKIN, PITIRIM (1889-1968) Russian-American sociologist.

SPANGLER, DAVID Lecturer, former co-director of Findhorn Foundation, New Age author, community organizer.

SPENCER, HERBERT (1820-1903) English philosopher.

SPINOZA, BENEDICTUS de (1632-77) Dutch philosopher.

STANDING BEAR (b. 1868) Lakota Sioux Indian chief. Also known as Chief Luther.

STARHAWK (b. 1940) Feminist, peace activist, high priestess, writer. Also known an Miriam Simos.

STEINDL-RAST, DAVID Vienna-born experimental psychologist, Benedictine monk, Celtic spiritualist.

ST. EXUPERY, ANTOINNE de (1900-44) French author.

STERRY, PETER (1613-72) Leading Cambridge Platonist.

STEVENSON, ADLAI E. (1900-65) American statesman, diplomat.

STOBAEUS, JOANNES (A.D. 5th century) Greek anthologist.

STOOKEY, PAUL American songwriter and member of popular folk group Peter, Paul & Mary.

SUN BEAR Chippewa medicine man, leader of Bear Tribe Medicine Society, teacher, lecturer.

SUSO, HEINRICH (1295-1365) German Dominican mystic, follower of Eckhart.

SUTHERLAND, J. (1862-1942) American politician, jurist, Associate Justice of the United States Supreme Court.

SUZUKI, DAISETZ TEITARO (1870-1966) Japanese Buddhist scholar, lecturer, popularizer of Zen Buddhism.

SWIMME, BRIAN Cosmic creation author.

SZEKELY, EDMUND BORDEAUX (d. 1979) Ph.D., professor of philosophy and religion, philologist in Sanskrit, Aramaic, Greek and Latin. Founder of International Biogenic Society, author of over 80 books, including Essene Gospel of Peace (ancient manuscript located in Secret Archives of Vatican).

TAGORE, DR. RABINDRANATH (1861-1941) Indian philosopher, poet, Nobel Prize winner.

TAKUAN (1573-1645) Zen master, poet, painter, abbot.

TAULER, JOHANNES (1300-61) Friar preacher of Strassburg, mystic, theologian.

TEILHARD de CHARDIN, PIERRE (1881-1955) French Jesuit priest, philosopher, paleontologist.

TENNYSON, LORD ALFRED (1809-92) English poet laureate.

TERESA OF AVILA, SAINT (1515-82) Spanish carmelite nun and mystic, leading figure in Catholic Reformation, associate of St. John of the Cross.

TERESA OF LISEUX, SAINT (1873-97) French carmelite nun, called "Little Flower of Jesus." Also known as Therese Martin.

THE MOTHER (1878-1973) French-born artist, mathematician, student of Sri Aurobindo, founder of Indian ashram. Also known as Mira Alfassa Richard.

THOMAS, SAINT (A.D. 1st century) Gnostic gospelist, apostle of Jesus of Nazareth. Also known as Didymus Jude Thomas.

THOMPSON, DOROTHY (1894-1961) American journalist.

THOMPSON, FRANCES (1859-1907) English poet.

THOREAU, HENRY DAVID (1817-62) American naturalist, mystic, author.

THOTH Legendary Atlantean priest-king, architect of the Great Pyramid of Giza, thrice-born immortal (including final incarnation as Hermes Trismegistus), deified as the God of Wisdom and The Recorder,

TILLICH, PAUL (1886-1965) Philosopher, theologian.

TINGLEY, KATHERINE (1852-1929) Theosophist, leader of Raj Yoga School.

TOCQUEVILLE, ALEXIS de (1805-59) French statesman, philosopher, author.

TOLSTOY, LEO NIKOLAEVICH (1828-1910) Russian-born novelist.

TORREY, BRADFORD (1843-1912) American naturalist, ornithologist, author.

TOV, BAEL SHEM (1700-60) Jewish religious leader, founder of Hasidic movement.

TOYNBEE, ARNOLD (1889-1975) English historian.

TRAHERNE, THOMAS (1637-74) English poet, religious writer, Platonist.

TREVELYAN, SIR GEORGE Orator, author, trustee of Findhorn Foundation, known as the father of the new age in Britain.

TRIBE, LAURENCE Harvard professor of constitutional law, legal scholar.

TRINE, RALPH WALDO Philosopher, author.

TRISMEGISTUS, HERMES (1399-1257 B.C.) Legendary ancient Egyptian Master and founder of Hermetic Teachings, instructor of Abraham, Father of Occult Wisdom, founder of astrology, discoverer of alchemy, member of early secret brotherhood -- "Illuminati." Also known as "Thoth" and as the "Scribe of the Gods."

TRUNGPA RINPOCHE CHOGYAM (1939-87) Tibetan Buddhist teacher and master, 11th incarnation of the Trungpa Tulku, founder of Vajradhatu.

TURGENEV, IVAN SERGEEVICH (1818-1883) Russian novelist, poet and playwright.

TUTU, DESMOND (b. 1931) South African religious leader, civil rights advocate, Nobel Peace Prize winner.

TWITCHELL, SRI PAUL (d. 1971) Eck master.

UNDERHILL, EVELYN (1877-1941) English poet, mystic, author, spiritual leader.

U THANT (1909-74) Burmese statesman, Secretary General of the United Nations.

VAN GOGH, VINCENT (1853-90) Dutch post-impressionist painter.

VAUGHAN, THOMAS (1622-66) English alchemical writer, twin brother of mystic poet Henry Vaughan.

VIRGIL (70-19 B.C.) Roman poet, author of epic poem "The Aeneid."

VIVEKANANDA, SWAMI (1863-1902) Disciple of Sri Ramakrishna.

VOLTAIRE, PATRIE (1694-1778) French writer, philosopher, historian. Also known as Francois Marie Arouet.

WALKER, ALICE (b. 1944) American author.

WALLACE, HENRY (1888-1965) Former Vice President of the United States.

WARREN, EARL (1891-1974) 14th Chief Justice of the United States Supreme Court.

WASHINGTON, GEORGE (1732-99) 1st President of the United States.

WEBER, RENEE Philosophy professor, author.

WEBSTER, DANIEL (1782-1852) American statesman, lawyer, orator.

WEIL, SIMONE (1903-43) French philosopher, mystic.

WELLS, H. G. (1866-1946) English novelist, historian.

WESLEY, JOHN (1703-91) English theologian, evangelist, founder of Methodism.

WHITE, DAVID Professor of philosophy, scholar of philosophies of India, author.

WHITE, SASHA Founder of the Campaign for the Earth Foundation.

WHITEHEAD, ALFRED NORTH (1861-1947) English-born philosopher, mathematician.

WHITMAN, WALT (1819-92) American poet, mystic.

WHITTIER, JOHN GREENLEAF (1807-1892) Abolitionist, Quaker, poet.

WILBER, KEN Scholar, author on consciousness, science, psychotherapy, philosophy and religion.

WILCOX, ELLA WHEELER (1850-1919) American poet.

WILLERS, BILL Professor of biology, environmental adviser, participant in Green Party movement, author.

WILLIAMS, PAUL (b. 1948) Writer, spiritual activist.

WILSON, WOODROW (1856-1924) 28th President of the United States, Nobel Peace Prize winner.

WINTHROP, JOHN (1638-1707) American statesman.

WOLFE, THOMAS (1900-38) American novelist.

WOOLGER, ROGER Ph.D., Past life therapist, author, speaker.

WORDSWORTH, WILLIAM (1770-1850) English poet laureate.

YARROW, PETER American songwriter and member of popular folk group Peter, Paul & Mary

YEATS, W. B. (1865-1939) Irish poet, dramatist, Nobel Prize winner.

YOGANANDA, PARAMAHANSA Indian disciple of Sri Yukteswarji, founder of Self-Realization Fellowship, author.

YOUNG, MEREDITH LADY Channel for Agartha, New Age author.

YWAHOO, DHYANI Cherokee healer, author, transmitter of Tsalagi teachings dating back 2,860 years.

ZIMMER, HEINRICH (1890-1943) German ideologist, thinker.

ZOHAR, DANAH Author on physics, philosophy and religion.

ZUKAV, GARY (b. 1943) Author on physics, Eastern mysticism and spirituality.

OTHER SOURCES

A COURSE IN MIRACLES (1965-71) Spiritual, self-study thought system consisting of text, workbook and teacher's manual. Course came to Helen Schucman, Ph.D., in series of symbolic dreams and imagery experiences culminating in hearing an inner voice. Assisted by William Thetford, Ph.D., the Course was taken down over a six year period, and it consists of over 1,200 pages. Schucman and Thetford were both psychologists on the faculty of Columbia University College of Physicians and Surgeons. Course was first published in 1976 by The Foundation for Inner Peace. As the Course states:

"[t]his Course was sent to open up the path of light to us, and teach us, step by step how to return to the eternal Self we thought we lost. . . . Your goal is to find out who you are."

A NALECTS (4th - 5th century B.C.) Collection of sayings or discourses of Confucius (551-479 B.C.) compiled over century following his death. Also known as Lun-Yu. Recognized as the most informative source on the life and teachings of Confucius.

A SHTAVAKRA SAMHITA (2d century B.C.) One of earliest works of literature of the Samhitas. Most ancient hymns which make up Vedas. Considered to be the work of Advaita Vedanta. Explores and describes perceptions and concepts of Vedanta. Text is attributed to Ashtavakra, crippled 2d century B.C. sage and principal teacher of Patanjali. Also known as Ashtavakragita.

A THARVA-VEDA (6th - 1st century B.C.) Fourth Veda, containing 731 hymns copied from the Rig Veda and other texts. Includes magical incantations and metaphysical speculations. Also deals with medicinal concerns. Original version had appendix known as Ayur Veda (Sanskrit "life science") -- named for India's traditional system of medicine. Included within work is beautiful prayer to the earth known as Hymn to the Earth.

*A*VATAMSAKA SUTRA (A.D. 5th century)   Short title for "Buddhavatamsaka Sutra" or "Sutra of the Garland of Buddhas." Vaipulya Sutra of Mahayana embodying sermons of the Buddha after reaching enlightenment. Came to become root text of Chinese Hua-yen School of Mahayana Buddhism. Teaches unity and oneness of all. Known in Japan as Kegon Sutra. Brought to Japan in A.D. 735.

*B*HAGAVAD-GITA (5th - 2d century B.C.) Sruti teachings of Sri Krishna. Name derived from Sanskrit word for "Song of the Lord." Constitutes 18 chapter section of Hindu epic, the Mahabharata. Consists of 700 verses. Forms body of the central texts of Hindu religion.

*B*OOK OF THE HOPI (orig. 3000 B.C. -) Sacred teachings and prophesies of ancient Hopis passed down orally from generation to generation to the present day Hopi (Hopituh), Shoshonean Pueblo Indian people living on mesas in Northern Arizona – the "peaceful ones." Includes teachings of Massau'u, the Great Spirit, prophesying on four ages or worlds preceding destruction of humanity.

*C*HANDOGYA UPANISHAD (8th - 7th century B.C.) Second oldest of the Upanishads associated with Sama Veda collection. Represents secret teachings of the Chandogya School, containing fundamental teachings of early Vedic Hinduism concerning cosmology, the individual, universal soul and the afterlife. Also referred to as Chhandogyapanishad.

*D*EAD SEA SCROLLS (200 B.C. - A.D. 70) Literature of the Essenes, Jewish ascetic sect living in desert of Judah on eastern shore of the Dead Sea from about 200 B.C. to destruction by Roman soldiers in A.D. 68. Ancient Scrolls were found in eleven caves at Qumran between 1947 and 1956. Included are texts forming part of Biblical Old Testament, hymns, philosophical treatises, and manual concerning life and discipline in the Essene community. Some believe that both John the Baptist and Jesus were members of the Essenes. Texts yet to be fully translated.

*D*HAMMAPADA (240 B.C.) Taken from the Pali word for "Path of True Doctrine." Collection of sayings attributed to the Buddha. Part of the Pali canon of Buddhist scriptures, the Tripitika. Contains favorite aphorisms garnered from other parts of the scripture and popular Buddhist wisdom. Also contains Four Noble Truths and Eightfold Path. Accepted by the Council of Ashoka.

*E*GYPTIAN BOOK OF THE DEAD (1600 B.C.) Egyptian title "Coming Forth by Day" and English "The Book of the Ever Deathless." Text contains collection of chants and magical spells designed to assist the departing soul in facing judgment by the gods Anubis, Thoth and Osiris. Texts said to have accompanied deceased to the tomb. Major revisions in text made in 664-525 B.C.

*E*MERALD TABLET OF HERMES (A.D. 2d - 3d century) Alchemical document containing sacerdotal wisdom of Egyptian antiquity attributed to Hermes Trismegistus (1399-1257 B.C.), said to contain very secrets of Creation of the world. Legend states it was Sara, wife of Abraham, who discovered the text in the tomb of Hermes Trismegistus. Also traced to Arabic sources such as Jabir claiming to quote from Apollonius of Tyana, and found in Greco-Egyptian Leyden Paprus at Thebes (A.D.300). Some believe that the Emerald Tablet is only a highly abreviated, lesser exposition of the Emerald Tablets of Thoth first made widely public within last century.

*E*MERALD TABLETS OF THOTH-THE-ATLANTEAN (36,000 B.C.) Represented to be a translation of twelve tablets of Emerald green substance created through alchemical transmutation which are imperishable, resistant to all elements, upon which are engraved chracters in the ancient Atlantean language. Said to be fastened together with hoops of a golden colored alloy suspended from a rod of the same material, the tablets are believed to have been written by Thoth (an Atlantean priest-king and builder of the Great Pyramid of Gizeh). It is said that the tablets were entrusted to and moved by pyramid priests from the Great Pyramid to

South America where they were placed beneath a Mayan temple until finally returned to the Great Pyramid.

ᕮSSENE GOSPEL OF PEACE (A.D. 1st - 2d century) Ancient manuscript of teachings of Essenes said to be stored in Secret Archives of the Vatican and, in part, the Royal Library of the Habsburgs. Translated to Hebrew and Aramaic by Edmond Bordeaux Szekely. Contains words and teachings of Jesus and the Elders of the Essene Brotherhood. Manuscripts preserved date back to A.D. 1st century, including letters from the Ancient Brotherhood, a society of ascetic Jews. The Gospel of Peace was published in four volumes between 1928 and 1981. Complete story told in The Discovery of the Essene Gospel of Peace published by the International Biogenic Society in 1975.

GRANTH SAHIB (A.D. 1604) Central holy book of the Sikh religion. Revered as living guru. Compiled by succession of Sikh gurus containing hymns, devotional songs, and writings of Hindu and Muslim saints from Northern India. Also known as Adi Granth or First Book.

HADITH (A.D. 100 - 1000) Compilation of deeds and utterances of Muhammad, the Prophet of Islam, as recounted by his companions. Passed down orally and in written form and collected in volumes for guidance of Muslim communities. Deals with contents of the Koran, social and religious life, and everyday conduct. Also contains stories about God, angels, Prophets, and the last judgment. First collections compiled in 1st century, followed by numerous other compilations in time-frame A.D. 800 - 1000. Accompanied by isnad ("Chain") listing line of sources transmitting the tradition.

HERMETIC WRITINGS AND PRINCIPLES (1200 B.C. - A.D. 300) Hidden Wisdom and Mystic Teachings of the Adepts and Masters of Egypt following Hermes Trismegistus, the "scribe of the gods." Early basic Hermetic Doctrines passed on from teacher to student, and sometimes referred to as The Kybalion. Passed by word of mouth, basic precepts constitute principles of "The Art of Hermetic Alchemy." Legend of

"Philosophers' Stone" was allegory relating to Hermetic Philosophy. Seven Hermetic Principles form the basis of Hermetic Philosophy. Writings consist of collection of short essays and dialogues by Egyptian Philosophers of the Neoplatonic School. Corpus Hermeticum is title for collection of seventeen chapters, or tractates, of Hermetic writings originating in Alexandria during 1st and 2d centuries, which were compiled in Greek between the 6th and 9th centuries. Some teachings believed to be of gnostic origin. Portion of texts also found among the Nag Hammadi Scriptures discovered in 1945, including Coptic texts written in 4th century, such as partial version of the Asclepius and On the Ogdoad and the Ennead on spiritual regeneration. Hermetic Teachings believed to form foundation for many of esoteric teachings throughout the world.

HOLY BIBLE:

OLD TESTAMENT (9th - 3d century B.C.) Diverse texts by many authors written in Hebrew, Greek and Aramaic, some representing and reflecting oral traditions dating back several thousands of years. Comprised of the Law, the Prophets, the Hagiographia, works of Wisdom, poetic Psalms (traditionally ascribed to King David) and Proverbs. First five books (Genesis, Exodus, Leviticus, Numbers and Deuteronomy) form basis of the Pentateuch included within Jewish Torah.

OLD TESTAMENT APOCRYPHA (200 B.C. - A.D. 100) Books declared "uninspired" and excluded from Hebrew Bible, as well as from many Christian versions of the Bible. Sometimes referred to as Deuterocanonical Books ("hidden things") of Old Testament consisting of 16 books written in Greek during last two centuries B.C. After canonization of texts by the Catholic Church in 1546, books were included in King James Version of the Bible between Old and New Testaments. Also sometimes referred to as intertestamental literature. Includes Books 3 and 4 of Ezra; the Book of Baruch; the Book of Judith; Ecclesiasticus (180 B.C.) written in Hebrew by Jeshua ibn Sirach of Jerusalem; and Songs of Solomon or Book of Wisdom (50 B.C.) written in Greek by unknown Jew living in Alexandria and, by custom, ascribed to King Solomon (10th century B.C.). Both Ecclesiasticus and Songs of Solomon provide poetic accounts of God's feminine aspect which the Greeks referred to as Sophia, described as pervading and permeating all things, and the source of all treasure in the universe ("Wisdom").

NEW TESTAMENT (A.D. 1st - 2d century) Collective name for 27 later books of the Bible concerned with the life and teachings of Jesus of Nazareth. Texts first written in Greek. Includes Gospels, Acts of the Apostles, Revelation of St. John, Epistles and Letters. Christian part of the Book of Books.

GNOSTIC GOSPELS and NEW TESTAMENT APOCRYPHA (A.D. 2d - 3d century) Gospel of Thomas (collection of sayings of Jesus), Gospel of Truth (homiletic exposition of the good news), Gospel of Philip (collection of Jesus' thoughts and sayings), and Gospel of Mary (visionary revelations of the risen Jesus received by Mary Magdalene). Fragments of original Greek texts discovered in Egypt in approximately 1900. Coptic writings found in 1945 in cave in the area of Nag Hammadi in ancient Egypt (the "Nag Hammadi Library"). Also included in writings discovered were apocryphal texts meant to remain hidden and secret, such as the Apocryphon of John or The Secret Book of John. Additional apocryphic texts include the Gospel of the Egyptians, Gospel of the Hebrews, Gospel of Petrus, Gospel of Nicodemus, Apocalypse of Adam and Hypostasis of the Archons. Writings said to include direct communications of Jesus during forty days spent with circle of chosen disciples after resurrection. The texts have never enjoyed canonical status. Due to similarities with gnostic teachings, the New Testament Gospel of John is likewise sometimes referred to as "gnostic gospel."

KATHOPANISHAD (6th century B.C.) One of principal Upanishads, writings of philosophical movement of ancient India. In explorations, great questions of meaning of life and relation of individual to the cosmos are examined. A pathway to the atman or soul is indicated in the image of a chariot and its driver.

_L_ANKAVATARA SUTRA (1st century B.C.) Sometimes referred to as Sutra on the Descent to Sri Lanka or Entrance to Ceylon Text. Mahayanist scripture and Mahayana Sutra stressing inner enlightenment and rising above duality and all distinctions. Relates experience possible through realization of "tathagata-garbha" immanent in all beings. One of few traditional Mahayana texts, along with Diamond Sutra. Translated for first time into Chinese in 5th century. Said to have been given by Bodhidharma, the first Chinese patriarch of Zen to his student Itviko.

_M_AITREYAVYAKARANA (5th century B.C.) Buddhist scripture regarding life of Maitreya, the "Coming Buddha," whose name is derived from mitra ("friend"), a basic Buddhist virtue akin to Christian "love." It is believed that Maitreya is now residing in Tushita heaven, but that he will undergo his last rebirth into a womb, at which time he will lead humanity as supreme sage into state of Dharma on earth which will endure for 10,000 years. Scripture describes the rebirth, the conditions which will exist at that time, and the way in which Maitreya will guide those blessed to be incarnated at that time. At end of his last incarnation, Maitreya will enter Nirvana. To be reborn in Maitreya's presence is greatest wish of many Tibetans and Mongols. Rocks of numerous mountains contain the inscription, "Come, Maitreya, come."

_M_UNDAKA UPANISHAD (6th century B.C.) Another principal Upanishad. All that exists is traced back to the supreme person, the Purusha. By series of progressively lower manifestations, known cosmos is called into being. Relates one's inner Self to the All. States that which separates man from perceiving unity is partial vision and suggests pathway to greater wholeness. Part of Atharva-Veda collection. Includes chant or prayer focusing on sacred syllable Om.

_P_HILOKALIA (A.D. 1st - 11th century) Writings of Fathers of the Eastern Orthodox Church over span of eleven centuries and compiled in 18th century. Collection of writings of monks and abbots applying Jesus' teachings to personal lives. One of the earliest works on basic practice of Christianity. Discusses how man may develop his inner powers and awaken from illusion to know God from personal experience. In Russian, Dobrotolubiye or "The Love of Spiritual Beauty."

QURAN (A.D. 6th - 7th century) In Arabic, "Recital." Also known as Koran. Islamic sacred scripture revealed by the angel Gabriel to the Prophet Muhammad. As written, a compilation of Muhammad's teachings ordered by Abu Bekr a year after Muhammad's death based on memory. Second edition compiled 11 or 12 years later by Caliph Othman after the originals were destroyed. Muslims believe to be the Word of God in the world, and many Muslims believe sacrilege to translate. Also contains 114 sutras divinely revealed from year 610 onward by Allah to Muhammad. Includes legal, ethical, theological, and sociological rules and guidelines, along with mythical and prophetic material.

RAMAYANA (4th - 3d century B.C.) Hindu epic of "Deeds of Rama." Ancient Hindu story of adventures of Rama and teachings of sage Visishtha to Prince Rama. Transcribed in 3d century B.C. by Valmiki under name Ramayana. One of two major national epics of Indian literature containing more than twenty thousand stanzas. Story of tragic love and dealing with asceticism. Repository of folklore, moral values and folk wisdom. Learned in India mainly through recitations and public readings. Primary source for religious and moral concepts.

SECRET DOCTRINE OF ROSICRUCIANS (3000 B.C. - ?) Body of esoteric teachings handed down for ages by those deeply versed in the esoteric doctrines and occult lore. The Wisdom of the Rosicrucians ("The Brothers of the Rosy Cross") is said to have originated in the Orient and, to this day, to comprise part of the Inner Teachings of the highest Oriental Brotherhoods. Also believed to be related to Secret Brotherhood of Egypt known as Illuminati, the Essene Brotherhood and other esoteric, mystical bodies which followed. Teachings incorporate alchemical laws and principles. Some of the original teachings of the Rosicrucians have been incorporated into higher degrees of Masonry. Unorganized "Order" with admission granted only upon request and recommendation of those attaining the esoteric knowledge and who keep alive the Sacred Flame of Truth. Modern Rosicrucians often linked with 14th to 16th century

European mystics. Little of the Secret Doctrine has been committed to writing until modern times, although parts of the Secret Doctrine are said to be contained in ancient Hermetic, Greek, Hindu, Hebrew and Eastern esoteric texts. Secret Doctrine also said to contain teachings preserved from legendary Atlantean civilization.

*S*HEKEL HAKODESH (A.D. 1150) Metrical Hebrew work of medieval Spanish Jewish Scholar, Joseph Kimchi of Narbonne (1105-70) based on maxims in Arabic by Nestorin Christian Honein (d. 873), and translated into Hebrew by Yehuda Alcharisi. Also referred to as The Holy Shekel.

*S*UTRAS (1st century B.C. - A.D. 6th century) Divine revelations and discourses of the Buddha. Sutra means "thread." Sutras are collected in second part of Buddhist canon Tripitaka, as well as in the Sutra-Pitaka or "Basket of the Teachings." Sutras preserved in Pali and Sanskrit, as well as in Chinese and Tibetan translations. Fundamental religious and sacred texts, each introduced by the words "Thus, have I heard" ascribed to Ananda, student of the Buddha. Style is simple, popular and didactically oriented. Rich in parables and allegories. In many sutras, songs are interspersed. Principal sutras divided into Hinayana Sutras and Mahayana Sutras.

*T*ALMUD (A.D. 4th - 6th century) Ancient body of Jewish Civil and Canonical law. Recordings of the oral Torah in over thirty large volumes, 2.5 million words, on 5,894 folio pages. Contains Mishnaic texts with long commentary called gemara. Major work of post-Biblical Jewish Literature. Compilation of commentaries on ancient, orally transmitted laws and customs. Represents written interpretation of the development of Hebrew thought and tradition, ethics, religion and folklore. Divided into sections covering differing aspects of traditions. Legends, poetry and anecdotes found in Aggada, as well as legal matters constituting Halakah.

*T*AO TE CHING (6th - 3d century B.C.) Earliest Taoist Classic containing collection of sayings gathered from writings of Chinese Sages. Traditionally attributed to Lao Tzu (604-531 B.C.). Contains paradox, word play, mystical visions, spiritual counseling, and political advice. Tells story of Tao ("way" or "the path"), and Te (manifestation of Reality). Ranks third in popularity only behind the Bible and Bhagavad-Gita in English translations. Also known as "The Book of The Way and Its Power."

*T*HEOLOGIA GERMANICA (A.D. 1350) Literary jewel and treatise of the Society of the Friends of God. Probably written in Frankfurt by a priest of Teutonic Order. Represents attempt to make mystic principles available for common person. Greatly loved by Luther who published incomplete edition in 1518. Also known as "Book of the Perfect Life."

*T*IBETAN BOOK OF THE DEAD (14th century B.C.) "Liberation Through Hearing in the In-Between State" or "Liberation by Hearing on the After-Death Plane." Also known as Bardo Thodol. Mayahana Buddhist text composed of group of instructions stemming from Padmasambhava elaborated into systematic teaching in form of a "terma" in the 14th century. First committed to writing in A.D. 8th century. In general use throughout Tibet as a funeral ritual, and, esoterically, as an initiate support. Sets forth process of death and rebirth as three phases or in-between states closely connected with three bodies of a buddha. All three phases offer possibility, through hearing appropriate instructions, for being able to recognize nature of own mind and attain liberation or Nirvana. Suggests that, following death, soul is faced with possibility of absorption into the pure light of mystical union with the godhead or Nirvana.

*T*ORAH (10th century B.C. - A.D. 2d century) Sacred Jewish Scripture including Book of Moses, the Pentateuch (first five books of Christian Old Testament) and 34 other books added to form the Hebrew Bible. Oral Torah is recorded in the Talmud, the Midrash, the Mishnah, the Books of the Prophets, the Aggadah, the Ketuvim and other writings. Scrolls kept in closet called "The Holy Ark." Also known as Tanakh.

*U*PANISHADS (8th - 5th century B.C.) Collection of diverse speculations regarding liberation, metaphysics and epistemology. Compilations date back to 1000 B.C., but systematic summary appeared in A.D. 8th century. Upanishads generally refers to collection of 108 texts on Secret Doctrine, but more specifically to thirteen classical texts which are authoritative sources of Vedic Wisdom. The texts include the Isa, Kena, Katha, Maitri, Prasna, Mundaka, Aitareya, Mandukya, Kavasitaki, Chandogya, Taittiriya, Svetasvatara and Brihadaranyaka. Word in Sanskrit means "knowledge," loosening bondage of the world and enabling pupil to realize the Self. Explains methods of attaining spiritual freedom and spiritual wisdom, including techniques and practices.

$\mathcal{A}$CKNOWLEDGMENTS, BIBLIOGRAPHY
AND RECOMMENDED READING

A Course in Miracles. © 1975 Foundation for Inner Peace. Mill Valley, CA.

A Testament of Hope: the Essential Writings of Martin Luther King Jr., edited by James Melvin Washington. San Francisco: Harper & Row, 1986.

A Treasury of Traditional Wisdom, presented by Whitall N. Perry. Cambridge: Quinta Essentia, 1971.

Abandonment to Divine Providence, translated by John Beevers. New York: Doubleday, 1975.

Abrams, M. H., The Mirror and the Lamp. London: Oxford University Press, 1953.

Adams, Brian, How to Succeed. California: Melvin Powers Wilshire Book Company, 1985.

Adler, Mortimer J., Six Great Ideas. London: Collier MacMillan Publishers, 1981.

Ahmad, Aijaz, The Ghazals of Ghalib, New York: Columbia University Press, 1971.

Aldridge, Alfred Owen, Voltaire and the Century of Light. Princeton: Princeton University Press, 1975.

Alexander, Cecil Frances, All Things Bright and Beautiful. New York: Charles Scribner's Sons, 1962.

Alighieri, Dante, The Divine Comedy, translated by Charles S. Singleton, 6 vols. Bollingen Series LXXX. Princeton, New Jersey: Princeton University Press, 1975.

Allen, Paula Gunn, The Sacred Hoop. New York: Beacon Press, 1986.

Aquinas, Saint Thomas, <u>Summa Theologica</u>. New York: McGraw-Hill Book Company, 1966.

Arguelles, Jose, <u>Surfers of the Zuvuya</u>. Santa Fe, New Mexico: Bear & Company, 1988.

Aristotle, <u>Nichomachean Ethics</u>. Salem, New Hampshire: Ayer Co. Publishers, 1909.

Armstrong, Edward A., <u>Saint Francis: Nature Mystic</u>. Berkeley, California: University of California Press, 1973.

Attenborough, Richard, <u>The Words of Gandhi</u>. New York: Newmarket Press, 1982.

Atwater, P.M.H., <u>Future Memory</u>. Carol Publishing Group, 1996.

Audubon, Maria, <u>Vol. I, Audubon and His Journals</u>. New York: Dover Publications, 1960.

Avedon, John, <u>An Interview With The Dalai Lama</u>. New York: Littlebird Publications, 1980.

<u>Awakening Osiris: The Egyptian Book of the Dead</u>, translated by Normandi Ellis. Grand Rapids, Michigan: Phanes Books, 1988.

Bach, Richard, <u>Illusions</u>. London: Pan Books, 1979.

Bach, Richard, <u>Jonathan Livingston Seagull</u>. New York: Avon Books, 1970.

<u>Baha'i World Faith: Selected Writings of Baha'u'llah and 'Abdu'l-Baha</u>. Wilmette, Illinois: Baha'i Publishing Trust, 1956 ed.

Bailey, Alice A., <u>Discipleship in the New Age</u>. London: The Lucis Trust Press, 1955.

Bailey, Alice A., <u>Education in The New Age</u>, New York: Lucis Publishing Company, 1954.

Bailey, Alice A., Esoteric Psychology I: A Treatise on the Seven Rays. New York: Lucis Publishing Co., 1962.

Bailey, Alice A., The Externalisation of the Hierarchy. London: The Lucis Trust Press, 1957.

Baker, Daniel B., Power Quotes. Detroit, Michigan: Visible Ink Press, 1992.

Bancroft, Anne, Weavers of Wisdom: Women Mystics of the Twentieth Century. New York: Viking Penguin, Inc., 1989.

Bates, Marston, The Nature of Natural History. New York: Macmillan Publishing Co., 1950.

Bateson, Gregory, Mind & Nature. New York: Bantam Books, 1980.

Bateson, Gregory, Steps to an Ecology of Mind. New York: Ballantine Books, 1972.

Becker, Ernest, The Denial of Death. New York: Free Press, 1985.

Beecher, Henry Ward, The Sermons of Henry Ward Beecher, Vol. 4. New York: J. B. Ford and Company, 1875.

Berg, Rabbi Philip S., Miracles, Mysteries and Prayer. Research Centre of Kabbalah, 1993.

Bergson, Henri, Creative Evolution, translated by A. Mitchell. New York: Modern Library, 1984.

Berman, Morris, The Reenchantment of the World. San Francisco: Sierra Club Books, 1988.

Berry, Thomas, Riverdale Papers. Riverdale Press 1974-1983.

Berry, Thomas, The Dream of the Earth. San Francisco: Sierra Club Books, 1988.

Berry, Wendell, A Continuous Harmony: Essays Cultural and Agricultural. New York: Harcourt Brace Javonovich, 1975.

Berry, Wendell, The Unsettling of America: Culture and Agriculture. New York: Avon Books, 1978.

Bhagat, Shantilal P., Creation In Crisis. Elgin, Illinois: Brethren Press, 1990.

Bhagavad Gita for Daily Living, translated by Eknath Easwaren. Petaluma, California: Nilgiri Press, 1975-85.

Blake, William, The Poems of William Blake. Cambridge: Howard University Press, 1969.

Blake, William, The Complete Poetry and Prose of William Blake, edited by David V. Erdman. New York: Doubleday, 1988.

Bly, Robert, The Kabir Book. Boston: Beacon Press, 1977.

Bly, Robert, News From the Universe. San Francisco: Sierra Club Books, 1980.

Bohm, David, Wholeness and the Implicate Order. London: Routledge and Kegan Paul, 1980.

Bohr, Niels, Essays, 1958-1962, Atomic Physics and Human Knowledge. Wiley, 1963.

Boissiere, Robert, Meditations with the Hopi. Santa Fe, New Mexico: Bear & Co., 1986.

Boone, J. Allen, Kinship With All Life. New York: Woodbridge Press, 1954.

Boyd, Doug, Rolling Thunder. New York: Delta Publishing, 1974.

Braden, Gregg, Walking Between the Worlds, The Science of Compassion. Radio Bookstore Press, 1997.

Brown, Joseph Epes, The Sacred Pipe: Black Elk's Account of the Seven Rites of the Oglala Sioux. Norman, Oklahoma: University of Oklahoma Press, 1953.

Brown, Joseph Epes, <u>The Spiritual Legacy of the American Indian</u>. New York: Crossroad, 1986.

Brown, Lester R., <u>State of the World</u>. New York: W. W. Norton, 1989.

Brown, Raymond E., <u>The Gospel According to John</u>. New York: Doubleday, 1970.

Brown, Robert McAfee, <u>Theology in a New Key</u>. The Westminster Press, 1978.

Browning, Robert, <u>Robert Browning's Poetry</u>. New York: W. W. Norton & Co., 1979.

Brunton, Paul, <u>The Quest of the Overself</u>. York Beach, Maine: Samuel Weiser, 1984.

Buber, Martin, <u>I and Thou</u>. Edinburgh: T. & T. Clark, 1937.

Bucke, Richard, <u>Cosmic Consciousness</u>. New York: E. P. Dutton, 1923.

Buddha, <u>Dhammapada</u>. Berkeley, California: Dharma Publishing, 1985.

<u>Buddhist Scriptures</u>, edited by Edward Conze. Harmondsworth, UK: Penguin, 1959.

Caddy, Eileen, <u>Footprints on the Path</u>. Findhorn, Forres, Scotland: Findhorn Press, 1976.

Caddy, Eileen, <u>The Dawn of Change</u>. Findhorn, Forres, Scotland: Findhorn Press, 1979.

Campbell, Eileen, <u>A Dancing Star: Inspirations to Guide and Heal</u>. London: The Aquarian Press, 1991.

Campbell, Joseph, <u>Myths to Live By</u>. New York: Viking Penguin Inc., 1972.

Campbell, Joseph, <u>The Hero With a Thousand Faces</u>. Princeton: Princeton University Press, 1949.

Campbell, Joseph, The Inner Reaches of Outer Space. New York: Alfred van de Marck Editions, 1985.

Campbell, Joseph, The Mythic Image. Princeton, New Jersey: Princeton University Press, 1974.

Campbell, Joseph, The Power of Myth. New York: Doubleday, 1988.

Camphausen, Rufus, The Divine Library. Rochester, Vermont: Inner Traditions International, Ltd., 1992.

Camus, Albert, Neither Victims Nor Executioners. New York: Continuum Publishing Co., 1980.

Camus, Albert, Resistance, Rebellion and Death. New York: A. A. Knopf, 1961.

Capra, Fritjof, The Tao of Physics, 2nd ed. New York: Shambhala Publications and Bantam Press, 1984.

Capra, Fritjof, The Turning Point: Science, Society, and the Rising Culture. New York: Simon & Schuster, 1982.

Caras, Paul, The Gospel of Buddha. La Salle, Illinois: The Open Court Publishing Co., 1973.

Carson, Rachel, Silent Spring. Boston: Houghton Mifflin Jovanovich, 1962.

Carson, Rachel, A Sense of Wonder. New York: Harper & Row, 1956.

Castenada, Carlos, The Teachings of Don Juan, A Yaqui Way of Knowledge. Harmondsworth: Penguin Books, Ltd., 1973.

Chesterton, G. K., All Is Grist: A Book of Essays. Freeport, New York: Books for Libraries Press, 1967.

Clark, Glenn, The Man Who Tapped the Secrets of the Universe. Saint Paul, Minnesota: Macalester Park Publishing Co., 1946.

Clark, James and John V. Skinner, <u>Meister Eckhart: Selected Treatises and Sermons Translated From Latin and German</u>. London: Faber & Faber, Ltd. 1958.

<u>Classic American Philosophers</u>. New York: Appleton-Century-Crofts, 1951.

Cohen, Alan, <u>Lifestyles of the Rich in Spirit</u>. Somerset, New Jersey: Alan Cohen Publications, 1987.

Cohen, Alan, <u>The Dragon Doesn't Live Here Anymore</u>. Somerset, New Jersey: Alan Cohen Publications, 1990.

Cohen, Alan, <u>Rising In Love: The Journey Into Light</u>. Somerset, New Jersey: Alan Cohen Publications, 1983.

Coleridge, Samuel Taylor, <u>Biographia Literaria</u>. London: Oxford University Press, 1954.

<u>Collection of Sundry Books</u>. Cincinnati, Ohio: B. C. Stanton, 1829.

Commoner, Barry, <u>The Closing Circle: Nature, Man & Technology</u>. New York: Bantam, 1972.

Conze, Edward, <u>Buddhist Scriptures</u>. New York: Penguin Books, 1959.

Coomeraswamy, Ananda K., <u>Am I My Brother's Keeper</u>? New York: John Day, 1947.

Coomeraswamy, Ananda K., <u>Hinduism and Buddhism</u>. New York: Philosophical Library, 1943.

Coomeraswamy, Ananda K., <u>Time and Eternity</u>. Ascona, Switzerland: Artibus Asiae, 1947.

Copeland, Lewis and Lawrence W. Lamm, <u>The World's Great Speeches</u>, 3rd Enlarged Edition. New York: Dover Publications, 1973.

Cornford, F. M., <u>Greek Religious Thought From Homer to the Ages of Alexander</u>. New York: E. P. Dutton, no date.

Corwin, Edward S., Liberty Against Government. Westport, Connecticut: Greenwood Press, 1948.

Dalai Lama, A Policy of Kindness: An Anthology of Writings By and About The Dalai Lama, compiled and edited by Sidney Piburn. Ithaca, New York: Snow Lion Publications, 1990.

Darwin, Charles Robert, The Origin of Species. London: J. M. Dent & Sons, 1972.

Dass, Ram, Journey of Awakening. New York: Bantam Books, 1978.

Davis, Paul, God and the New Physics. New York: Simon & Schuster, 1983.

Day, Clarence Shepard, This Simian World. New York: A. A. Knopf, 1968.

Devall, Bill, and George Sessions, Deep Ecology: Living as if Nature Mattered. Salt Lake City, Utah: Peregrine Smith Books, 1985.

Dharma Gaia: A Harvest of Essays in Buddhism and Ecology, edited by Allan Hunt Badiner. Berkeley, California: Parallax Press, 1990.

Dickinson, Emily, Final Harvest. Emily Dickinson's Poems. Boston: Little, Brown & Co., 1961.

Donne, John, Satyre, III, Complete Poetry and Selected Prose. Bloomsburg, England: Nonesuch Press Ltd., 1929.

Doreal, The Emerald Tablets of Thoth the Atlantean. Nashville: Source Books, 1994.

Dossey M.D., Larry, Recovering Soul: A Scientific and Spiritual Search. New York: Bantam Books, 1989.

Dworkin, Ronald, Law's Empire. Cambridge: The Belknap Press of Harvard University Press, 1986.

Dylan, Bob, Lyrics 1962-1985. New York: Alfred A. Knopf, Inc., 1985.

Dyson, Freeman, Infinite in All Directions. New York: Harper & Row, 1988.

Early Fathers from the Philokalia, translated by E. Kadloubovsky and G.E.H. Palmer. London: Faber and Faber Limited, 1954.

Easwaran, Eknath, The Compassionate Universe. Petaluma, California: Nilgiri Press, 1989.

Easwaran, Eknath, Gandhi the Man. Petaluma, California: Nilgiri Press, 1978.

Easwaren, Eknath, God Makes The Rivers To Flow: Selections From the Sacred Literature of the World. Tomales, California: Nilgiri Press, 1991.

Eckhart, Meister, Die deutschen Werke, edited by Josef Quint. Stuttgart: 1958-76.

Einstein, Albert, Out of My Later Years. Secaucus, New Jersey: The Citadel Press, 1974.

Einstein, Albert, Ideas and Opinions. New York: Crown, 1982.

Einstein, Albert, The World As I See It. New York: Philosophical Library, 1949.

Eliot, T. S., Four Quartets. New York: Harcourt Brace Javanovich, 1971.

Eliot, T. S., The Complete Poems and Plays. New York: Harcourt Brace Jovanovich, 1952.

Emerson, Ralph Waldo, Works of Ralph Waldo Emerson. Edinburgh: Nimmo, Hay & Mitchell, 1906.

Emerson, Ralph Waldo, Conduct of Life. Boston: J. R. Osgood & Co., 1873.

Emerson, Ralph Waldo, Emerson's Essays. New York: Thomas Y. Crowell Company, 1926.

Emerson, Ralph Waldo, Society and Solitude. Boston and Cambridge: Houghton Mifflin Co., 1904.

Emerson, Ralph Waldo, The Complete Works of Ralph Waldo Emerson. Cambridge: Harvard University Press, 1962.

Eriugena, John Scotus, The Voice of the Eagle: Homily on the Prologue to the Gospel of St. John, translated by Christopher Bamford. Hudson, New York: Lindisfarne Press, 1990.

Essays on Jurisprudence From the Columbia Law Review. New York: Columbia University Press, 1963.

Exeter, Michael, Living at the Heart of Creation: Practical Wisdom for Extraordinary Times. Loveland, Colorado: Foundation House Publications, 1990.

Everson, William, Earth Poetry. Berkeley, California: Oyez, 1980.

Fabre, Jean Henri, The Wonders of Instinct. New York: The Century Company, 1918.

Fabre d'Olivet, Antoine, The Golden Verses of Pythagoras, translated by N. L. Redfield. New York: Weiser, 1975.

Ferguson, Marilyn, The Aquarian Conspiracy: Personal and Society Transformation in the 1980's. Los Angeles: J. P. Tarcher, 1980.

Fischer, Louis, The Life of Mahatma Gandhi. New York: Harper & Row, Harper Colophon Books, 1983.

For the Love of Good, edited by Benjamin Shield and Richard Carlson. San Rafael, California: New World Library, 1990.

Fosdick, Harry Emerson, Riverside Sermons. New York: Harbor & Brothers, 1958.

Foster, Steven and Meredith Little, The Roaring of the Sacred River: The Wilderness Quest for Vision and Self-Healing. New York: Prentice Hall Press, 1989.

Fox, George, The Journal of George Fox, edited by John L. Nickalls. London: Religious Society of Friends, 1975.

Fox, Matthew, Creation Spirituality: Liberating Gifts for the Peoples of the Earth. HarperSanFrancisco, 1991.

Fox, Matthew, <u>Hildegard of Bingen's Book of Divine Works, With Letters and Songs</u>. Santa Fe, New Mexico: Bear & Co., 1987.

Fox, Matthew, <u>Meditations with Meister Eckhart</u>. Santa Fe, New Mexico: Bear & Co., 1982.

Fox, Matthew, <u>Original Blessing</u>. Santa Fe, New Mexico: Bear & Co., 1983.

Fox, Matthew, <u>Sheer Joy: Conversations with Thomas Aquinas on Creation Spirituality</u>. New York: HarperCollins Publishers, 1992.

Fox, Matthew, <u>The Coming of the Cosmic Christ</u>. San Francisco: Harper & Row, Publishers, 1940.

Free, Ann Cottrell, <u>Animals, Nature, and Albert Schweitzer</u>. Barrington, Massachusetts: The Albert Schweitzer Center, 1982.

Fritz, Robert, <u>The Path of Least Resistance</u>. Salem, Massachusetts: DMA, Inc. 1984.

Fromm, Erich, <u>The Art of Loving</u>. London: Allen & Unwin, 1957.

Fromm, Erich, <u>The Sane Society</u>. Greenwich, Connecticut: Fawcett, 1955.

Fulghum, Robert, <u>All I Really Need to Know I Learned in Kindergarten</u>. New York: Villard Books, 1988.

Fuller, R. Buckminster, <u>Critical Path</u>. New York: St. Martin's Press, 1981.

Gadon, Elinor W., <u>The Once and Future Goddess</u>. San Francisco, California: Harper & Row Publishers, 1989.

Galloway, Allan D., <u>The Cosmic Christ</u>. London: Nisbet, 1951.

Gandhi, Mohandas K., <u>My Religion</u>. Ahmedabad, India: Navajivan, 1955.

Gawain, Shatki, <u>Creative Visualization</u>. Mill Valley, California: Whatever Publishing, 1978.

Ghose, Sri Aurobindo, <u>The Life Divine</u>. Wilmot, Wisconsin: Lotus Light, 1980.

Ghose, Sri Aurobindo, The Human Cycle in Social and Political Thought. Pondicherry, India: Sri Aurobindo Ashram Press, 1970.

Ghose, Sri Aurobindo, Essays on the Gita. Pondicherry, India: Sri Aurobindo Ashram Press, 1972.

Ghose, Sri Aurobindo, Savitri. Pondicherry, India: Sri Aurobindo Ashram Press, 1970.

Ghose, Sri Aurobindo, The Future Evolution of Man: The Divine Life Upon Earth, compiled by P. B. Saint-Hilaire. Wheaton, Illinois: The Theosophical Publishing House, 1974.

Ghose, Sri Aurobindo, The Mind of Light. New York: E. P. Dutton, 1971.

Gibran, Khalil, Sand And Foam. New York: A. A. Knopf, 1926.

Gibran, Khalil, The Prophet. New York: A. A. Knopf, 1962.

Gibran, Khalil, The Voice of The Master. New York: Carol Publishing Group, 1990.

Gilson, E., The Christian Philosophy of Saint Augustine. London: Gollancz, 1961.

Godwin, Joscelyn, Paul Brunton Essential Readings. London: The Aquarian Press, 1990.

Goethe, Johann Wolfgang von, Faust, A Tragedy. New York: Random House, 1967.

Goodman, Michael Harris, The Last Dalai Lama. Boston: Shambhala Publications, 1986.

Goodman, Paul, The Society I Love in Is Free. New York: Horizon Books, 1962.

Govinda, Lama, Foundations of Tibetan Mysticism. New York: Samuel Weiser, 1972.

Govinda, Lama, Creative Meditation and Multi-Dimensional Consciousness. Wheaton, Illinois: Theosophical Publishing, 1976.

Graham, A. C., The Books of Lieh-Tze. London: Mandala, 1991.

Granville, David, Song of Songs. Oakland, California: Friends of Creation Spirituality, 1988.

Gray, Glenn, The Warriors. New York: Harper & Row, 1956.

Greenstein, George, The Symbiotic Universe: Life and the Cosmos in Unity. William Morrow & Co., 1989.

Gregorios, Paulos Mar, The Human Presence. New York: Amity House, 1987.

Griffin, Susan, Woman and Nature: The Roaring Inside Her. New York: HarperCollins Publishers, 1978.

Guru, R. H. H., Talk Does Not Cook the Rice, Series 2 - A Commentary on the Teachings of Agni Yoga. York Beach, Maine: Samuel Weiser, Inc., 1985.

Hadfield, J.A., The Psychology of Power. New York: The Macmillan Co., 1919.

Hamilton, Alexander, The Papers of Alexander Hamilton. New York: Columbia University Press, 1961.

Hamilton, Michael, This Little Planet. New York: Charles Scribner's Sons, 1970.

Hammarskjold, Dag, Markings, translated by Leif Sjoberg & W. H. Auden. New York: Ballantine Books, 1964.

Hanh, Thich Nhat, Being Peace. Berkeley, California: Parallax Press, 1987.

Hanh, Thich Nhat, Present Moment, Wonderful Moment, Mindfulness Verse for Daily Living. Berkeley, California: Parallax Press, 1990.

Harman, Willis, Global Mind Change. Indianapolis, Indiana: Knowledge Systems, Inc., 1988.

Harman, Willis and John Hormann, Creative Work. Indianapolis, Indiana: Knowledge Systems, Inc., 1990.

Harvey, Andrew, The Way of Passion -- A Celebration of Rumi, Berkeley, California: Frog, Ltd. 1994.

Hays, Edward, Prayers for a Planetary Pilgrim. Leavenworth, Kansas: Forest of Peace Books, Inc., 1989.

Hayward, Susan, A Guide for the Advanced Soul. Avalon, Australia: In-Tune Books, 1984.

Hayward, Susan, Begin it Now: A Book of Motivation. New South Wales, Australia: In-Tune Books, 1987.

Heidegger, Martin, Being and Time. New York: Harper & Row, 1962.

Heschel, Abraham Joshua, God in Search of Man: A Philosophy of Judaism. New York: Farrar, Straus & Giroux, 1955.

Heschel, Abraham Joshua, The Prophets. New York: Harper & Row, 1962.

Heschel, Abraham Joshua, Who Is Man? Stanford, California: Stanford University Press, 1965.

Heschel, Abraham Joshua, The Earth is the Lord's. New York: Farrar Straus Giroux, 1978.

Hill, Carol, The Eleven Million Mile High Dancer. New York: Penguin Books, 1986.

Hitchcock, John, The Web of the Universe: Jung, the "New Physics," and Human Spirituality. New York: Paulist Press, 1991.

Holmes, Oliver Wendell, Collected Legal Papers. New York: Harcourt, Brace and Howe, 1920.

Houston, Jean, Godseed: The Journey of Christ. Wheaton, Illinois: Quest Books, 1992.

Houston, Jean, Search for the Beloved. London: The Aquarian Press, 1990.

Houston, Jean, The Possible Human. Los Angeles, California: J. P. Tarcher, Inc., 1982.

Hudson, William Henry, The Book of a Naturalist. New York: George H. Doran Co., 1919.

Human Rights Reader, edited by Walter Laqueur and Barry Rubin. New York: New American Library, 1989 ed.

Huxley, Aldous, The Perennial Philosophy. New York: Harper Colophon Books, 1945.

Huxley, Thomas H., Life and Letters of Thomas H. Huxley. New York: D. Appleton & Co., 1901.

Inaugural Addresses of the Presidents of the United States, Bicentennial Edition. Washington, D.C.: U. S. Government Printing Office, 1989.

Incognito, Magus, The Secret Doctrine of The Rosicrucians. Chicago, Illinois: The Yogi Publication Society, 1949.

Ingram, Catherine, In the Footsteps of Gandhi: Conversations with Spiritual Social Activists. Berkeley, California: Paralax Press, 1990.

In Praise of Nature, edited by Stephanie Mills. Washington, D.C.: Island Press, 1990.

Iyer, Raghavan, The Moral and Political Thought of Mahatma Gandhi. New York: Oxford University Press, 1973.

Jacob, Jolande and R.F.C. Hull, C. G. Jung: Psychological Reflections. Princeton, New Jersey: Princeton University Press, 1978.

James, William, The Energies of Men. New York: Longmans, Green & Co., 1911.

James, William, The Will To Believe. New York: Dover Publications, 1956.

Jantsch, Erich, The Self-Organizing Universe. New York: Pergamon Press, 1980.

Jayakar, Pupul, Krishnamurti - A Biography. New York: Harper & Row, 1986.

Jeans, Sir James, The Mysterious Universe.   Cambridge, Massachusetts: Cambridge University Press, 1931.

Jefferson, Thomas, The Papers of Thomas Jefferson. Princeton, New Jersey: Princeton University Press, 1950.

Jefferson, Thomas, The Writings of Thomas Jefferson.   New York: The Knickerbocker Press, 1892-1899.

Jones, Mary Hoxie, Rufus M. Jones. London: Friends Home Service Committee, 1955.

Jones, Rufus M., An Interpretation of Quakerism. London: Friends Home Service Committee, 1930.

Jones, Rufus M., Spirit in Man. Berkeley, California: Peacock Press, 1962.

Jones, Rufus M., The Faith and Practice of the Quakers. Richmond, Indiana: Friends United Press, 1991.

Joyce, James, A Portrait of the Artist as a Young Man. London: Jonathen Cape, Ltd., 1916.

Jung, C. G., Memories, Dreams, Reflections. New York: Vintage, 1968.

Jung, C. G., Collected Works. Princeton, New Jersey: Princeton University Press, 1990.

Jung, C. G., Psyche and Symbol. Garden City, New York: Doubleday, 1958.

Jung, C. G., The Secret of the Golden Flower. New York: Harcourt Brace Jovanovich, 1962.

Kammen, Michael, The Origins of the American Constitution: A Documentary History. New York: Penguin Books, 1986.

Kant, Immanuel, Groundwork of the Metaphysics of Morals. New York: Harper Torchbooks, 1964.

Keats, John, <u>Letters of John Keats to His Family and Friends</u>. London: Macmillan & Co., 1921.

Keen, Sam, <u>Fire in the Belly: On Being a Man</u>. New York: Bantam Books, 1991.

Keen, Sam and Anne Valley-Fox, <u>Your Mythic Journey</u>. Los Angeles: Jeremy P. Tarcher, Inc., 1973.

Keiser, Melvin R., <u>Inward Light and The New Creation</u>. Wellingford, Pennsylvania: Pendle Hill Publications, 1991.

Kempis, Thomas A., <u>The Imitation of Christ</u>. Garden City, New York: Image Books (Doubleday & Company), 1955.

Kidder, Rushworth M., <u>An Agenda for the 21st Century</u>. Cambridge: MIT Press, 1987.

Kierkegaard, Soren, <u>Sickness Unto Death</u>. New York: Doubleday Anchor Books, 1954.

Kierkegaard, Soren, <u>The Journals of Kierkegaard 1834-1854</u>. Huntington, New York: Fontana Publishing, 1958.

King, Alexander and Bertrand Schneider, <u>The First Global Revolution: A Report by the Council of the Club of Rome</u>. New York: Pantheon Books, 1991.

King, Martin Luther, <u>Stride Towards Freedom: The Montgomery Story</u>. New York: Harper & Row, 1958.

King, Martin Luther, <u>Why We Can't Wait</u>. New York: Mentor, 1964.

Kipling, Rudyard, <u>Just So Stories</u>. Mattituck, New York: Amereon Ltd., 1976.

Koller, J.M., <u>Oriental Philosophy</u>. New York: Charles Scribner's Sons, 1985.

Kuhn, Thomas, <u>The Structure of Scientific Revolution</u>. Chicago: University of Chicago Press, 1962.

Kumar, Sehder, <u>The Vision of Kabir</u>. Concord, Ontario, Canada: Alpha & Omega, 1984.

La Violette, Wesley, The Creative Light. Los Angeles, California: DeVorss & Co., 1968.

La Violette, Wesley, Wings Unfolding. Los Angeles, California: DeVorss & Co., 1971.

Laing, Ronald D., The Politics of Experience and the Bird of Paradise. Harmondsworth: Penguin Books, Ltd., 1984.

Lao Tzu, Tao Te Ching. New York: Macmillan Publishing Co., 1989.

Lao Tzu, Tao Te Ching, A New Translation. New York: Viking Press, 1972.

Lao Tzu, The Way of Life. New York: Capricorn Books, 1962.

Laszlo, Erwin, A Strategy for the Future: The Systems Approach to World Order. New York: George Braziller, 1974.

Laszlo, Erwin, Evolution, The Grand Synthesis. Boston: Shambhala, 1987.

Law, William, The Selected Mystical Writings of William Law, edited by S. Hobhouse. London: 1938-49.

Lawless, Gary, First Sight of Land. Nobleboro, Maine: Blackberry Books, 1990.

Lawrence, D. H., Apocalypse. Harmondsworth: Penguin Books, Ltd., 1980.

Learning to Listen to the Land, edited by Bill Willers. Washington, D.C.: Island Press, 1991.

LeFlesche, Francis, "The Osage Tribe: Rite of the Chiefs, Sayings of Ancient Men," 36th Annual Report of the Bureau of American Ethnology. Washington, D.C.: Government Printing Office, 1921.

Leonard, George, The Silent Pulse. London: Wildwood House Ltd., 1978.

Leopold, Aldo, A Sand County Almanac. New York: Oxford University Press, 1949.

Levi, <u>The Aquarian Gospel of Jesus The Christ</u>. Marina Del Ray, California: DeVorss & Co., 1907.

Lewis, C. S., <u>The Weight of Glory and Other Addresses</u>. New York: Macmillan, 1980.

Lhalungpa, Lobsang P., <u>The Life of Milarepa</u>. New York: E. P. Dutton, 1977.

Lloyd, Donna H., <u>The View from Olympus: A New Gnostic Gospel</u>. Sedona, Arizona: Deltaran Publishing Co., 1991.

Lynd, Staughton, <u>Nonviolence in America</u>. New York: Bobbs-Merrill, 1966.

Macy, Joanna Rogers, <u>Despair and Personal Power in the Nuclear Age</u>. Philadelphia: New Society Publishers, 1983.

Macy, Joanna Rogers, <u>Thinking Like a Mountain: Toward a Council of All Beings</u>. Philadelphia: New Society Publishers, 1989.

Malone, Dumas, <u>Jefferson and the Rights of Man</u>. New York: Little, Brown, 1951.

Maltz M.D., Maxwell, <u>Psycho-Cybernetics</u>. Englewood Cliffs, New Jersey: Prentice-Hall, Inc., 1960.

Marcel, Gabriel, <u>The Mystery of Being</u>. Chicago, Illinois: Henry Regnery Company, 1960.

<u>Marcus Aurelius: Meditations</u>, translated by Maxwell Staniforth. New York: Penguin Books, 1964.

Margenau, Henry, <u>Open Vistas</u>. New Haven, Connecticut: Yale University Press, 1961.

Margenau, Henry, <u>The Miracle of Existence</u>. Woodbridge, Connecticut: Ox Bow Press, 1984.

Maslow, Abraham H., <u>The Farther Reaches of Human Nature</u>. New York: Viking Press, 1971.

Maslow, Abraham H., <u>Toward A Psychology of Being</u>. Van Nostrand, 1962.

Maslow, Abraham H., <u>The Further Reaches of Human Nature</u>. New York: Viking Press, 1971.

Maurer, Armand A., <u>Master Eckhart: Parisian Questions and Prologues</u>. Toronto: Pontifical Institute of Medieval Studies, 1974.

May, Rollo, <u>The Courage to Create</u>. New York: W. W. Norton & Co., 1975.

McKeever, Porter, <u>Adlai Stevenson: His Life and Legacy</u>. New York: Quill William Morrow, 1989.

McMurphy Ph.D., John H., <u>Secrets from Great Minds</u>. Dallas, Texas: MRA, Inc., 1991.

McNamara, M. Frances, <u>2,000 Famous Legal Quotations</u>. New York: Aqueduct Books, 1967.

Merkle, John C., <u>Abraham Joshua Heschel: Exploring His Life and Thought</u>. New York: Macmillan, 1985.

Merton, Thomas, <u>Conjectures of a Guilty Bystander</u>. New York: Doubleday Image, 1968.

Merton, Thomas, <u>The Collected Poems of Thomas Merton</u>. New York: New Directions Publishing Corp. 1968.

Miller, Alan S., <u>Gaia Connections</u>. Savage, Maryland: Rowman & Littlefield Publishers, 1991.

Miller, Alice, <u>The Drama of the Gifted Child</u>. New York: Basic Books, 1981.

Miller, Alice, <u>For Your Own Good</u>. New York: Farrar Straus Giroux, 1984.

Miller, Alice, <u>Thou Shalt Not Be Aware</u>. New York: New American Library, 1986.

Miller, Henry, <u>The Colossus of Marouss</u>. Harmondsworth: Penguin Books, Ltd., 1985.

Miller, Ronald S., <u>As Above So Below: Paths to Spiritual Renewal in Daily Life</u>. Los Angeles, California: Jeremy P. Tarcher, Inc., 1992.

<u>Mother Earth: Through the Eyes of Women Photographers and Writers</u>, edited by Judith Boice. San Francisco, California: Sierra Club, 1992.

Moyers, Bill, "The Power of Myth: An Interview with Joseph Campbell," <u>New Age Journal</u> (July/August 1988)

Muir, John, <u>My First Summer in the Sierra</u>. Boston: Houghton Mifflin Co., 1916.

Muktananda, Swami, <u>I Have Become Alive</u>. South Fallsburg, New York: SYDA Foundation, 1985.

Muller, F. Max, <u>The Upanishads</u>. New York: Dover Publications, 1962.

Muller, Robert, <u>A Planet of Hope</u>. New York: Amity House, 1985.

Muller, Robert, <u>New Genesis: Shaping a Global Spirituality</u>. New York: Doubleday & Co., 1982.

Mumford, Lewis, <u>The Transformations of Man</u>. New York: Harper Brothers, 1956.

Murray, W. H., <u>The Scottish Himalayan Expedition</u>. J. H. Dent & Sons, Ltd., 1951.

Naimy, M., <u>The book of Mirdad</u>. New York: Penguin Books, 1962.

Nair, Keshavan, <u>Beyond Winning</u>. Phoenix, Arizona: Paradox Press, 1988.

Nash, Roderick Frazier, <u>The Rights of Nature: A History of Environmental Ethics</u>. Madison, Wisconsin: University of Wisconsin Press, 1989.

<u>Native American Wisdom</u>, edited by Kent Nerburn and Louise Menglekoch. San Rafael, California: New World Library, 1991.

<u>Nature, Man, and Society: Main Currents In Modern Thought</u>. New York: Nicholas Hays, Ltd., 1976.

Neihardt, John G., Black Elk Speaks. New York: Washington Square Press, 1972.

Notes of Debates In the Federal Convention of 1787 Reported By James Madison. Athens, Ohio: Ohio University Press, 1987 ed.

Open Secret: Versions of Rumi, translated by John Moyne and Coleman Barks. Putney, Vermont: Threshold Books, 1984.

Ornstein, Robert, and Paul Ehrlich, New World, New Mind. New York: Doubleday & Co., 1989.

Ortega y Gasset, Jose, The Revolt of the Masses, Man and Crisis. New York: Norton, 1964.

Otto, Rudolf, Mysticism East and West. New York: Meridian, 1957.

Ouspensky, P.D., In Search of the Miraculous: Fragments of an Unknown Teaching. London: Routledge & Kegan Paul, 1977.

Paine, Thomas, Rights of Man. Buffalo, New York: Prometheus Books, 1987.

Parfit, Derek, Reasons and Persons. Oxford: Oxford University Press, 1984.

Paths to Peace, edited by John Matthews. Rutland, Vermont: Charles E. Tuttle Company, Inc., 1992.

Peat, F. David, Philosopher's Stone: Chaos, Synchronicity, and the Hidden Order of the World. New York: Bantam Books, 1991.

Penington, Isaac, The Way of Life and Death. In Works. London: Benjamin Clark, 1681.

Pfeiffer, Franz, Meister Eckhart, translated by C. de B. Evans, 2 vols. London: John W. Watkins, 1947.

Picard, Max, The World of Silence. Gateway Book, 1961.

Plato: The Republic, translated by Benjamin Jowett, M.A. New York: Prometheus Books, 1986.

Plaut, W. Gunther, <u>The Torah, Genesis, A Modern Commentary</u>. New York: Union of American Congregations, 1974.

Prem, Sri Krishna and Sri Madhava Ashish, <u>Man, the Measure of All Things</u>. Wheaton, Illinois: The Theosophical Publishing House, 1969.

Prem, Sri Krishna, <u>The Yoga of the Kathopanishad</u>. London: John Watkins, 1955.

Price, John Randolph, <u>The Super Beings</u>. Austin, Texas: Quartus Books, 1981.

Prigogine, Ilya, <u>From Being to Becoming</u>. New York: W. H. Freeman & Co., 1980.

Rain, Mary Summer, <u>Phoenix Rising: No-Eyes' Vision of the Changes to Come</u>. Norfolk, Virginia: The Donning Co., 1987.

Raines, Howell, <u>My Soul Is Rested</u>. New York: Putnam, 1977.

Rajneesh, Bhagwan Shree, <u>Roots and Wings: Talks on Zen</u>. Poona, India: Rajneesh Foundation, 1975.

Rajneesh, Bhagwan Shree, <u>The Discipline of Transcendence</u>, 2 vols. India: Rajneesh Foundation, no date.

Ramacharaka, Yogi, <u>Mystic Christianity: The Inner Teachings of The Master</u>. Chicago, Illinois: The Yogi Publication Society, 1908.

Ramacharaka, Yogi, <u>The Spirit of The Upanishads</u>. Chicago, Illinois: The Yogi Publication Society, 1907.

<u>Ramtha</u>, edited by Steven L. Weinberg. Eastsound, Washington: Sovereignty, Inc. 1986.

<u>Ramtha - An Introduction</u>, edited by Steven L. Weinberg. Eastsound, Washington: Sovereignty, Inc. 1988.

Rank, Otto, <u>Beyond Psychology</u>. New York: Dover Publications, 1958.

Rank, Otto, <u>Art and Artist</u>. New York: Agathon Press, 1975.

Ravindra, Ravi, <u>Science and Spirit</u>. New York: Paragon House, 1991.

Ray, Michael and Rochelle Myers, <u>Creativity In Business</u>.   New York: Doubleday, 1989.

Reich, Charles, <u>The Greening of America</u>. New York 1970.

<u>Reflections on the Art of Living: A Joseph Campbell Companion</u>, selected and edited by Diane K. Osborn. New York: HarperCollins Publishers, 1991.

<u>Respectfully Quoted, A Dictionary of Quotations Requested From the Congressional Research Service</u>. Washington, D.C.: Library of Congress, 1989.

Rilke, Rainer Maria, <u>Poems From the Book of Hours</u>, translated by Babette Deutsch. New York: New Directions Publishing Corp., 1941.

Rilke, Rainer Maria, <u>Letters To A Young Poet</u>, translation by Joan M. Burnham. San Rafael, California: New World Library, 1992.

Rodegast, Pat and Judith Stanton, <u>Emmanuel's Book: A Manual for Living Comfortably in the Cosmos</u>. New York: Bantam Books, 1985.

Roszak, Theodore, <u>Person/Planet</u>. New York: Anchor Books, 1978.

Roszak, Theodore, <u>The Making of a Counter Culture</u>. Garden City, New York: Doubleday & Co., 1969.

Roszak, Theodore, <u>Where the Wasteland Ends: Politics and Transcendence in Postindustrial Society</u>. Garden City, New York: Doubleday & Co., 1972.

Rousseau, Jean-Jacques, <u>The Social Contract and Discourse on the Origin and Foundation of Inequality Among Mankind</u>, edited by Lester G. Crocker. New York: Washington Square Press, 1967.

Rumi, Jelaluddin, <u>The Ruins of the Heart: Selected Lyric Poetry of Jalal-ud-Din Rumi</u>. Putney, Vermont: Threshold Books, 1981.

Russell, Bertrand, <u>The Conquest of Happiness</u>.   George Allen & Unwin Paperbacks Ltd., 1985.

Russell, Peter, The Awakening Earth - The Global Brain. London: ARK PAPERBACKS, 1985.

Russell, Walter, The Secret of Light. Waynesboro, Virginia: University of Science and Philosophy, 1947.

Sagan, Carl, The Dragons of Eden - Speculations on the Evolution of Human Intelligence. New York: Ballentine Books, 1984.

Salk, Jonas, Anatomy of Reality. New York: Praeger, 1985.

Salt, Henry S., Animal's Rights Considered in Relation to Social Progress. Clarks Summit, Pennsylvania: Society for Animal Rights, 1980 ed.

Sangharakshita, A Survey of Buddhism. Boulder, Colorado: Shambhala, 1980.

Satin, Mark, New Age Politics: Healing Self and Society. New York: Delta, 1979.

Satprem, Sri Aurobindo, or the Adventure of Consciousness. New York: Harper & Row, 1968.

Satprem, The Mind of the Cells. New York: Institute for Evolutionary Research, 1982.

Schell, Jonathan, The Fate of the Earth. New York: A. A. Knopf, 1982.

Schell, Jonathan, The Abolition. New York: A. A. Knopf, 1984.

Schopenhauer, Arthur, The Complete Essays. New York: Willey Book Co., 1942.

Schrodinger, Erwin, What is Life? London: Cambridge University Press, 1969.

Schweitzer, Albert, Out of My Life and Thought: An Autobiography. New York: Henry Holt, 1933.

Schweitzer, Albert, Reverence for Life. New York: Harper & Row, 1966.

Schweitzer, Albert, The Philosophy of Civilization. New York: The Macmillan Company, 1932.

Schweitzer, Albert, The Problem of Peace in the World of Today. New York: Harper & Brothers, 1954.

Seattle, Chief, Chief Seattle's Testament. Leicester, U.K.: St. Bernard Press, 1977.

Selders, George, The Great Quotations: A unique anthology of the wisdom of the centuries and dedicated to "the illimitable freedom of the human mind". Secaucus, New Jersey: Citadel Press, 1983 ed.

Seligmann, Kurt, The Mirror of Magic. New York: Pantheon Books, 1948.

Shakespeare, William, Complete Works. London: Cambridge Text, 1983.

Snyder, Robert, Buckminster Fuller. New York: St. Martin's Press, 1980.

Soelle, Dorothee, Beyond Mere Obedience. New York: Pilgrim Press, 1982.

Solara, 11:11 Inside the Doorway. Charlottesville, Virginia: Star-Borne Unlimited, 1992.

Sorensen, Theodore, Kennedy. New York: Harper & Row, 1965.

Sorokin, Pitirim, The Ways and Power of Love. Boston: Beacon Press, 1954.

Sorokin, Pitirim, The Crisis of Our Age. E. P. Dutton, 1941.

Spangler, David, Revelations: The Birth of a New Age. Elgin: Lorian Press, 1979.

Spaulding, Baird, The Life and Teachings of the Masters of the Far East. Marina Del Ray, California: DeVorss & Co., 1972.

Stein, Diane, Dreaming The Past, Dreaming The Future: A Herstory of the Earth. Freedom, California: The Crossing Point, 1991.

Suzuki, D. T., Manual of Zen Buddhism. London: Rider, 1950.

Suzuki, D. T., Mysticism Christian and Buddhist. London: Allen & Unwin, 1957.

Swimme, Brian, The Universe is a Green Dragon: A Cosmic Creation Story. Santa Fe, New Mexico: Bear & Co., 1985.

Szekely, Edmond Bordeaux, The Essene Gospel of Peace. British Columbia: International Biogenic Society, 1981.

Tagore, Dr. Rabindranath, Collected Poems and Plays. New York: Macmillan & Co., 1937.

Tagore, Dr. Rabindranath, Glorious Thoughts of Tagore. New Book Society of India, 1965.

Tagore, Rabindranath, Sadhana. New York: Macmillan, 1913.

Taylor, Charles, Sources of The Self. Cambridge, Massachusetts: Harvard University Press, 1989.

Teilhard de Chardin, Pierre, The Divine Milieu. New York: Harper Colophon Books, 1960.

Teilhard de Chardin, Pierre, The Heart of Matter. New York: Harcourt Brace Jovanovich, 1978.

Teilhard de Chardin, Pierre, Human Energy. New York: Harcourt Brace Jovanovich, 1969.

Teilhard de Chardin, Pierre, The Phenomenon of Man. New York: Harper & Row, 1959.

Teilhard de Chardin, Pierre, Man's Place in Nature. New York: Harper & Row, 1966.

Teilhard de Chardin, Pierre, Hymn of the Universe. New York: Harper & Row, Fontana Religious Books, 1970.

Teilhard de Chardin, Pierre, Toward the Future. London: Collins, 1975.

Teilhard de Chardin, Pierre, The Future of Man. London: Collins, 1965.

Tennyson, Alfred Lord, The Complete Poetic Works of Tennyson. Boston: Houghton Mifflin Co., 1898.

Terres, John K., Things Precious & Wild: A Book of Nature Quotations. Golden, Colorado: Fulcrum Publishing, 1991.

Thakar, Vimala, The Eloquence of Living. Berkeley, California: Vimala Programs, 1981.

The Animal World of Albert Schweitzer, translated by Charles R. Joy. Boston: Beacon Press, 1950.

The Basic Writings of Bertrand Russell, edited by Robert E. Egner and Lester E. Dennon. New York: Simon and Schuster, 1961.

The Bhagavad Gita, translated by Eknath Easwaran. Petaluma, California: Nilgiri Press, 1985.

The Bible of the World, edited by Robert O. Ballou. New York: Viking Press, 1939.

The Complete Writings of Thomas Paine, edited by Philip Foner. New York: The Citadel Press, 1945.

The Courage of Conviction, edited by Phillip L. Berman. New York: Ballentine Books, 1986.

The Dhammapada, translated by Eknath Easwaren. Petaluma, California: Nilgiri Press, 1985.

The Dhammapada, translated by P. Lal. New York: Farrar, Straus and Giroux, 1967.

The Enlightened Heart: An Anthology of Sacred Poetry, edited by Stephen Mitchell. New York: Harper & Row Publishers, 1989.

The Founders' Constitution: Volume One, Major Themes, edited by Philip B. Kurland and Ralph Lerner. Chicago: The University of Chicago Press, 1987.

The Gospel According to Thomas, Coptic text, translated by A. Guillaumont, H.-Ch. Puech, G. Quispel, W. Till, and Yassah'abd al Masih. Leiden: E. J. Brill, 1959.

The Great Quotations. New York: Pocket Books, 1976 ed.

The Gospel of Sri Ramakrishna, translated by Swami Nikhilananda. New York: Ramakrishna - Vivekananda Center, 1942.

The Kybalion: The Hermetic Philosophy of Ancient Egypt and Greece, by Three Initiates. Chicago, Illinois: Publication Society, 1912.

The Little Book of Eternal Wisdom, translated by James M. Clark. London: Faber & Faber, 1953.

The Mystics of Islam, translated by Reynold A. Nicholson. London: Arkana, 1989.

The Mystique of Enlightenment - The Unrational Ideas of a Man Called U.G., edited by Rodney Arms. India: Dinesh Vaghela, 1982.

The Nag Hammadi Library, edited by J. M. Robinson. New York: Harper & Row, 1977.

The Nobel Peace Prize and The Dalai Lama, compiled and edited by Sidney Piburn. Ithaca, New York: Snow Lion Publications, 1980.

The Other Bible, edited by Willis Barnstone. New York: HarperCollins Publishers, 1984.

The Portable Tolstoy, edited by John Bayler. New York: Penguin Books, 1978.

The Pythagorean Sourcebook And Library, compiled and translated by Kenneth Sylvan Guthrie. Grand Rapids, Michigan: Phanes Press, 1988.

The Rule of Law, edited by Robert Paul Wolff. New York: Simon and Schuster, 1971.

The Thirteen Principal Upanishads, translated by Robert Ernest Hume. London: Oxford University Press, 1921-1934.

The Tibetan Book of the Dead, translated by W. Y. Evans-Wentz. London: Oxford University Press, 1927-1951.

The Upanishads: Breath of the Eternal, translated by Swami Prabhavananda and Frederick Manchester. Hollywood, California: Vedenta Press, 1968.

The Words of Albert Schweitzer, selected by Norman Cousins. New York: Newmarket Press, 1984.

The Words of Martin Luther King, Jr., selected by Coretta Scott King. New York: Newmarket Press, 1983.

The Words of Peace: Selections from the Speeches of the Winners of the Nobel Peace Prize. New York: Newmarket Press, 1990.

The World's Great Speeches, edited by Lewis Copeland and Lawrence W. Lamm. New York: Dover Publications, Inc., 1973 ed.

Thoreau, edited by Carl Bode. New York: Penguin Books, 1947.

Thoreau, Henry David, The Journal of Henry David Thoreau. Cambridge: Houghton Mifflin Co., Riverside Press, 1887.

Thoreau, Henry David, The Writings of Henry Thoreau, edited by Bradford Torrey. Boston, 1906.

Tillich, Paul, The Courage to Be. Yale University Press, 1952.

Tillich, Paul, The Shaking of the Foundations. New York: Charles Scribner's Sons, 1948.

Timms, Moira, Prophesies and Predictions: Everyone's Guide to the Coming Changes. Santa Cruz, California: Unity Press, 1980.

Toffler, Alvin, The Third Wave. New York: Bantam, 1981.

Toynbee, Arnold, A Study of History. New York: Oxford University Press, 1947.

Treasury of Religious Quotations, compiled and edited by Gerald Tomlinson. Inglewood Cliffs, New Jersey: Prentice Hall, 1991.

Trevelyan, George, Magic Casements: The Use of Poetry in the Expanding of Consciousness. London: Coventure, 1980.

Trevelyan, George, Summons to a High Crusade. Scotland: Findhorn Press, 1986.

Trine, Ralph Waldo, <u>In Tune With the Infinite</u>. London: G. Bell, 1930.

Trine, Ralph Waldo, <u>TWO By Ralph Waldo Trine, In Tune With The Infinite</u>. Connecticut: Keats Publishing, Inc., 1986.

True, Michael, <u>Justice Seekers, Peace Makers</u>. Mystic, Connecticut: Twenty-Third Publications, 1990.

<u>TWO SUNS RISING</u>, translated and compiled by Jonathan Star. New York: Bantam Books, 1991.

Underhill, Evelyn, <u>Mysticism</u>. New York: New American Library, 1974.

Van Doren, Carl, <u>The Great Rehearsal: The Story of the Making and Ratifying of the Constitution of the United States</u>. New York: Viking Penguin, Inc. 1948.

<u>Voices of Struggle, Voices of Pride</u>, compiled by John Beilenson and Heidi Jackson. White Plains, New York: Peter Pauper Press, Inc., 1992.

Wagner, Jane, <u>The Search for Signs of Intelligent Life in the Universe</u>. New York: Harper and Row, 1986.

Wall, Steve and Harvey Arden, <u>WisdomKeepers: Meetings with Native American Spiritual Elders</u>. Hillsboro, Oregon: Beyond Words Publishing, Inc., 1990.

Ward, Barbara and Rene Dubos, <u>Only One Earth: The Care and Maintenance of a Small Planet</u>. New York: W. W. Norton & Co., 1972.

Waters, Frank, <u>Book of the Hopi</u>. New York: Ballantine Books, 1963.

Watson, Lillian Eichler, <u>Light From Many Lamps: A Treasury of Inspiration</u>. New York: Fireside edition of Simon & Schuster, 1988.

Weber, Renee, <u>Dialogues with Scientists and Sages: The Search for Unity</u>. London: Routledge and Kegan Paul, 1986.

<u>Webster's Unabridged Dictionary of the English Language</u>. New York: Portland House, a division of deLithium Press, Ltd., 1989.

Weisskopf, Victor, <u>The Joy of Insight: Passions of A Physicist</u>. New York: Basic Books, 1991.

Whelan, Richard, <u>Self-Reliance -- The Wisdom of Ralph Waldo Emerson as Inspiration for Daily Living</u>. New York: Bell Tower, 1991.

Whitman, Walt, <u>Song of Myself, Leaves of Grass</u>. New York: Doubleday, Doran & Co. 1940.

Whitman, Walt, <u>The Works of Walt Whitman</u>. New York: Minerva Press, 1969.

Wilber, Ken, <u>Quantum Questions</u>. Boston, Massachusetts: New Science Library, 1984.

Wilber, Ken, <u>The Holographic Paradigm and Other Paradoxes</u>. Boulder, Colorado: Shambhala, 1982.

Wilkinson, Sir Denys, <u>Our Universe</u>. New York: Columbia University Press, 1991.

<u>William Wordsworth, Selected Poems and Prefaces</u>, edited by Jack Stillinger. Boston: Houghton Mifflin, Riversdale ed., 1965.

Williams, Paul, <u>Das Energi</u>. Warner Books, 1978.

Woodruff, Sue, <u>Meditations with Mechtild of Magdeburg</u>. Santa Fe, New Mexico: Bear & Co., 1982.

Yatri, <u>Unknown Man: The Mysterious Birth of A New Species</u>. New York: Simon & Schuster Inc., Fireside Div., 1988.

Yeats, W. B., <u>The Collected Poems of W. B. Yeats</u>. New York: Macmillan Publishing Company, 1924.

Young, Meredith Lady, <u>Agartha: A Journey to the Stars</u>. Walpole, New Hampshire: Stillpoint Publishing, 1984.

Yutang, Lin, <u>The Wisdom of Confucius</u>. New York: Carlton House, 1938.

Zimmer, Heinrich, <u>Philosophies of India</u>, edited by Joseph Campbell. New York: Pantheon, 1951.

Zinn, Howard, <u>Declarations of Independence: Cross-Examining American Ideology</u>. New York: Harper Collins Publishers, 1990.

Zohar, Danah, <u>The Quantum Self: Human Nature and Consciousness Defined by the New Physics</u>. New York: Quill/William Morrow, 1990.

Zukav, Gary, <u>The Seat of the Soul</u>. New York: Fireside edition of Simon & Schuster, 1990.

Index

G

H

ℐ

𝒥

K

L

M

𝒫

S

CREDITS

Grateful acknowledgment is made to the following for permission to reprint previously published material:

Excerpts from *Fire in the Belly* by Sam Keen. Copyright © 1991 by Sam Keen. Used by permission of Bantam Books, a division of Bantam Doubleday Dell Publishing Group, Inc.

Excerpts from *Myths to Live By* by Joseph Campbell. Copyright © 1972 by Joseph Campbell. Used by permission of Viking Penguin, a division of Penguin Putnam Inc.

Excerpts from *The Compassionate Universe* by Eknath Easwaran, founder and director of the Blue Mountain Center of Meditation, © 1989. Reprinted with permission. of Nilgiri Press. To receive a catalog of books by Eknath Easwaran, call 800-475-2369.

Excerpts from *Letters to a Young Poet* by Rainer Maria Rilke © 1995. Reprinted with permission of New World Library, Novato, CA.

Excerpts from Alice Bailey's works including *Discipleship in The New Age* (Copyright © 1972), *Education in The New Age* (Copyright © 1954), *Esoteric Psychology I: A Treatise on the Seven Rays* (Copyright © 1962) and *The Externalisation of the Hierarchy* (Copyright © 1957) reprinted with permission of Lucis Trust.

Excerpts from *The Creative Light* by Dr. Wesley La Violette © 1968, reprinted with permission from Dr. La Violette's grandson, James O'Halloran.

Excerpts from *In Tune with the Infinite* by Ralph Waldo Trine. Copyright © 1990 by Ralph Waldo Trine. Published by Keats Publishing, Inc., New Canaan, CT 06840. Reprinted with permission.

Excerpts from *The Hero with a Thousand Faces* by Joseph Campbell. Copyright © 1949 by Bollinger Foundation, renewed 1976 by Princeton University Press. Reprinted by permission of Princeton University Press.

Excerpts from *The Secret of Light* by Walter Russell, copyright © 1947 and from Glenn Clarke's biography of Walter Russell, *The Man who Tapped the Secrets of the Universe*, copyright © 1946. Reprinted with permission from University of Science and Philosophy (Formerly the Walter Russell Foundation).

Portions from *A Course in Miracles* © 1975. Reprinted by permission of the Foundation for Inner Peace, Inc., P.O. Box 598, Mill Valley, CA 94942-0598.

Excerpt reprinted with permission from *Prayers for a Planetary Pilgrim* by Edward Hays. Copyright Forest of Peace Publishing, Inc., 251 Muncie Rd., Leavenworth KS 66048.

Excerpts reprinted with permission from *Lifestyles of the Rich in Spirit (formerly The Healing of the Planet Earth)* (Copyright © 1987), *The Dragon Doesn't Live Here Anymore* (Copyright © 1990) and *Rising in Love: The Journey Into Light* (Copyright © 1983), Alan Cohen Programs & Publications, 430 Kukuna Road, Haiku, HI 96708.

Excerpts reprinted with permission from *Surfers of the Zuvuya* by Jose' Arguelles, Copyright © 1989, Bear & Co., Sante Fe, NM.

Excerpts reprinted with permission from *Original Blessing* by Matthew Fox, Copyright © 1983, Bear & Co., Sante Fe, NM.

Excerpts reprinted with permission from *The Voice of the Master* by Khalil Gibran, Copyright © 1990, Carol Publishing Group.

Also from Wings of Spirit Foundation

Soular Reunion (book)

Return of the Dove (book & audio tape)

Twin Soul Reunion (video tape)

Holy Spirit Regeneration (audio tapes)

It is a time of tribulation, confusion, chaos, fear and monumental change as the foundations of the past are crumbling beneath our feet to give way to a new beginning — a New Genesis.

As we pause in contemplation of our passage, let us not allow the shadows of our former selves to darken the path of Light beckoning us to the birth of our awakened, boundless Self.